A Soldier's Best Friend

Scout Dogs and Their Handlers in the Vietnam War

John C. Burnam

CARROLL & GRAF PUBLISHERS
NEW YORK

A SOLDIER'S BEST FRIEND:

Scout Dogs and Their Handlers in the Vietnam War

Carroll & Graf Publishers

An Imprint of Avalon Publishing Group Inc.

161 William St., 16th Floor

New York, NY 10038

Copyright © 2000 by John C. Burnam

First Carroll & Graf trade paperback edition 2003

First cloth edition published in 2000 under the title *Dog Tags of Courage*

Library of Congress Cataloging-in-Publication Data is available.

ISBN: 0-7867-1137-X

Book design by Sue Canavan

Printed in the United States of America

Distributed by Publishers Group West

This book is dedicated to the exceptionally brave and loyal war dogs and their handlers and to all the men and women who lost their lives in Vietnam; to every military serviceman who was wounded in action, but found the strength to carry on; and to every dog lover who shares in my grief over those German shepherds and Labrador retrievers that we were forced to abandon in the Republic of Vietnam.

Let us NEVER forget our military servicemen still missing in action (MIA) or prisoners of war (POW).

Table of Contents

Preface	ix
Prologue	xvii
Camp Alpha	1
Gary Owen	7
Ia Drang Valley	17
Bong Son	38
Wounded in Action	75
106 General Hospital	84
Sentry Dog Platoon	93
Return to Vietnam	121
Dau Tieng Base Camp	127
44th Scout Dog Platoon	136
Timber and Ambush	144
Clipper	173
Death in the Kennel	180
Trapped	194
Booby Traps	227
The Capture	256
Life between Missions	262
Short-Timer	275
TET and Convoy	291
Good-bye Clipper	313
Leaving Vietnam	318
Epilogue	327
Glossary	334
Acknowledgments	336
Appendix: Gone But Not Forgotten	337
Index	355

Preface

I am proud to have served my country in South Vietnam from March 1966 to March 1968. As a nineteen-year-old, U.S. Army enlisted man at the rank of private first class (PFC), I went on my first twelve-month tour of duty with other young combat infantrymen from all over the United States. My first assignment was with the 2nd Platoon of Company B, 1st Battalion, 7th Cavalry "Gary Owen." I was a replacement for a young soldier who was killed during the battle of the Ia Drang valley in November 1965, which is now depicted in a movie titled *We Were Soldiers*.

My survival depended on a combination of basic military training, streetwise instincts, luck, and the bravery of the teenaged men in my platoon. At times, I begged for deliverance in heaven while my jungle boots grounded me in hell. During my first tour of duty, I learned the full meaning and significance of the word *brotherhood* in a place called Bong Son on a hot day, May 6, 1966.

Before my next twelve-month tour in South Vietnam, I trained and patrolled with a German shepherd sentry dog named Hans on the island of Okinawa. When I arrived in South Vietnam for the second time, I served as a German shepherd scout dog handler with the 44th Scout Dog Platoon. I led combat infantry patrols from behind the leash of magnificent scout dogs named Timber and Clipper. My life depended on how effectively I read the dogs' natural reactions and alerts to danger. I came to know the full meaning of the saying: *A dog is a man's best friend.*

Because of my U.S. Army military service, I received a Combat Infantry Badge, Paratrooper Wings, Purple Heart, Bronze Star medal, Vietnamese Cross of Gallantry, Legion of Merit medal, two Meritorious Service Medals, Army Achievementl, and a personal letter of appreciation from the former President of the United States, Jimmy Carter.

Approximately ten thousand infantry war dog handlers and four thousand war dogs served during the ground war in South Vietnam. Their number was quite small compared to the several million American and allied men and women who rotated in and out of that country from 1960 to 1973 when all the ground forces withdrew. However, the war dog team mission and record for saving lives was quite significant.

German shepherds became the dogs of choice for military scouting and sentry duty. Labrador retrievers were selected for tracking. These two breeds were well-suited to their tasks because of their accommodating dispositions, ability to work with multiple handlers, innate intelligence, learning ability, and adaptability to variable climates, terrain, and working environments.

Each dog's ear was branded with a four character, alphanumeric service number for identification and accountability. Each dog had an official military medical, training, and service record established upon entry into military service. The records were maintained by veterinarians or veterinarian technicians assigned to support the individual war dog units.

By war's end, the Americans had gained a grudging respect for the enemy—the North Vietnamese Army (NVA) and the Viet Cong (VC), or Charlie, as we called these fierce and savvy Asian warriors. They constantly surprised the Americans with their hit-and-run guerilla tactics. Over the course of the Vietnam War, Charlie inflicted thousands of casualties on American and allied soldiers. They destroyed tons of war material worth billions of dollars. The enemy was adept at hiding invisibly under cover within local civilian population or in neatly camouflaged positions and remote jungle base camps. The enemy was exceptionally difficult to find or surprise.

Courageous, well-trained, and disciplined war dog teams were called on to counteract the success of the hit-and-run tactics of the enemy. Their deployment in South Vietnam dramatically improved the infantry's ability to search, locate, engage, and eradicate the enemy's capacity to surprise and inflict casualties or destroy equipment. Due to the extraordinary success of the war dog teams walking point, tracking, or guarding, the enemy placed price tags on their heads and used a variety of means to eliminate them.

A war dog team consisted of one dog and one handler. The following are the various types of K-9 units that supported the army, air force, marines, and navy during the Vietnam War:

1. **Infantry Platoon Scout Dogs (IPSD):** A handler and his German shepherd scout dog performed as a team in the mission of leading combat patrols and providing early silent warning of danger. A scout dog team was deployed out front as "point man," which is the most vulnerable and dangerous position of a

tactical formation moving through enemy territory. The handler interpreted his scout dog's alerts on enemy movement, noise, airborne and ground scents of booby traps, land mines, base camps, underground tunnel complexes, and underground caches of weapons, food, and medical supplies. The U.S. Army had the highest number of scout dog units deployed in South Vietnam and consequently suffered the highest number of scout dog casualties. Fort Benning, Georgia, was the primary training center. Formal scout dog training was twelve weeks long. Upon graduation the entire class was formed into a numbered K-9 unit, fully equipped, and shipped to South Vietnam to support infantry ground operations. Veterinarians and veterinarian technicians were assigned to support their medical needs.

2. Combat Tracker Dog Teams (CTT): Labrador retrievers were used to track the enemy's scent or blood trail after contact had been broken. A CTT consisted of a dog and handler, cover man, visual tracker, and team leader. The dog handler concentrated on the dog for signs of danger. The dog's naturally heightened ground-scent instincts could be relied upon to locate the target. The team was equipped with a radio for communication and support. CTTs were highly trained and effective in locating the enemy, as well as wounded or dead American soldiers, in all types of weather and terrain conditions. CTTs received most of their training in Malaysia at the British Jungle Warfare School (JWS).

3. Sentry Dog Teams: A handler and his German shepherd sentry dog performed as a team in the mission of defending aircraft, airfields, supply depots, ammunition dumps, defensive perimeters, and many other strategic military facilities throughout South Vietnam. Sentry dog teams were usually deployed as the first line of defense of an American base camp and they patrolled day and night. Sentry dog teams received their initial training at Lackland Air Force Base, in San Antonio, Texas.

4 Patrol Dog Teams: A handler and his German shepherd patrol dog were deployed as a team to patrol and protect air bases. The patrol dog team normally operated along the perimeter and many times outside the wire to search the surrounding area and villages. Patrol dog teams were trained to track, search buildings, and attack if necessary. Oftentimes, they rode in jeeps with military law enforcement officers and assisted as required. The patrol dog teams proved to be very effective in South Vietnam.

5. Mine, Booby Trap, and Tunnel Dog Teams: A handler and his German shepherd mine and booby trap dog were usually deployed with the infantry and combat engineer units. They were trained to sniff out mines and booby traps, search underground tunnel complexes, and search Vietnamese villages and other populated communities considered a threat for hiding the enemy, as well as caches of arms, ammunition, and other war supplies. Their deployment successfully reduced the enemy's supply of hidden war material.

6. Water Dogs: The navy successfully used German shepherd dogs on patrol boats to alert on the breath scent of enemy underwater divers breathing through reeds, snorkels, and other underwater apparatuses operating throughout the American-patrolled waterways of South Vietnam. The water dogs proved to be quite successful in saving lives and equipment as well as reducing the enemy's capacity to conduct underwater sabotage operations.

If a war dog handler was killed, wounded, injured, or lucky enough to complete his twelve-month tour of duty in South Vietnam, his dog was reassigned to another handler. In what turned out to be a tragic decision, the U.S. Defense Department designated war dogs as military surplus equipment. Their mission was to serve in South Vietnam until they died in combat, were overcome by disease, or became the victims of some other unfortunate circumstance. They weren't expected to survive the war and die of old age. When a young man had to say good-bye to his best friend, parting brought on deeply felt emotions. How do you tell a beloved dog you are going home and he isn't going with you?

As each military war dog unit pulled out of South Vietnam, the K-9 units were instructed to crate and ship the surviving war dogs to specific quarantine locations for processing and redeployment to other military bases outside of Vietnam. The surviving dog handlers did not necessarily get the privilege of escorting their four-legged partners to the quarantine location. The handlers had assumed that the military would honor its word to care for their dogs and ship them out of the country after each dog completed the quarantine process.

Many of the dog handlers who departed Vietnam years or months before the American withdrawal operations ended in 1973 had no idea what had happened to their dog. Most of us thought that the military got all the surviving war dogs out of Vietnam alive, but we had no idea where they were redeployed.

In my case, thirty years after the war, I joined the Vietnam Dog Handler Association, which was established in 1996. The founding members had already completed some research on the official military war dog records archived at Lackland Air Force Base. Their work revealed that only a little more than two hundred war dogs made it through the quarantine program and were redeployed for duty outside of South Vietnam. The rest of those brave Vietnam war dogs were either put to sleep or given to the South Vietnamese Army (ARVN), which meant that most likely, according to Vietnamese cultural practices, the dogs could be slaughtered for food. No one knows how many war dogs, if any, were smuggled out of South Vietnam by determined handlers.

During that final quarantine of these courageous animals and at their final moment of death, no one played taps, none held a twenty-one-gun salute, no special burial ceremony was performed, no white crosses marked their gravesites.

However, I am directly involved in an organized movement sponsored by the Vietnam Dog Handler Association (*www.vdhaonline.org*) to get the U.S. Government to mandate a National War Dog Memorial in Washington D. C.

While writing this book, I often became tearful, touching upon deeply rooted emotions as I recalled the vivid details about my life, the truth of what happened in Vietnam, the death of comrades, and the sheer horror of the situation I'd encountered in South Vietnam. In the pages that follow, I have tried to describe my experiences as best as I could from an infantryman's viewpoint, an ant's-eye view, and not from a command, strategic, or politically motivated perspective.

I made my story as historically accurate as I could, but much is based on my own memory and perspectives, personal notes, and recollections, along with letters, military documents, memorabilia, tactical military maps, war citations, photographs, and some interviews and discussions with a few of the men I served with in South Vietnam.

Soldiers wear dog tags for identification, to make sure they're accounted for on the battlefield, remembered, and honored properly. It's my goal that *A Soldier's Best Friend: Scout Dogs and Their Handlers in the Vietnam War* will help to secure a place in history for the Vietnam war dogs who earned their dog tags through unconditional loyalty and bravery in the face of war.

Prologue

We were on the last leg of our combat mission and heading home to our base camp at Dau Tieng. Our final objective was to form a long, on-line sweeping formation to cover as much ground as possible and hunt for VC hideouts. After my scout dog, Clipper, and I moved past a few rows of rubber trees, we were ordered to halt our progress.

We waited for several minutes for the rest of the platoon behind us to clear the hamlet and join the main element inside the rubber trees. Finally, the signal was given to move out again. Clipper and I carefully moved out on-line among the tall rows of trees. The rest of the platoon slowly strung out to the left, right and rear.

As Clipper and I passed between two trees, I heard a shattering explosion to our immediate right. I hit the ground and dragged Clipper down beside me. We didn't hear any shots being fired, but then I heard the sounds of a hurt soldier a few feet away from me. I quickly crawled over to him. He was lying on his back rocking in pain with his legs and boots covered in blood.

I yelled, "Medic! Medic!"

When the medic arrived, he cut the young black soldier's boots off and treated the wounds on his legs and feet. Looking around on the ground, I discovered a broken tripwire attached to a short stick that was stuck in the ground. The other end of the wire was tied to a rubber tree. I immediately thought, *That could have been me, if I'd moved one more tree over before I stopped. Would Clipper have alerted on that booby trap?* I'd never know the answer to that question.

I decided that it was time to put to the test all the training that Clipper and I had gone through. Clipper had shown in our recent training sessions that he knew how to detect booby trap tripwires. He'd have to do it for real now, or more of these men would be injured or killed.

After the wounded soldier was medevaced, I told the platoon leader that I'd take the lead. I asked him to move the rest of the platoon into a column and follow behind me. I didn't give the platoon leader a chance to respond as I turned away. Out front, I slowly moved forward and began to follow Clipper's lead. As I glanced behind, I noticed that the platoon leader had ordered the troops to form a single column.

I thought, *Clipper is in charge now, even if he doesn't realize it. If anyone can do it, Clipper can get us through this area and safely home to Dau Tieng.*

With the outer perimeter of our Dau Tieng base camp less than a half-mile away, I kept my attention glued to Clipper's head and ears while he guided me forward. Clipper gave a faint alert to the left, briefly hesitated, and then moved right. I glanced in that direction and saw nothing, so I didn't stop. I had to trust Clipper because my field of vision was only clear at eye level. The ground below was overgrown with knee-high weeds and grass. It was easy to walk through, and Clipper didn't have a problem negotiating a path.

Clipper gave another weak alert to his right and then moved

left. He performed that maneuver again and again without much hesitation or stopping. A short time later a voice from behind had ordered me to stop. As I looked back, I saw a long column of American troops snaking through the rubber trees behind me. We only stopped briefly and then moved out again. That stop-and-go situation occurred several times during the journey. I wasn't completely sure why we were stopping. No one behind me said anything about it, and I didn't ask because I was too far forward. They could have been checking something out or reviewing the map for direction of travel. Someone may have spotted tripwires or booby traps. I had no way of knowing.

I didn't think Clipper's alerts were strong enough for me to worry about danger. The way he was moving, it looked as if he was deliberately going around things that could be tripwires or booby traps. Clipper had performed that kind of maneuver during our training sessions in base camp, but now when he'd move from one direction to another, I couldn't see anything out of the ordinary. I decided to focus on watching Clipper instead of trying to figure out why he was walking from left or right so much. I was grateful that there had been no more explosions; Clipper was leading us on a safe path.

We finally reached the outskirts of Dau Tieng's base camp. I stopped short of the concertina wire and spotted soldiers standing on the other side next to their sand-bagged bunkers and staring at us. I dropped to one knee and waited for the rest of the platoon to catch up. My right knee was aching again, but I knew that I'd soon be safe inside the K-9 compound.

While I knelt and rubbed my right knee, several soldiers caught up with us. One of them stopped and told me to wait for the platoon leader. Another soldier smiled as he passed by. The soldiers moved along the fence of concertina wire in a column toward the base camp's entrance gate.

The lieutenant I had worked with throughout the mission finally showed up. I stood up to greet him and he smiled and thanked me for getting his men through all the other booby traps. Then he knelt and gave Clipper a hug and told him what a great dog he was.

I was puzzled, so I asked, "What other booby traps?"

The platoon leader looked at me, as though I should have known the answer to that question. He told me that when Clipper had changed directions for the first time, one of his men had spotted a grenade tied to the base of a rubber tree, right where the dog had changed directions.

He said, "After you and your dog changed directions several times, my men got wise to what was going on so they started searching for booby traps. The times we had stopped were used to mark the booby traps Clipper had avoided." He explained that the marked booby traps would be detonated after the entire company was safely through the area.

I was happy to hear that I'd been right. Clipper had been deliberately going around booby traps and tripwires. I hadn't seen any of them because I didn't stop to search.

The platoon leader told me that it had been brave of me to take the lead when I didn't have to. He said that if it hadn't been for Clipper some of his men could have been wounded or killed by those booby traps. He also said that he was going to recommend us for a Bronze Star. Then he shook my hand. As he walked away, he turned to me and said, "I'm going to ask for you the next time I need a scout."

That was the finest compliment I'd ever received for doing my job.

I smiled, waved, and gave the lieutenant a thumbs-up signal. I looked down at Clipper and tapped my chest. Clipper jumped up and rested his front paws on my shoulders. I looked into his big brown eyes and gave him a bear hug. I told him what a great warrior he was and how proud I felt to have him as my friend and scout.

I thought about the lieutenant's words. That was the first time anyone had ever wanted to recommend me for a medal. I felt honored but knew that all the credit belonged to my dog. He'd been the hero of the day. I was the lucky guy behind the leash and grateful to have such a wonderful companion to lead us to safety. I felt that there was nothing more valuable or rewarding than knowing that others had lived because of my dog. My trust and confidence in Clipper increased dramatically that day.

Clipper and I moved out behind the rest of the troops through the gate entrance. I walked with my head and shoulders high and smiled all the way home to the 44th Scout Dog Platoon. On the way, I thought about the trip-wire training I'd put Clipper through. I remembered how Clipper had given faint alerts and avoided the trip wires by going around them. The training had paid off. Lives had been saved. I was relieved that another mission was over. As I watched my dog walk ahead of me I thought to myself, *Thanks again for another safe mission, Clipper!*

Camp Alpha

It was March 1966, a few days before my nineteenth birthday. I had five months of U.S. Army service under my belt, all of which was spent training to be an infantryman. I was now aboard a commercial passenger jetliner for the long trip from San Francisco to South Vietnam to fight in a war I knew nothing about.

American soldiers took up every seat on the plane. Sleeping was difficult, so I catnapped most of the way. Finally, the pilot announced our arrival at Tan Son Nhut airport near Saigon. It was daylight outside as I strained my neck and eyes to peer through the small porthole for my first glimpse of the foreign land below. I heaved a sigh of relief at the familiar sound of screeching rubber on pavement. The long ride was over.

Armed military policemen (MPs) boarded the plane and ushered us off into awaiting military buses with bars and thick wire mesh replacing glass windows. For the first time, I saw a beautiful German shepherd sentry dog and his handler in combat gear standing a short distance from the aircraft. I thought, *Wow! I didn't know they had dogs over here.* Little did I know then that this quick sighting of a Vietnam war dog was a glimpse into my future.

The driver told us that the wire mesh over the windows was to protect us from being hit by grenades that might be hurled at the bus while we traveled through the crowded city of Saigon. I smelled the hot, sticky air with its peculiar odor of stale fish. Raised in the Denver suburb of Littleton, Colorado, I had never experienced a climate or permeating smell like this. Where I came from, the air was dry, fresh, and clear, the land a mile above sea level.

As the bus slowly maneuvered its way through the crowded streets, I stared at the foreign cars, bicycle riders, and pedestrians. Most of the people wore black or white pajamas, straw hats, and flip-flop sandals. During the ride I didn't hear any shooting, witness any explosions, or see any buildings on fire. In fact, I didn't see anything in the city of Saigon but Vietnamese civilians and soldiers going about their business in peace.

I thought, *Where is the war?*

The bus finally stopped at the front gate, where a sign read "Camp Alpha." It was a U.S. Army replacement center. Armed MPs quickly herded us into a large wooden building to be in-processed. After handing over our assignment orders, personnel files, finance and medical records, we were moved into another part of the building. No one talked much. I felt like a robot following orders: "Stop! Wait here! Follow me! That's far enough!"

The camp commander arrived wearing a clean starched khaki uniform with polished brass, shined shoes, and silver leaves on his collar designating the rank of a lieutenant colonel (LTC). He greeted our group with a smile and gave a "Welcome to Vietnam" orientation. He briefed us on the Vietnamese culture and why we had been sent to help stop the spread of Communism from

North to South Vietnam. Our military presence was stated as no more than a "police action," because the United States had not declared war on North Vietnam.

I whispered to the soldier next to me, "What the hell is the difference between a *declared war* and a *police action* if both sides are killing each other?" I didn't get a response, so I shut up and continued to listen. Fresh out of high school with only a few months of military service and training, I was not sure what to expect next.

Camp Alpha consisted of long rows of wooden buildings with tin roofs and screens for windows. It reminded me of the infantry training centers I had stayed in at Fort Leonardwood, Missouri, Fort Ord, California, and Fort Benning, Georgia. I was housed in a numbered wooden building with a concrete slab floor and several rows of metal bunk beds lining the inside walls. Each building accommodated about fifty men and had electric lights but no air conditioning. I doubted that I would ever adjust to the heat, humidity, or the persistent smell of stale fish in Vietnam.

Most of the replacements were bewildered teenagers like me, fresh out of training with a quarter inch of hair on their heads, wearing new fatigue uniforms and army-issue baseball hats. A tall barbed-wire fence surrounded the camp and armed guards were stationed in towers. I felt like I was living in a small prison.

Camp Alpha had a small store where one could buy soft drinks, candy, cigarettes, toothpaste, and other assorted sundries. A small service club featured live music sung by a Vietnamese rock-and-roll band. I thought it was hilarious that the musicians couldn't speak English and butchered the words of Rolling Stones and Beatles songs. The club was always crowded, sticky hot, and filled with cigarette smoke. There was nowhere else to unwind except a small chapel with posted notices for religious services.

Being a gregarious person by nature, I usually started conversations by asking a soldier where he was from or what his job or Military Occupational Specialty (MOS) was. I met guys from almost every state in the Union. There were truck drivers, medics, helicopter and vehicle mechanics, personnel and supply clerks, military police, cooks, and construction engineers. Most of them had trained for jobs other than infantry.

During my stay at Camp Alpha, I met Kenny Mook, a twenty-one-year-old draftee from the farmlands of northern Pennsylvania. I had no idea at the time that we would soon be fighting for our lives in a place called Bong Son, an experience that would bond us for life.

Both Kenny and I were in excellent health and physical condition. Before joining the army, I had played varsity football and baseball at Littleton High School. I had also placed first in several conference and invitational wrestling tournaments in the 122-pound class. Kenny wasn't an athlete but he was strong from farming in northern Pennsylvania.

We felt a certain kind of chemistry between us and quickly became friends. And we were both infantrymen, destined to fight in the jungle, defend a base camp, and protect supply roads, airfields, motor pools, and hospitals. Although our mission was a little scary, we liked to talk about how important our jobs were.

Kenny was what paratroopers call a *Leg*—a nickname for an infantryman who was not trained as a paratrooper to jump out of airplanes at twelve hundred feet. To become a paratrooper, a soldier had to be a volunteer and pass a three-week training course that was both physically and mentally taxing and had a high rate of dropouts.

I said, "I didn't go to three weeks of jump school hell to be assigned to an infantry Leg unit. I'm sure the army will assign me to an elite paratrooper outfit."

Kenny replied, "The only things that fall out of the sky are bird shit and fools. Besides, after you land, you're a Leg, too."

Throughout our infantry marksmanship training, Kenny and I had both trained on the M14 rifle. We didn't know what the standard issue M16 rifles looked like until we saw camp guards carrying them. I asked one of the sergeants who ran the camp if I'd be issued one. The sergeant looked at me with a smile on his face and said, "No!" He told me that Camp Alpha was well protected, and I'd get an M16 when I arrived at my combat unit.

As replacements, we were all unarmed and vulnerable if the enemy attacked Camp Alpha. I worried that by the time I'd be issued a weapon and ammunition during an attack, provided there were enough to go around, I'd be dead. Many frightening thoughts like that ran through my mind while I waited for an assignment to an infantry combat unit.

Less then a week after my arrival, I heard my name called over the loudspeaker to report to the personnel office. Kenny's name was also called. By a stroke of good luck, Kenny and I were assigned to the 1st Air Cavalry Division located in the central highlands about 250 miles northwest of Saigon.

Kenny and I were sick of replacement centers, both stateside and in-country, and we were always happy to leave them. We knew their routine all too well: "Hurry up and wait." I'd been waiting six months to get assigned to an active unit that was not a training or replacement center. Now, by late March 1966 my training was over, the travel had ended, and replacement centers were about to be history. I relished my new prospect of fighting in real combat as an elite paratrooper.

There would be some life-and-death experiences before my adventures with German shepherd war dogs. But now, at last, Kenny and I were heading for the mountains of South Vietnam. I wondered how it would feel jumping out of a plane with a parachute in a war zone for the first time.

Gary Owen

In the early morning light, Kenny and I hauled our duffel bags up the ramp of a C130 military transport plane that quickly filled with troops and supplies. The pilot wasted little time getting airborne. For the first time since I'd arrived in Vietnam, I felt cool air.

It was incredibly noisy riding inside of that plane and almost impossible to carry on a conversation without yelling. The aircraft flew north of Saigon for several hours before the pilot banked the plane left and began his descent. As I peered through the small window, I saw an airstrip and rows and rows of green military tents and equipment below. Camp Radcliff, home of the 1st Cavalry Division, was directly below us. Kenny pointed out a large yellow and black 1st Cavalry Division shoulder patch painted on the mountainside above the camp.

I thrilled at the thought that we would soon be wearing that patch.

The circular base camp was surrounded by dense jungle and mountains. The small Vietnamese village of An Khe rested near the camp's outer perimeter. Trucks, jeeps, and troops moved along the dirt roads that ran through the camp. Helicopters sat idle in neat rows along the airstrip, which was called "The Golf Course" because it was so enormous. The 1st Cavalry Division, nicknamed "The First Team," had more helicopters than any other division in Vietnam.

From the air, the camp appeared well fortified. The vegetation around the outer edges of the camp was bulldozed, leaving a 360-degree dirt buffer that separated the heavily guarded perimeter from the surrounding jungle. It made for clear lanes of fire in all directions. Three or four heavily fortified bunkers were evenly spaced between lookout towers. Strategically positioned artillery pieces and tanks dotted the perimeter.

After the plane landed, we were hustled to the division's personnel and administration building. A clerk collected our individual personnel, finance, and medical records to process us into the division. We had to show our two metal dog tags hanging from chains around our necks. If a soldier was killed, the medic would take one dog tag from the chain and lodge the other one between the dead man's teeth. One dog tag went to the unit commander for accountability and the other to the morgue with the body for identification.

The personnel clerk congratulated us as he handed over a set of orders officially promoting us from private to private first class. The army's policy at the time was to make such a promotion effective on a soldier's arrival in South Vietnam. That meant a monthly pay increase of at least $50. We also got another $60 per month as combat pay. At the time, I made $300 a month and didn't have to pay taxes. If I was assigned to a paratrooper outfit, I'd get an additional $55 monthly.

An infantry division's organizational structure is layered in the shape of a pyramid. At the top is the division commander, a two-star general, who had the ultimate power and authority. The division commander's subordinate commanders, in order of power, are the brigade commander, battalion commander, company commander, and then the platoon leader. These are all command positions occupied by commissioned officers.

There may be three brigades in a division, three battalions in a brigade, and four companies in each battalion. In each company, there may be four platoons made up of four squads of enlisted men. There are eleven enlisted men in a squad at full strength. Each squad has two fire teams commanded by a squad leader and two fire team leaders. A platoon at full strength has a total of forty-four infantrymen.

The enlisted structure is layered in authority starting with the division sergeant major, brigade sergeant major, battalion sergeant major, company first sergeant, platoon sergeant, squad leader, fire team leader and then the riflemen. Kenny and I were riflemen—peons with no authority.

We were assigned to Company B, 1st Battalion, 7th Cavalry Regiment. George Armstrong Custer had commanded the 7th Cavalry Regiment in 1876 at Little Big Horn. Whenever we passed an officer outside the cover of a building, the 7th Cavalry tradition was to say "Gary Owen" as we saluted. "Gary Owen" was the title of General Custer's favorite Irish marching song, which he liked to have the 7th Regiment band play at parades and other festive military functions. I felt a sense of pride that this historical tradition had continued to be observed through the years.

Our new home was a skimpy old green canvas tent surrounded

with sandbags stacked waist-high and held up by two wooden center poles and wooden tie-down stakes. Several empty canvas cots stood on a dirt-packed floor inside. I couldn't believe that this dark and misty tent would be my home for the next twelve months.

Kenny said, "Well, Johnny, we're finally here."

"Yeah, but I wonder where in the hell the platoon is. All I saw when we flew in were mountains and very little civilization."

"We're not in Saigon anymore," Kenny said. "We're in a war zone. The platoon is probably out in the jungle hunting for the enemy."

The dining hall, or *mess hall* as we called it, was a large wooden building not far from our tent. Just outside it were large green canvas bags full of drinking water. We ate from metal trays and sat on picnic tables. Breakfast consisted of powdered eggs, powdered milk, fresh baked bread, and bitter coffee. Lunch and dinner were nothing to write home about.

After we ate breakfast that morning and were on the way back to our tent, we passed an officer, saluted him, and said, "Gary Owen, sir!"

The officer returned the salute and replied, "All the way!"

After the officer had passed, Kenny and I looked at each other and chuckled. We thought it was really cool to say "Gary Owen!" instead of "Good morning, sir!"

Kenny and I were introduced to the company supply sergeant. He lived in a tent that was packed and stacked high with supplies. The supply sergeant told us that he had everything we'd ever need for fighting a war. He issued us backpacks, water canteens, ammunition pouches, medical field dressings, a plastic poncho, a nylon poncho liner, a helmet (steel pot), a helmet liner, an entrenching tool (field shovel), and a bayonet. The supply sergeant also gave us several division patches like the one we saw on the mountainside when we flew into the base. The cloth insignia on these patches meant that we were no longer trainees in transit without a unit—we now belonged to a fighting unit.

The supply sergeant told us we'd get weapons, ammunition, grenades, claymores (mines), trip flares, and other goodies after the platoon returned from its mission in the field. He advised us that our new platoon sergeant would decide when we'd be ready to go on S and Ds.

I asked, "What are S and Ds?"

The supply sergeant smiled and shook his head and said, "Search and destroy missions. That's what we do for a living around here, young trooper!"

Kenny and I wondered what it would be like to meet the other members of the 2nd Platoon due to arrive within the hour aboard helicopters. I was nervous yet eager to see real combat infantrymen for the first time. *Would the other soldiers accept us?* I wondered. Kenny appeared to be calm, but his eyes showed that he too was a little nervous.

The sounds of helicopters filled the air outside. I ran out of the tent for a look. Fifteen or twenty ships drifted into view.

Fully equipped soldiers clutched their weapons and sat inside the open doors. The door gunners held M60 machine guns mounted on posts.

Dirt kicked up as the first group of ships touched down about one hundred feet away from us. The wind from the helicopters' rotating blades rippled our fatigues and almost whipped the caps off our heads. The dust was swirling all around me as I watched with excitement as the men climbed out and slowly walked in my direction. The door gunners stayed aboard as the empty ships lifted off the road and flew away.

I watched, awestruck, while the men walked past me as if I were invisible. Under their steel helmets, I could see the soldiers' tired faces and eyes. Their dirty fatigues and boots looked as if they hadn't been polished since they were issued. The men carried various types of shoulder weapons, some of which I'd never seen before. They wore backpacks filled with items that I couldn't see. As the men walked by, I noticed that they looked and smelled as if they hadn't taken a bath in a month.

Some of the soldiers entered the tent Kenny lived in. I was too nervous to follow them inside. Finally, I gathered up enough courage, walked in, and sat on my cot like a little kid, silently watching the soldiers unpack their gear. Kenny sat on his cot too and quietly observed everyone. It was easy to see that they were happy to be back in base camp.

A short time later, two men walked into the tent and called our names: "PFC Kenneth L. Mook and PFC John C. Burnam."

Kenny and I jumped to our feet and answered, "Here!"

The men approached us, stopped, and looked us over in silence. We remained standing to show respect as we'd been taught during training. The men looked at one another, smiled, and told us to sit down and relax. They were amused at our innocent behavior. One man introduced himself as Sergeant Savage. He was five-feet-seven inches, about twenty-three-years old, and huskily built; he had a hardened darkly tanned face. Sergeant Savage introduced Sergeant Dorman to us as our new squad leader, then he excused himself.

Sergeant Dorman smiled and said, "I'm your squad leader. Welcome to the 2nd Platoon and 4th Squad, better known as the *weapons squad.*"

Sergeant Dorman was a thin, twenty-two-year-old man, five-feet-eight inches tall, with bright blue eyes, brown hair, and a deep tan. Even though he hadn't cleaned up yet, Sergeant Dorman had the appearance and presence of a leader who spoke with confidence. He reached into his breast pocket and took out a little green notepad. He asked us for our full names, ranks, ages, service numbers, types of training we'd had, hometowns, next of kin, and the dates we had arrived in Vietnam. He recorded our answers in his notebook.

Sergeant Dorman explained that a weapons squad had two five-man machine gun teams. Each machine gun team had one M60 machine gun. Each team consisted of one gunner, an assistant gunner, and three riflemen/ammunition bearers.

He said, "That's an ideal, fully manned squad. The problem is that I only have two M60 machine gunners and one assistant M60 machine gunner. My squad is critically undermanned. You men are a sight for sore eyes. Forget whatever you were taught in the States about machine gun deployment. Even though my squad is undermanned, it's still the primary firepower of the 2nd

Platoon. When the shit hits the fan there's nothing better than the M60. Counting you two, I now have three men on the number two gun and two men on the number one gun."

As Sergeant Dorman continued, I gathered that the number one gun provided firepower to the front and the number two gun provided firepower and security at the rear of the platoon.

We met the number one M60 gunner, Specialist Four (SP4) Engles, and his assistant gunner, Private Wildman, and the number two M60 gunner, SP4 Bob Dunn. Sergeant Dorman appointed Kenny as Bob's assistant gunner and I was assigned as Bob's ammo-bearer.

Bob Dunn was five-foot-seven inches tall, weighed about 170 pounds, with blond hair and blue eyes, and wore a crusty mustache. Bob was from New York and spoke in a heavy accent. He had arrived in Vietnam in early January 1966.

I asked Bob where the platoon had been. He said that they'd searched the jungle for a week but had made no contact with the Gooks.

I said, "You mean the enemy?"

Bob then translated some new terminology for me. He explained that *VC* meant Viet Cong, *NVA* was the North Vietnamese Army, and *PAVN* meant the Peoples Army of Vietnam. *Cong, Dinks,* and *Charlie* were other terms used to describe the enemy. The NVA, he said, were the toughest of all to fight.

As we started talking about our duties, Bob explained the importance of keeping the M60 machine gun clean and oiled at all times. Out in the jungle, he told us, the gun got dirty quickly. The rain and humidity caused any part that wasn't oiled to rust and possibly malfunction.

SP4 Dunn explained what the squad's job was. "We get an operations order for a mission. We pack up and leave base camp for a week or so. We hunt and kill some Gooks. After that, we come home for a few days to shower, rest, and get some hot food. Then it starts all over again. Believe me, you guys will get your share of the action and then some."

When Bob gave me my first M16 rifle, I acted like a little kid with a new Christmas toy. Kenny and I test-fired our weapons at a safe location on the camp's perimeter. Bob taught us how to take them apart, put them together, and showed us where to put the most oil.

My previous training had taught me how to maintain sight alignment, control breathing, and squeeze the trigger. I was surprised that the M16 had little or no kick. As with all military rifles and pistols, the M16 was designed for right-handed people. When the guns are fired, hot brass casings eject to the right and away from the right-handed shooter. Because I was left-handed, the hot brass casings ejected across my face and body. Not a big problem, but on a rare occasion, I'd get a hot casing blown down my collar.

During training in the States, Kenny and I had been awarded Expert Rifle badges for consistently scoring hits in the center of targets with M14 rifles. The different qualification levels of marksmanship were, from lowest to highest ranking: expert, sharpshooter, and marksman. The targets, positioned at various ranges, had been both pop-up and stationary. Shooting positions—standing, prone, or kneeling—also varied based on target range. Hitting a target dead center was all in the sight alignment, breathing, and trigger squeeze. Kenny had also scored at the expert level with the M60 machine gun. Most soldiers qualified as sharp-shooters or marksmen, but you were very well-respected when you qualified as an expert with two types of weapons. This is probably why Kenny got to be Bob's assistant machine gunner.

As we trained in camp, SP4 Dunn gave us some pointers on how to conserve ammunition. He said, "Never switch to full automatic unless there's no other choice. Always carry your own supply of ammunition. The quicker you use it up, the less you'll have when you need it most." The training sessions boosted my self-confidence. As each day passed, Kenny and I felt more like members of the platoon team. We would need this camaraderie, because soon we'd be meeting Charlie face-to-face for the first time.

Ia Drang Valley

A few days before my first mission, Sergeant Dorman told a story to Kenny and me to fill us in on the history of our new platoon. It was about a mission that took place in the middle of November 1965.

The 2nd Battalion, 7th Cavalry had gone looking for a fight and flew into the Ia Drang valley—a remote area in the northern highlands of South Vietnam, at the base of the Chu Pong Mountain, close to the Cambodian border. Lieutenant Colonel Moore, the battalion commander, had led the battalion into the valley with the 2nd Platoon, making it one of the first on the ground. Immediately, the landing zone, known as LZ XRAY, was saturated with American artillery.

Sergeant Dorman held us spellbound as he recounted the events of that day:

> When our platoon landed, we rushed into the woods with our guns firing. Lieutenant Colonel Moore directed our leader to move the 2nd Platoon about 100 meters and set up a new position. The platoon fanned out and ran forward toward the base of Chu Pong Mountain. We spotted two or three enemy soldiers moving across our front, and the platoon leader ordered us to chase and capture them. We pursued the enemy

for fifty meters and ran into 150 NVA soldiers dressed in khaki uniforms, wearing pith helmets, and coming down off the mountain shooting at us.

These were hard-core troops from North Vietnam, not your ordinary black pajama, part-time soldier/ farmer. When they attacked us, we took casualties before we could hit the dirt and return their fire. We tried to get behind anything that would provide cover, but we were pinned down by heavy fire and cut off from the rest of the company.

The platoon spread out. We took cover behind clumps of bushes and trees. Communication was nearly impossible above the noise of blazing machine guns, rifle fire, and grenade explosions. Totally out-numbered, we fought for our lives.

We were so overwhelmed. Many of our men were already wounded or dead. The Gooks screamed at the top of their lungs while they came at us shooting. A few missions before Ia Drang, a member of the 2nd Platoon had died after drowning in a river. The men in the platoon had blamed our platoon leader for the man's death, but he hadn't been relieved of his com-mand. It was no secret that many of us had lost our respect for him, but in this battle, during one of the enemy's human wave attacks, this platoon leader was badly wounded and died bravely, fighting alongside his men.

The weapons squad suffered so many casualties that the squad leader took over one of the M60s. He fired it until he was overrun and killed. Then the Gooks turned our M60 machine gun on us. We had several more casualties before we took it back. Low on ammunition and grenades, we gathered what we could from our own dead.

I don't know how we made it after losing the platoon leader, the platoon sergeant, and the squad leaders. Sergeant Savage was the only sergeant left, so he took over the platoon. He got on the radio and found cover behind a log while he called for artillery strikes. We fought, on and off, all day and into the night. Sergeant Savage continued to send periodic situation reports over the radio. We received radio reports that the entire battalion was under heavy ground attack by the NVA. Hundreds of enemy soldiers were storming down from the mountain to join the fight. We were too far out for any immediate rescue attempts. Our orders were to hold our ground until help arrived the next day.

It was very dark that first night, but none of us slept. We kept quiet and tried to comfort the wounded as we waited to be attacked again. During that night, I heard a bugle call coming from the mountain, and then all hell broke loose again. We withstood several attacks and survived until sky troopers from a sister company rescued us in the afternoon of the second day. The 2nd Platoon became known as the *Lost Platoon* because we'd been the only platoon outside the battalion lines of defense.

The battle raged for a third day. B52 bombers dropped tons of bombs on Chu Pong mountain and the surrounding area. When the fighting was over, our battalion had taken heavy casualties; our company had forty men left out of 115. The North Vietnamese Army had lost over a thousand men. At the time, I was a rifleman in the 2nd Squad of the 2nd Platoon. I don't know how I survived without getting killed. There were bodies all over the place. The Gooks and Americans were lying dead next to each other. That was how close the fighting had become.

Our battered troops were relieved by a sister battalion—2nd Battalion, 7th Cavalry. We were flown out by helicopter for much-needed rest. The 2nd Battalion, 7th Cavalry moved on foot a mile or so away to LZ Albany. They marched in columns, strung out through the woods. We figured the fight and cleanup was over, but the North Vietnamese Army had other plans. They had fresh battalions in reserve—men who were waiting to join the action and kill Americans. The enemy paralleled the American movement until they were in a position to do the most damage. In a matter of several hours, they cut to ribbons and wiped out an entire American battalion of several hundred men.

Most of our battalion had been in-country for a little over two months before that battle during which hundreds of them were wounded or killed in Ia Drang valley. Afterward, I was promoted to sergeant and became the weapons squad leader.

After losing so many men, the replacements we needed in the weapons squad didn't arrive until January. First, SP4 Engles, SP4 Dunn, and PVT Wildman arrived. You and Kenny are the second set of replacements. It's now the first week of April and my weapons squad is still short-handed.

I only have to make it a few more months before I go home in August. We haven't been back to Ia Drang since November. I hope that I never have to see the place again.

With tears in his eyes, Sergeant Dorman got up, excused himself, and quickly left. I was wide-eyed, astounded, and speechless. What could I say to someone like him? I felt honored and humbled to know this brave man who had such an extraordinary story, but frightened too. I'd been stateside in Uncle Sam's army for about a month at the time of the Ia Drang valley battle. Now I was assigned to a platoon that had been almost wiped out there.

Would I be brave in the face of the enemy or too scared to fight? Would I be killed instantly, severely wounded, or survive like Sergeant Dorman? I wondered. I found it difficult to sleep the night after Sergeant Dorman told us his story. Instead, I stayed awake, thinking about the Lost Platoon.

A few days later, Sergeant Dorman came into our tent and said, "Wake up and listen. After you clean up and get some breakfast, meet me here for an operations order."

I got out of my cot, grabbed my shaving gear, and slipped on my *rice-paddy-racers* (our nickname for rubber flip-flops). I headed for the showers, which consisted of several green fifty-gallon drums welded together, sitting on top of a wood frame with canvas siding. Flat wooden pallets underneath the showerheads provided a place to stand above the moldy, wet, mosquito-infested ground underneath. A trench was dug around the wooden pallets for water drainage. Towels and clothes hung on nails hammered into the posts holding the shower frame together. A faucet attached to a pipe controlled the flow of cold water. There was no hot water. We took quick showers to conserve water for others and shaved outside the shower, using our steel helmets as sinks. Water tankers filled the shower water containers daily when the troops were in from the field.

After showers and shaves, it was time for breakfast. Kenny and I sat at a picnic table with our new team leader, Bob Dunn. He couldn't tell us anything more about our upcoming mission or operations order. I ate fast and returned to my tent. A few minutes later, everyone else in the weapons squad came back from breakfast.

Sergeant Dorman arrived and gathered us together. He took out his green notebook, glanced at his notes, and began to talk in a serious tone.

"We are going back to Ia Drang valley," he said.

From the story he'd told us only a few days before, Kenny and I knew how Sergeant Dorman must have felt about returning to Ia Drang, but he didn't betray his emotions. Instead, he put his military field map down and pointed to a grid that he knew all too well. The terrain appeared wooded and flat until it reached the base of Chu Pong Mountain. Inside the wooded area, near the base of the mountain, LZ XRAY was clearly marked on the map in grease pencil. The Cambodian border was within walking distance from the LZ. The entire area was completely isolated from any roads or villages.

Sergeant Dorman said, "S2 Battalion Intelligence reported small concentrations of enemy troops operating in this area. Our mission is to engage the enemy but not pursue them across the Cambodian border.

"We'll link up with the rest of the company when we get to LZ XRAY, and set up in a company-sized perimeter. Our objective is to check out the area, hike up Chu Pong Mountain, and look for enemy base camps. Then we'll sweep the Ia Drang valley, southeast to LZ Victor, spend the night there, and come back home the next day. We'll be supported by field artillery, gunships, and jet fighters, if necessary.

"Pack a basic load and enough food for three days. We'll be resupplied in the field. Be ready to move out to the road for pickup in an hour. Are there any questions?"

Sergeant Dorman looked at Kenny and me and said, "You two are about to get your cherries busted." He knew, and now we knew, that we were going to lose our innocence on this mission.

Bob Dunn turned to Kenny and said, "Don't forget to pick up the M60 machine gun spare parts bag from my tent."

The spare parts bag contained one extra gun barrel, an asbestos glove used to grab and change the barrel when it got too hot, cleaning rods, metal chamber, bore brushes, small oil cans, and cleaning cloths. It had a shoulder strap and weighed about twelve pounds.

I grabbed my pack and filled it with several pairs of socks, underwear, and T-shirts. I checked my shaving kit to make sure I had a toothbrush, shaving cream, soap dish with a new bar of soap, a bottle of aftershave lotion, a hand towel, and a razor. I decided to pack writing paper and envelopes in case I had time to write letters home. With my small canvas pack already full, Bob directed me to go with Kenny to the supply tent to pick up a basic load of M16 rifle ammunition (three 100-rounds), two grenades, two trip flares, one claymore mine, and eight 100-rounds of machine gun ammunition.

I thought, *Damn! That's a hell of a lot of extra shit to carry.*

When I got back with everything, I had twenty M16 magazines and twenty boxes of ammunition. I loaded each magazine and discarded the empty cartons, inserted several clips in a bandolier with a shoulder strap, and crammed the rest of the M16 clips into my pack. I rolled my poncho as small and tight as I could and strapped it underneath the pack.

The M60 machine gun ammunition was issued in a 100-round belt per box. Every fifth round was a red tracer, which lit up when it left the barrel. Tracers were used to help zero in on a target and for night firing. Each box came with a green cloth bag and a strap so it could be carried slung from the shoulder.

Kenny put two boxes of M60 machine gun ammunition in the spare parts bag. He set the other two boxes aside to be carried over his shoulder. I brought two 100-round boxes and Bob attached a 100-round belt to the feeding mechanism of the M60 machine gun. My pistol belt held two canteens of water, two ammunition pouches, two grenades, one bayonet, and a field shovel. We attached adjustable shoulder straps to the backpack and pistol belt to help distribute the weight more evenly between the small of the back and shoulders. Medical field bandages, attached to metal D rings, were sewn to the shoulder harness. We placed a plastic bottle of mosquito repellent inside the elastic headband on top of the steel pot.

I lifted the pack onto my back. When I bent over to pick up my M16 rifle and steel pot, the weight shifted forward. I nearly fell on my face. Soaking wet, I may have weighed 130 pounds, but the pack added at least fifty pounds. My feet pressed heavily into the soles of my boots. I didn't know how I was going to carry all that stuff for any great distance, let alone climb Chu Pong Mountain with it. Kenny looked surprised at the weight of his load as well.

When I thought I had everything packed, Bob told me to put my gear down and get three days of C rations. Each soldier was issued a case of C rations that contained twelve meals. A case of C rations was a little larger than a case of beer and about as heavy. When I got back to the tent, there was little time before I had to be at the road for pickup.

I complained, "How am I going to carry nine meals when my pack is full and I have all this other stuff to carry?"

Bob looked at my gear and asked, "What the hell did you pack?"

"Extra clothes, shaving gear, and ammunition," I replied.

Bob laughed. "Take the extra clothes out and use the room to pack essentials. Put cans of food in your long green socks and tie them to your shoulder harness. By the way, John, I know your pack is heavy. Mine is too. Pack only the bare necessities and as much ammunition as you can carry. Also, take only what you think you'll eat for three days and leave the rest here."

Although I felt like a complete moron, I did everything Bob said. It was my first mission, so what the hell did I know?

Sergeant Dorman spoke in a loud voice, "Saddle up!"

I looked awkward in my new gear. When I walked, it sounded as if I were carrying pots and pans. Kenny seemed a little uncomfortable, too. The other soldiers in the platoon looked at us as if we were recruits, but didn't say a word. When we reached the road, we joined the other members of the weapons squad. We sat and waited for the choppers that morning in the hot sun.

———————

Sergeant Dorman briefed the squad on the loading plan. We were to split into machine gun teams—one on each side of the road. When the choppers landed, soldiers were to simultaneously board from both sides of the ship.

The first group of choppers landed and SP4 Engles and PFC Wildman climbed aboard with members of another squad. The ships quickly took off and another group of slicks landed. Sergeant Dorman ordered our machine gun team to board the closest ship. When it touched down, I ran a short distance and climbed aboard. I sat down against the inside wall away from the open door. I felt a little uncomfortable because the doors remained open during flight.

As the ship lifted off the ground, I felt the metal floor vibrate and rattle. I braced myself. I thought I'd slide across the floor and out of the open door. My stomach was full of butterflies. It felt as if I were going down the first steep drop of a roller-coaster ride. As the aircraft gained altitude, it joined a column formation of other ships. I was still a little tense when the helicopter reached cruising altitude a few thousand feet up. As I looked down, I watched the base camp slowly disappear. Several gunships flew escort at a lower altitude barely above the treetops.

At least thirty ships were in the air. I could see men sitting inside the helicopters flying alongside us. Despite my nervousness, I thought that riding inside a fully armed formation of flying warships was an awesome view and feeling.

The cool air felt good against my face. As I looked around, I noticed that no one talked. Everyone stared out of the open doors of the ship. The door gunners had their machine guns loaded and tilted down. They wore green flight crew helmets with intercoms so they could communicate with the two pilots. The formation of ships traveled for about an hour before descending. Then the treetops came closer and closer.

Green smoke swirled up from the ground of LZ XRAY in the Ia Drang valley, indicating that the LZ was cleared for landing. The gunships buzzed around the zone as the choppers approached the landing area. In the near distance, Chu Pong Mountain stuck out like a pyramid covered with tropical vegetation. When our chopper got ready to land, I noticed the other soldiers scooting closer to the open doors. As soon as the landing gear touched the earth, everyone quickly jumped out. Kenny and I followed Bob and we created a small perimeter around the ship until it lifted away.

Sergeant Dorman barked, "Bob, get your gun over to those trees and cover our asses."

Bob ran. Kenny and I followed to a tree line about fifty yards out. My adrenaline spiked. My eyes were wide open scanning for anything unusual. Bob put the gun down on its bipod. He loaded the chamber for firing. He told me to move to my left and link up with the next man in the platoon. I reacted without saying a word. About twenty yards away, I spotted another member of the platoon. After we made eye contact, I dropped down on one knee and faced out into the surrounding trees.

The helicopters kept landing with more troops. Bob and Kenny manned the M60 machine gun about forty yards from the landing zone and about five yards to the left of my position. Knee-high grass, dried by the hot sun, surrounded the trees. I nervously tapped the bottom of the magazine inserted into the M16 rifle. I loaded a round into the chamber and made sure the selector switch was on "safe." Everyone lay quietly in a prone position on the hard dry grass. I scanned my front, trying to see and listen for anything resembling enemy movement. Minutes passed. Nothing happened. Sergeant Dorman was busy going from man to man, checking that each of us was present and in correct position.

Sergeant Dorman ordered Bob to follow him to a better location. Kenny and I briskly moved behind them in a crouched position. As I walked, my helmet felt loose on my head and kept moving in front of my eyes. When we finally stopped, Sergeant Dorman pointed where he wanted the M60 machine gun set up. The position he picked faced Chu Pong Mountain.

He instructed Bob, "Before you dig in, check in front of your position about thirty yards to make sure you know there's nothing out there."

Bob took Kenny with him but ordered me to stay back to

cover them. They slowly walked around with the machine gun at the ready and returned with nothing to report.

Over one hundred men were on the ground by then. The gunships still buzzed around but weren't firing. Gunships didn't have door gunners but were heavily armed with machine guns and aerial rocket artillery, controlled by the pilots. I felt safe but still didn't know what I was doing or what to expect.

The order was given to dig in. Bob stood guard behind the M60, while Kenny and I dug a three-man foxhole. Sergeant Dorman said he normally didn't put three men in one position, but since we were new, he wanted Bob to teach us how to set up a machine gun position.

After we dug the foxhole, Bob showed Kenny and me how to set up a claymore mine. He said, "The first thing to remember is that the claymore has FRONT printed in large letters on one side. Be sure to point that side in the direction of the enemy. Claymores are real easy to set up, but if you don't do it right, Charlie will turn the mines around and place them closer to your foxhole. When it's time to squeeze the trigger, you'll blow up your own ass. Remember, surprise is important. Camouflage the mine without disturbing the natural look of the surrounding vegetation. A claymore mine has a fifty-foot wire. One end has the blasting cap attached. It screws inside a well in the claymore. The other end has the trigger mechanism. There's also a circuit tester to make sure it's armed.

"Don't set trip flares out during the day. Do it right before dark. Trip flares are a little touchy, but you want them that way. When the enemy trips the wire, the pin should easily pop out and ignite the flare. To keep Charlie from tampering, attach a second trip wire to the bottom of the claymore. Charlie will be caught by surprise like a deer in headlights. Then we'll kill him."

Patrols were scheduled for the next morning to search the area and climb Chu Pong Mountain. The sun was setting. I went out with Bob to assemble the claymores and trip flares while Kenny watched from behind the machine gun. When we got back, I boasted to Kenny with a big smile and said, "It's a cinch!"

Kenny replied, "Good, then you can do it all the time."

Bob laughed and said, "Kenny, tomorrow it's your turn."

Sergeant Dorman came by to remind us to keep alert and to make sure someone manned the M60 machine gun at all times. He also gave us the password for the night. We would use the password, which changed daily, to get back through friendly lines if people got split up during a fire fight at night.

Bob scheduled two-hour guard shifts. Everyone ate supper before the first watch. I used a tiny can opener, called a P38, to open a warm can of beefsteak and potatoes. It tasted terrible, but I ate every bit of it.

Each box of C rations had a dark brown plastic bag full of goodies—a plastic spoon; a tiny roll of toilet paper; a sample-size box of four cigarettes; little packets of sugar, creamer, salt, and pepper; one book of matches; and a packet of instant coffee.

To cover our exposed skin, we used mosquito repellent. It was powerful enough to keep the bugs from biting us at night. Each man carried a green plastic poncho to sleep on. By then, I'd concluded that sleeping in a foxhole was like sleeping in a grave.

At first light, everyone awoke. We used water from canteens to brush our teeth, wash up, and mix powdered coffee. We were required to have a clean-shaven face, even though no one but the army cared what we looked like. When I finished shaving, I slapped on some Mennen Skin Bracer.

To my surprise, Bob blurted, "Who the hell has the aftershave lotion on?"

I confessed, and Bob ripped into me. He said, "You can't go on patrol smelling like a whore. Charlie will smell you a mile away. Charlie has instincts like a fucking animal. He lives out here, for crying out loud. What the hell is wrong with you? You don't need to fucking help him out."

I was stunned and so embarrassed that I didn't say a word. I also knew the smell would take time to wear off. I quietly dug a hole and buried that bottle of Mennen Skin Bracer and wiped my face with dirt, trying to get rid of the smell. When Sergeant Dorman found out what I did, he couldn't stop howling. Before long, I was the topic of conversation throughout the platoon. They called me "The Mennen Boy."

What a way to start my first full day in the field with a bunch of veterans!

Bob and Kenny went to retrieve the trip flares and claymores. Our orders were to hike to Chu Pong Mountain and scout for enemy base camps. Sergeant Dorman directed the number two machine gun to bring up the rear of the platoon. He ordered the number one machine gun team to get behind the point man. The platoon spread out and traveled in a column formation. Flank guards were placed on each side of the column about twenty-five yards out. With a flat terrain, visibility was good. We walked slowly and cautiously through the trees and knee-high brown grass while avoiding large termite mounds.

I was close to the last man in the formation. We traveled at a slow pace through a clearing. I stepped over a branch and crushed two huge millipedes crawling near my boot. Red ants, called fire ants, covered the trees. When they bit, it stung like hell, so I quickly learned to avoid them.

The patrol halted before reaching the base of the mountain. Nearby, I spotted a helmet on the ground a short distance away. I picked it up. It had a large bullet hole in the front. I examined the inside and saw a piece of dried scalp stuck to the back of the helmet liner. The name on the headband read "Sgt. Bernard." I put it down and wondered about the man who had worn it, feeling sorry that an American had been killed out here in the middle of nowhere. I looked around and noticed that other soldiers were finding remnants of a battle that had previously taken place there.

Shallow foxholes, overgrown with grass, appeared everywhere. Military web gear from a backpack stuck out from a mound of dirt. Tarnished brass from all types of spent shells littered the area around the foxholes. The positions of everything indicated that the fighting had been fierce, possibly hand-to-hand combat.

Kenny located a splintered human jawbone and a skull with a bullet hole in it. Near me, the rains had partly washed away the dirt and exposed what appeared to be human bones. Bob told me that these weren't American remains, because we don't leave our men behind. I wondered how this had all happened. Never in my young nineteen years had I seen this kind of devastation.

The patrol moved out again, and we eventually reached the base of the mountain, which was rugged, dense with vegetation, and dark. The point man used a machete to cut a path. The sunlight barely penetrated to the jungle floor as we started to climb at a snail's pace up the mountain. My pack snagged on vines every step of the way.

We didn't travel far before someone at the head of the platoon spotted a huge enemy base camp built in a large bamboo forest. A few soldiers checked for booby traps before we entered the camp. The entire platoon slowly moved inside. The sunlight reflected off the bamboo, creating a yellow glow. We were warned to watch out for snakes, especially bamboo vipers. I shuddered because I'd always hated the sight of snakes.

We set up a defensive position inside the enemy base camp. Half the platoon spread out and searched the camp, but it was empty. However, we uncovered a huge cache of ammunition, mortars, and rockets, hidden in camouflaged holes in the ground. We found cooking utensils, a meeting area, and a small hospital with a few medical supplies. Bunkers and tiny one-man foxholes dotted the area. Small piles of grenades with wooden handles and strings dangling from them were scattered throughout the camp that looked as if it could have held several hundred North Vietnamese soldiers.

I thought, *This had to be one of the base camps that the enemy used to launch attacks on our company.*

Sergeant Dorman couldn't believe the B52 bombers had missed this place, although it couldn't be seen from the air. There wasn't a crater anywhere inside the base camp. The platoon leader got on the radio to speak with the company commander. They decided to set charges and blow up the enemy munitions.

When we returned to our foxholes that evening, we were dirty and tired. I had to take a shit real bad so I asked Kenny, "Where do you think I should go?"

"Out in the woods, I guess. I haven't had to go yet."

Bob overheard us and said, "We'll cover your ass!"

He and Kenny broke into laughter. It would have been terrible for the enemy to catch me by surprise with my pants down, so I put up with the sarcasm and accepted their protection.

At a creek beside the mountain and about 150 yards from my foxhole, we set up an ambush that night. Sergeant Dorman teamed me with SP4 Johnson, a twenty-five-year-old black soldier and a survivor of the battle of Ia Drang. He spoke in a tense and nervous voice about not being very happy to be in this place again. After we talked for a few minutes, he set up the trip flares and claymores in front of our foxhole.

That night, while on guard duty in the foxhole, I heard rifle and machine gun fire coming from the direction of the creek. Johnson woke up and jumped in the foxhole with me. We pointed our weapons into the darkness and listened and waited to be attacked.

Johnson blurted out, "I hope them Gooks trip the flare so I can blow their asses to hell with the claymore."

He instructed me to put my ammunition in front of me so I could reload as fast as possible. The firing in the distance lasted about a half minute. Then, total silence. Nothing else happened the rest of the night.

The next morning, Sergeant Dorman told us that the 1st

Platoon had killed two enemy soldiers at the creek. He said that the company commander was pissed because someone had sprung the ambush too soon, and the main element had gotten away. The two kills were NVA who had been armed with AK-47 rifles.

Later that morning, the entire company swept the valley to LZ Victor a few miles southeast of LZ XRAY. Our route followed the east side of Chu Pong Mountain parallel to the Cambodian border. I walked next to Kenny. It seemed to get hotter and hotter as we pushed in the direction of LZ Victor. The water inside my canteen was so hot from the sun that it was unbearable to drink, but I forced it down anyway. The temperature must have been over 115 degrees. My fatigue jacket was soaked with sweat.

Almost out of water, with my legs weakening under the heavy load on my back, I kept walking as Kenny pointed out nearby bomb craters. Helicopters flew around to cover our advance through the lightly wooded area. After the platoon stopped for a break, Kenny saw that I was slowing down. Determined not to give in to the heat, I wanted to make it to LZ Victor on my own.

When the platoon stopped again, I drank the last of my water but was unable to stand. I felt dizzy and went down on one knee. I stayed in that position for a moment. Then, struggling to stand, I felt a hand on my shoulder and heard a voice ask, "Are you okay, trooper?"

Without looking up, I replied, "I feel a little dizzy and weak."

"How long have you been in-country?"

I finally looked up and recognized Lieutenant Colonel Moore, the battalion commander who had led the ill-fated battle of Ia Drang valley that Sergeant Dorman had told us about before we'd left.

I tried to steady my legs, but fell against the tree. LTC Moore grabbed me under the arm and held me up. I thanked him and confessed that this was my first mission.

He gave me some water from his canteen and said, "Where are you from, trooper?"

"Littleton, Colorado, sir."

"It's going to take you awhile to get used to this type of heat and humidity, but it's an unusually hot day."

LTC Moore didn't have a pack on, only a belt with a .45-caliber pistol and two canteens of water. He looked fresh, as if he'd just arrived, and he'd hardly broken a sweat. He instructed me to take off the pack.

"Now you'll cool down faster. Grab your rifle and follow me."

LTC Moore picked up my pack and carried it. We walked at a brisk pace, and I finally cooled down. When we got to LZ Victor, I followed my commander to the command post. He gave me my pack and ordered one of his men to fill my canteens and have the medic check on me.

LTC Moore turned and began to walk away, so I said, "Gary Owen, sir!"

He turned and smiled, "All the way, Sky Trooper!"

I made it back to my platoon and didn't see LTC Moore again, but I knew that I'd be forever grateful for that act of kindness from my commander.

Our mission to Ia Drang valley was over. The helicopters lifted us off LZ Victor and we headed home to An Khe. My first mission had taught me valuable lessons about packing gear, riding in troop assault helicopters, moving in a tactical formation, and setting up a defensive position even though I never fired a single shot. My thoughts of not getting an assignment to an elite paratrooper unit didn't seem to matter anymore. I felt lucky to be with the men in the 2nd Platoon.

Later on, I'd learn the value of relying on a German shepherd scout dog to lead me through more treacherous enemy territory in South Vietnam. But my next mission would teach me the reality of combat, which was nothing I could have ever imagined.

Bong Son

By the last week of April 1966, we'd been running patrols every day and had been out in the field for seventeen days guarding Highway 19, a major supply road to An Khe. Although Kenny and I didn't make enemy contact, we continued to learn and gain valuable experience.

Living in a tent was now a luxury compared to how I had to live, eat, sleep, and hunt in the heat, rain, and mud of the Vietnam countryside. But that luxury didn't include companionship with my tent mates. It wasn't easy for me to make friends. Other than Kenny and Bob, I hardly knew the guys who shared my tent. When we moved in a tactical formation, each man maintained a comfortable distance from one another and remained silent for the most part. Riding in loud helicopters made it hard to talk. At night platoon members teamed up in foxholes strategically spaced apart and visiting was not a good idea, so the only men we got to know were the ones with whom we shared a foxhole. I began to realize that getting to know others and making lots of friends wasn't encouraged in a combat zone. The men we befriended one day might be killed in the next battle, so friendships often ended in pain and loss.

Although I didn't think of him as my friend, I looked up to Sergeant Dorman for his leadership. He commanded respect from every member of the platoon and his fellow squad leaders.

Sergeant Dorman always smiled and asked how Kenny and I were getting along. He teased me for being a *cherry jumper*—a paratrooper who had recently graduated from jump school but hadn't made a parachute jump since then. I'd earned my parachute wings by going through a physically rigorous, three-week course at Fort Benning, Georgia, where the dropout rate was traditionally high. There were three levels of paratrooper qualification: basic, senior, and master jumper.

I was proud to wear my paratrooper wings, even though I was not working in a paratrooper outfit. My aspirations of getting assigned to an elite paratrooper unit had diminished since joining the 7th Cavalry. My platoon was my new home and I was going to make the best of it.

Sergeant Dorman advised Kenny and me that soon we'd be eligible to earn a Combat Infantry Badge (CIB), which was awarded only to infantrymen. To qualify for a CIB, a soldier had to have been officially schooled as an infantryman and awarded an 11B Military Occupational Specialty. Ultimately, a soldier had to serve in a combat infantry unit for at least thirty days during wartime. The CIB was considered the badge of courage. Only a small percentage of soldiers in the entire army were authorized to wear a CIB. When a soldier earned it, he wore it with pride.

The CIB, about three inches long and an inch wide, was designed with a long silver rifle inlaid in a small, rectangular, blue-enameled background. An oval silver wreath surrounded the inlaid silver rifle. The CIB was worn above the left breast pocket and above all other service medals, ribbons, and badges. Sergeant Dorman once said, "A CIB is only for men with enough guts to be infantrymen and the balls to hunt Charlie for a living." Sergeant Dorman had already earned his CIB in the battle of Ia Drang valley in November 1965. His combat awards included a Purple Heart for combat wounds, Bronze Star for valor, and an Air Medal for making combat air assaults from Huey helicopters into enemy-held territory while under enemy fire.

Sergeant Dorman was a man you wanted by your side in battle, but there were a couple of men in our squad whom Kenny and I tried to avoid. There was one guy who had a real chip on his shoulder and enjoyed pulling pranks. He seemed to relish getting people agitated. Ever since I'd seen him break a young Vietnamese girl's soft drink bottle for no good reason, sleep on guard duty, and throw a dummy grenade at me, I had no respect for him as a man or soldier. I suppose every platoon had a guy like him. It's strange how the army threw men together and hoped for the best. I worried that this guy would cause someone to get hurt or killed. I didn't have much contact with him in the field and wanted to keep it that way.

But most of the men were all right. Rodriguez (Rod) was a guy Kenny and I got to know the day he showed us how to mix and spice up C rations. A large man of Hispanic descent, Rod was well liked by everyone. He carried himself with a sense of confidence, toughness, and experience. Rod was being considered for the next available promotion to squad leader.

Doc Bell, platoon medic, was not an infantryman, but was highly respected by everyone in the platoon. Doc Bell was a stocky black man with the biggest of smiles. He was a trained combat medical specialist. His job was to take care of casualties, save lives, and issue survival basics such as malaria and salt tablets. Doc Bell's field gear consisted of a large green shoulder bag, containing field medical supplies and .45-caliber pistol. During combat missions, Doc Bell was positioned near the platoon leader and radio/telephone operator. He wasn't eligible for a CIB. Instead, he had earned a Combat Medical Badge, which very few soldiers in the medical field were eligible to receive. Like the CIB, the CMB could only be earned during combat. When in base camp, Doc Bell's quarters were with the medical staff at the battalion aid station. Doc Bell had already experienced combat with the platoon and would soon see more of the same in a place called Bong Son.

By the first week of May 1966, we'd been back in base camp for only a few days when Sergeant Dorman gathered the squad to brief us on a new operations order. He told us we were going to the Bong Son plains. For that mission, dubbed *Operation Davy Crockett,* our entire battalion was to sweep Bong Son from the mountains to the South China Sea.

Sergeant Dorman put his map down on a cot and pointed out the location of the Bong Son plains. The map showed hundreds of rice paddies dotted with hamlets. Our 2nd Platoon would be settling on top of the mountain range bordering the Bong Son for the night. Choppers would pick us up in the morning and fly us into the valley.

S-2 (Battalion Intelligence) reported that Bong Son was a major North Vietnamese Army stronghold. For years, Charlie had used its heavily populated villages as safe havens. Several thousand heavily armed NVA regulars were reported to have been operating in small groups throughout the area of our operation. We were told it was *hot,* meaning that some firefights were already under way between the enemy and our battalion's advance units.

The entire 1st Battalion, 7th Cavalry was to air-assault and eradicate Bong Son of enemy forces. A convoy of troop trucks would be used to transport the battalion from An Khe to Bong Son before loading onto the choppers. Everyone had to pack supplies and ammunition for three days. Sergeant Dorman informed the 4th Squad that when we reached the beach of the South China Sea, we'd be rewarded with a day off to swim in the ocean and eat hot food.

After Sergeant Dorman left the tent, I turned to Kenny and said, "Did you hear him say fighting is already going on?"

"Yes, I did."

"Well, I guess this is it, Kenny. We're finally going to see combat."

For a few seconds, Kenny and I stared at one another. Neither of us said a word.

Then I said, "Kenny, if anything happens to me, please write my family and tell them how it happened. I want them to know from you."

"Johnny," he replied, "if anything happens to me, you write my folks."

At that moment we exchanged addresses and stuffed them into our pockets.

Shortly afterward, I asked Kenny, "Hey, buddy! How do you feel?"

Kenny turned and looked at me with a smile and simply replied, "Fine!"

Having never experienced combat before, I hoped that all the missions leading to this had prepared me to be brave in the face of the enemy.

While I packed my basic load, Bob Dunn came by and asked me how many more belts of M60 ammunition I could carry. Between Bob, Kenny, and me, we had ten belts, a total of one thousand rounds. I told Bob that I would add two more 100-round belts to my load. I also packed several grenades. When I finished packing, my total load weighed at least seventy pounds. I decided not to lighten the load and risk being sorry about my decision later. I was learning to just deal with the weight I had to carry and not complain.

A few more new men had been assigned to the 2nd Platoon since we had returned from our last mission of guarding Route 19. I figured that the new men probably felt the same way Kenny and I had when we prepared for our first mission. They were probably wondering if the veterans would accept them. With our platoon pumped up to twenty-five men, morale was high-spirited. We talked and joked while waiting for orders to move to the pickup point on the road.

A loud voice sounded, "Saddle up!"

We lifted gear onto our shoulders and headed toward a long column of trucks lining the road, bumper to bumper, as far as the eye could see. Each two-and-one-half-ton truck was stripped of its canvas top, except for the cab area. The drivers stood behind the dropped tailgates of their trucks. The smell of diesel fuel was in the air. One by one, soldiers climbed into the beds of the trucks and sat on foldout wooden bench seats, resting their feet on a solid sheet of steel flooring. The squad leader accounted for his men and then climbed into a cab with a driver.

Each truck slowly rolled down the dirt road. As the convoy moved, more trucks linked up from other roads that led out of An Khe. The distance between the trucks increased as they drove out of the gate.

An M60 was positioned on the top of each truck's cab. Every other man sitting inside faced out with weapons at the ready. Overhead, gunships and helicopters flew escort. If Charlie were to attack, the battalion could retaliate with troops, gunships, artillery, and fighter jets. It was quite an impressive sight to see so much military firepower assembled for this mission.

The convoy motored ahead, winding through the mountains with thick vegetation on each side of the road. Several men cat-napped, while others watched the trees and road for signs of danger. Riding in the back of an open truck made us easy targets. If Charlie wanted to snipe or spring an ambush, he could easily cause a lot of casualties and bring the convoy to a confusing halt.

The ride was long. As day turned into night, the drivers turned on tiny night-lights that limited the enemy's ability to see the vehicles at great distances. The tiny lights gave the drivers enough visibility to see the vehicle in front and behind, as long as they slowed the pace and tightened the distance between vehicles.

Kenny kept poking the weary driver of our truck, who would veer left and then right. I wondered if these drivers, unlike infantrymen, weren't used to working many hours without sleep.

Early the next morning, the vehicles stopped on a huge mountain plateau covered with short vegetation and dense jungle. We dismounted and moved away from the convoy. My platoon secured an edge of the mountain high above the Bong Son plains.

The sun shone early that morning as we overlooked the mountain into rice paddies below. The steep cliff, thick with vegetation, made the mountain appear impossible to climb. I could see no path or man-made road leading down into the Bong Son plains. What I saw below my position in the dirt was the water in the rice paddies reflecting the sunlight like tiny rectangular mirrors. Bong Son appeared like a giant checkerboard of colorful rice paddies dotted with small straw hut villages all the way to the South China Sea. It was a beautiful sight.

A steep ravine separated us from another company of the 1st Battalion, 7th Cavalry Regiment occupying the ridge on the other side. After we settled in, I accompanied a patrol to check out the ravine between the mountains. It was another breathtaking view. The ravine was terraced with rice paddies, and a rushing river wound its way into the mouth of the plains. It must have taken hundreds of years to carve this mountainside into giant terraced rice paddies. There were no Vietnamese farmers working anywhere in sight. Kenny quipped, "It looks like a picture straight out of a *National Geographic* magazine."

In spite of all that beauty, a war raged in the valley below. I spotted several navy warships in the waters off the coast of the South China Sea. From my vantage point the tiny vessels appeared to be firing their deck guns inland. Puffs of smoke blew from the stationary ships. Seconds later flashes of light and a billow of smoke from the exploding rounds appeared on the ground below. The sound was muffled.

To the right, air force jets dropped bombs and fired their twenty-millimeter cannons, which can only fire on full automatic at the expense of two thousand rounds per minute. When the pilot presses the trigger, the air is filled with a burping sound that lasts several seconds. One twenty-millimeter bullet, from casing to tip, is about five inches long and is as big around as a fat cigar. I could only imagine what was happening when those huge bullets hit their targets.

Above the valley floor, I could hear helicopter gunships firing M60 machine guns and launching rockets at the trees and rice paddies. On and off during that night, I saw bright flares in the sky above the valley and fire flashes from explosions. The whole situation was unlike anything I'd seen in my two months in Vietnam.

I commented to no one in particular, "There must be a hell of a lot of enemy troops down there to get the navy, air force, and the cavalry involved."

Bob replied, "The reason for all the fireworks is to prepare the valley for our air assault tomorrow morning."

Kenny and I didn't get much sleep that night, knowing that in the morning we would be flying into that valley of death.

Everyone stirred as the sun rose in a blue sky clear of rain clouds. I wiped the morning dew from my weapon, gave it a quick mechanical check, and oiled the exposed metal parts. Breakfast was C rations and water. Within minutes, everyone in the 2nd Platoon was prepared to move at a moment's notice.

Soon, a long stream of choppers flew in and landed not far behind our positions. Every chopper was empty except for two pilots and two door gunners. With doors locked in the open position, the rotors turned at an idle speed. The first load of infantrymen from another platoon climbed into the slicks, lifted off, and headed down into the valley.

A familiar voice called, "Saddle up!" which brought the 2nd Platoon to scramble to their feet. A few minutes later, twenty choppers roared to a landing. Following Bob and Kenny, I ran to our designated chopper. As soon as everyone was aboard, it swiftly lifted off and flew fifteen feet above the ground. When the chopper reached the ravine, the pilot made a sharp right banking maneuver and down we went. I thought I was going to fall out through the open doors as the ground looked parallel to the chopper. When the pilot leveled us out, he dove down the ravine at breakneck speed. The air escaped from my lungs as I held on for dear life. The chopper swooped so close to the tree-tops, I could almost reach out and touch the leaves.

We flew into the valley like a swarm of bees above the rice paddies. This was the fastest helicopter ride I'd ever had. The chopper suddenly slowed down to land in a huge, dry rice paddy a mile or so away from the mountain we'd left behind.

A stream of red smoke—signaling that enemy contact was imminent—marked the landing zone for the pilots. As the choppers prepared to land in the hot LZ, they slightly lifted the noses of the ships and briefly touched down. Everyone was out lickety-split and rushing for cover. I looked around and saw more and more choppers dropping men into the dry paddies. Eventually, the entire battalion of around five hundred combat infantrymen would join in the tactical sweep to the South China Sea.

Bob and Kenny were ahead of me on the ground in prone position, behind their M60. Suddenly, a loud voice bellowed, "Move out!"

I rose to my feet and felt the extra-heavy weight of my pack pulling me down and cutting into my shoulders. Rice paddies surrounded us in every direction. The men spread out about fifteen to twenty feet apart as the platoon began to cautiously step forward. I kept my eyes on the uneven ground in front of me and tried to keep my footing.

American soldiers on the left and right of our platoon slowly faded into the distance. After a while, my platoon was moving as a single unit. The valley seemed a lot bigger and much different from how it had looked from the mountaintop. I couldn't see the ocean or the navy ships anymore. The mountain we'd left was at least a mile behind.

A shot rang out overhead and broke the silence. We hit the ground at once. The shot sounded as though it had come from a wall of trees to my front. We waited a minute, but nothing more happened, so we were ordered to move out. One by one, we got up, then crouched and carefully advanced toward the tree line where the shot was fired.

As the 2nd Platoon continued its sweep, I was positioned close to the rear. Someone spotted two enemy soldiers in the distance running across our front. The platoon leader ordered us not to shoot or pursue, because the soldiers were too far out of our range and we had other Americans in the area we could not see. He didn't want a repeat of the situation that had trapped the 2nd Platoon in the Ia Drang valley after they'd chased a few fleeing enemy soldiers. We didn't encounter any resistance as the platoon continued to move closer to the wall of trees.

By late afternoon, my platoon had pushed deep into the Bong Son plains. We halted inside a lightly treed area surrounded by rice paddies. The platoon leader decided to set up a perimeter around it and partly encompass a nearby dry rice paddy. Bob found a good spot to set up the M60 machine gun.

After the platoon sergeant was satisfied with each platoon's defensive positions, he ordered us to dig foxholes for the evening. I had excellent visibility to the front of my position and clear lanes of fire on flat ground. I could easily see and communicate with adjacent fighting positions.

Before dark, I was about twenty-five yards away from my position setting up the claymore mines and trip flares when a loud explosion filled the air no more than one hundred feet behind me. I reacted by sprawling on the dirt and looking in the direction of the sound. I saw a small billow of white smoke.

Someone yelled, "Incoming!"

Seconds later, a second explosion ripped through the same spot.

I quickly crawled on my belly back to the foxhole. Kenny and Bob were already inside and preparing for the worst. From the direction of the explosions, I heard men repeatedly crying, "Medic!" In total silence, we waited for the enemy to attack. Several minutes passed. Nothing happened. Not one bullet was fired. Except for the commotion behind us, where someone had been hit, a strange quiet hung in the air.

Bob said that the first explosion was white phosphorous or *Willy Peter*, as it was commonly called. The second was a high explosive or *H.E.* Bob explained that Charlie didn't use Willy Peter; Americans did as spotter rounds to mark targets with smoke before firing a volley of rounds.

The mortars had been launched accidentally by an American mortar squad from another company that didn't know friendly troops were operating in their target area. Our platoon leader, platoon sergeant, a squad leader, and two riflemen had been wounded. All of them had been meeting at the command post (CP) when the two mortar rounds exploded. They suffered severe lower torso and leg wounds, but no one had been killed. A medical evacuation chopper landed and lifted the wounded to a field hospital. The 2nd Platoon was reduced to nineteen men and Sergeant Dorman took over as platoon leader.

Early the next morning, May 6, 1966, I went out to disarm and retrieve the claymore mines and trip flares. The sun was heating up as I packed my gear and buried the trash from the food I'd eaten. It was time to saddle up and continue the mission of sweeping on foot to the South China Sea. As the platoon moved out, the men began to put some distance between themselves. I positioned myself with Bob and Kenny's M60 at the rear of the platoon formation.

As the last man in the platoon formation, my job was to keep an eye on the rear. As we moved across the rice paddies, I spotted the flank guards about fifty yards to the left and right of the column. I visually searched my surroundings and saw no other friendly units.

The platoon crossed several large rice paddies before pausing at a dike. I knelt on one knee and heard jet aircraft in the distance. Soon the jets were flying about two hundred feet directly over our heads. Their engines screamed as they flashed by and headed toward the trees in front of us. Bombs released from their wings exploded with tremendous force in the wood line ahead. If they had dropped the bombs one hundred yards closer, they would have exploded on top of us. Someone had called in those air strikes, and I assumed it must have been Sergeant Dorman.

Gunships suddenly appeared and fired aerial rocket artillery into the trees ahead. After the air strikes, I visually searched for signs of the enemy but saw nothing.

The platoon sergeant positioned the platoon in a circular defensive perimeter. We were told to keep looking for the enemy. Each rice paddy was surrounded by dikes, roughly two feet high on all four sides, which held in the water for the Vietnamese who rotated their crops by manual water irrigation. The platoon happened to be set up in a dry rice paddy, although there were many wet ones in the area. These dikes presented excellent cover from the shrapnel of exploding bombs.

In the distance, other American troops halted and took cover from the air strikes. Our front was clear of obstacles all the way to the tree line, which was less than one hundred yards away. The platoon held tight until the air force and the air cavalry gunships ceased their strafing runs.

Kenny and Bob positioned the M60 machine gun on the corner of the dike and aimed at the trees ahead. I set up a short distance to their right side and without thinking, I had pointed my M16 rifle toward inside the perimeter. An F-102 screamed from behind us, a few hundred feet above, and dropped two bombs simultaneously.

The bombs fell into the trees and made an earth-shattering explosion. The ground underneath my feet shook violently, and at that very instant I had my finger on the trigger of my M16 rifle. As the bombs exploded, I flinched and jerked the trigger back. My M16 rifle was on full automatic and fired a long burst of rounds into the center of the perimeter. I watched with fright as the bullets kicked up clumps of dirt and soldiers scrambled for cover. As my finger released the trigger, I realized instantly what I'd done, but it was too late. Everything had happened in seconds.

Sergeant Dorman rushed over in a crouched position and asked where the shots had come from. Kenny and Bob looked at him and said nothing. I confessed that it was my fault and tried to explain what had happened. Sergeant Dorman interrupted and screamed, "Are you fucking nuts? Do you have any fucking idea what you did? You just about fucking killed me and the other squad leaders!"

I froze while looking into the rage of Sergeant Dorman's eyes.

"Next time you check your fucking weapon always keep it pointed out and away from anyone. Do I make myself clear?"

"Yes, Sergeant!"

Sergeant Dorman turned and stomped away while cussing and shaking his head. I'd almost killed someone by mistake. I'd never felt so humiliated and embarrassed in all my life. I told Kenny and Bob that I must have left the selector switch on the *auto* setting after I'd oiled my M16 that morning. Kenny saw that I was completely dejected by the whole event. He put his arm around my shoulder and said, "Hey, buddy, it's okay. Besides, this could have happened to anyone. Shake it off!"

I reflected back to the aftershave lotion incident in the Ia Drang valley and thought, *Man, am I prone to make mistakes or what?*

After the bombing stopped, the platoon ended up not going in the direction of the strikes anyway. Instead, we headed back the way we'd come and circled to the left toward what appeared to be a village in the distance. We spread out and walked very cautiously, looking into the trees and on the ground in front of us. My load kept shifting. This made it difficult to walk on the uneven ground.

I kept watching the ground and thinking about what had happened back at the rice paddy. Then I felt something blunt hit my helmet and a voice said, "Keep your head and eyes up; Charlie's not in the dirt." I looked up and recognized one of the other squad leaders. It really was an art to learn to walk on uneven soil with a heavy load and keep your head up with your eyes constantly scanning around for signs of danger. I was beginning to realize that my months of intensive stateside infantry training hadn't adequately prepared me for the real thing. I was learning to be a combat soldier on the job, and my mistakes didn't make it any easier to gain the confidence of the other members of the platoon.

Our platoon, now somewhere in the middle of the Bong Son plains with rearward mountains dwarfing us, was about to enter a Vietnamese village. The lead element stopped and everyone dropped to one knee. A squad of men was signaled to enter the village first. The men separated from the platoon and went forward with their weapons at the ready. Bob lay behind his M60 machine gun with Kenny at his side. I held my position at the tail end of the platoon and faced the rear.

The squad entered the village and checked out the straw huts inside it, while the rest of the platoon waited nearby. From a distance, the village appeared to be deserted. Not long into the search, however, someone uncovered several Vietnamese hiding inside spider holes and bunkers. Spider holes were very narrow and deep enough to hide and protect a single person. They were usually covered with a lid of vegetation and difficult to spot. The rest of our platoon quickly moved into the village to support the search and provide security.

We trained our weapons on the Vietnamese and ordered them to move into a group as we rounded up ten old and unarmed women and some young children. They squatted and huddled nervously in a group. It was easy to see the fear in their eyes and on their faces. An older woman cradled her crying infant. They wore black pajamas and no shoes; the babies didn't have a stitch of clothing covering them.

An American soldier spoke in Vietnamese, saying that we wouldn't harm them. He asked where the Viet Cong were hiding. An elderly woman kept crying out, "No VC! No VC!" Several men continued the search and uncovered nothing else.

We stayed in the village for lunch. The occupants appeared to be simple peasant farmers and the village was completely surrounded by rice paddies. I was impressed with how clean the area was and by the beautiful palm trees, coconut trees, and several fruit-bearing banana trees. I wondered where all the men and boys were. I speculated that maybe these captives were families of Viet Cong soldiers. Bob surmised that we hadn't found young men, women, and boys, because the Vietnamese thought we'd take the young men as prisoners, rape the women, and kill the boys. Bob went on to say that the men and boys were probably hiding somewhere nearby. When the platoon left, they'd return to their families—a typical reaction when American troops invaded a village.

We eventually released the Vietnamese to carry on with their daily lives. After their release, several women showed their hospitality by offering us fresh coconuts and bananas. The soldiers accepted the gifts with gratitude. I felt safe and didn't think Charlie was anywhere near the village as we relaxed in the shade of the trees.

Some of the guys started to horse around by chasing chickens through the village. The Vietnamese children laughed at those crazy Americans. After we ate and rested, it was time to move again. When we departed the village, an older Vietnamese woman bowed as each soldier passed.

Our platoon headed across another rice paddy, continuing the tactical sweep to the South China Sea. I spotted gunships overhead firing rockets and machine guns into a treed area just ahead of us. As we neared another village, I heard a machine gun that didn't sound like an M60 or anything else I'd heard before. It had a slower, thudding, firing rhythm. Bob quickly pointed out that this was the sound of an NVA heavy machine gun exchanging fire with our helicopter gunships.

Because Bob had been in other firefights with Charlie, I valued his knowledge and combat experience. This was his second mission in Bong Son. The first time had been in February—a month before Kenny and I had arrived in Vietnam.

While we marched, my mind filled with crazy thoughts of how I could sneak up with a grenade and knock out that enemy machine gun nest. I wanted to make up for my earlier mistakes and regain the respect that I thought I'd lost from my fellow squad members. My fantasy quickly disappeared when we were ordered to move right and away from the enemy machine gun nest.

Yet another village lay ahead in our path. The platoon entered it much the same way as the previous one. The lead squad approached the village and nothing happened. The rest of the platoon followed in three-man fire teams. One team crouched and rushed about fifty feet and knelt down. The other team moved in the same manner. The advance alternated until we were all inside cover of the village. Specialist Four Engles manned the number one machine gun for the platoon. He was positioned to provide firepower for the few men who searched the straw huts for possible enemy hiding places.

As the platoon poked around outside, they were completely surprised when several Vietnamese men, with hands held high over their heads, came running out of an underground hiding place. Some of the Vietnamese wore black pajamas, while others were dressed in khaki shirts and trousers. American weapons quickly trained on the unarmed men. One of the Vietnamese repeated loudly, "*Chieu Hoi! Chieu Hoi!*" He was referring to the "open arms" program, promising clemency and financial aid to Viet Cong and North Vietnamese soldiers and cadres who stopped fighting and returned to live under South Vietnamese authority.

In short, it meant, "I surrender."

The one man in our platoon who could speak some Vietnamese made the men lay facedown on the ground so they could be searched. The soldiers found no weapons or documents. The hands of each prisoner were immobilized and a rope linked them together for security. Bob, Kenny, and I were given the responsibility of guarding them. After a short while, the platoon captured several other Vietnamese men who were hiding in the village. We now had eight Vietnamese male prisoners. After a short interrogation, they confessed to being deserters from a battalion of NVA regulars operating in that area.

For the first time, Kenny and I faced the enemy up close. I wasn't afraid to guard them and they didn't appear to be afraid of me, either. They stared at me and probably wondered what I was going to do with them. The platoon stayed in the village for about an hour but didn't find anything else. With all eight prisoners now roped together, a squad leader positioned them near the center of our formation.

I asked, "What if they try to escape?"

Sergeant Dorman replied, "Shoot first and ask questions later."

The platoon headed out of the village to the edge of a clearing with the prisoners in tow. The prisoners had to be evacuated as soon as possible. The platoon sergeant used the radio to call for a chopper and to make contact with the company commander. Since I was in the center of the platoon, I heard what was going on over the radio and could see the point man leading the formation. We spotted a chopper nearby. Sergeant Dorman popped green smoke in the air to mark a landing site. The chopper, already crammed with gear, took all but two of the prisoners.

I was then given sole responsibility to watch over the remaining two prisoners. I walked behind them as they followed Kenny and Bob. Not long into the journey, across a clearing, a sniper fired several shots at the platoon. We hit the ground and got into a prone position. The front of the platoon quickly returned fire. Engles's M60 machine gun let go several short bursts. I didn't fire my weapon. Instead, I watched the prisoners to make sure they remained tied up and didn't try to escape. I wasn't going to make another mistake. If they ran, I'd shoot them, as ordered.

The sniper had shot our point man. Doc Bell assisted the wounded man, while Sergeant Dorman radioed for a medevac. With the platoon still in the middle of a rice paddy, we crawled on our bellies to form a hasty perimeter. A few minutes later the medevac hovered overhead. We popped red smoke and the medevac descended close to the ground with its nose up.

An enemy machine gun fired at the chopper. The ship must have gotten hit, because it took off before the wounded man could be loaded. As soon as it was airborne, the enemy stopped firing. Sergeant Dorman thought that the platoon's counterfire had silenced the enemy's machine gun. It was quiet for a while and the medevac was radioed to return for pickup. As soon as it started to touch down, the enemy opened fire again. I couldn't believe what I was witnessing. Here was an unarmed medevac with easily visible bright red crosses painted on its doors, and Charlie was determined to knock it out with complete disregard for the rules of the Geneva Convention. The medevac had to take off again and leave our wounded comrade behind.

The front of the platoon opened fire again to try to silence the enemy in the trees. A short time later, two air force F-102s appeared directly overhead. I checked my M16 to ensure I'd secured the safety and pointed my weapon away down range. One jet dived down no more than a few hundred feet above our heads and released two silver-colored canisters. The aircraft was so close that I could see the pilot in the cockpit.

Kenny and I watched in amazement as those canisters tumbled over our heads. When they hit the trees, they exploded into a huge wall of orange and red flames. Bob told me that this was napalm—a jellylike substance, mixed with fuel, that sticks to and burns everything it touches. I could feel the intense heat fifty yards away. A few seconds later, a second F-102 zoomed over and fired twenty-millimeter cannons, shattering tree limbs and kicking up dirt everywhere. I thought nothing living could have survived the barrage. The trees and village, not far from where we had captured the prisoners, were ablaze and smoking.

After the blaze had died down, we advanced across the clearing and into the burning village without a shot being fired. Our wounded point man had his arm in a sling and was positioned in the center of the formation with Doc Bell for maximum protection. Smoke billowed everywhere with small fires burning all around us. I kept my weapon trained on the two prisoners, who looked emotionally shaken and remained silent as they moved forward.

As I passed a burning hut directly in front of me, a dark figure stumbled out of a haze of smoke. I froze dead in my tracks and I yelled, "Oh my God, it's a woman!" Her clothes had been burned off and her body was charred and smoking. Her face was badly burned and bleeding as she raised her hands and cupped them to her mouth as if asking for water or help. She stood in front of me and spoke softly in Vietnamese. There was nothing I felt I could do for her. I actually thought of shooting her to put her out of her misery. She took a few more steps and fell facedown on the ground. I stared at her charred and smoking motionless body.

The entire incident caused me to briefly lose my concentration. I soon realized where I was and quickly composed myself. The prisoners hadn't moved and were still securely tied. The other members of my platoon were not far ahead, so I moved the prisoners at a quick pace away from the scene and didn't turn back to look.

When I caught up with Kenny and Bob, Kenny asked me if I'd shot the woman. I told him that I'd thought about it but hadn't. Kenny asked what had happened to her, and I told him that she'd fallen down and died. Kenny said that there was nothing anyone could have done for her.

A deep and wide ditch with muddied water halted the platoon's advance to its destination, the shores of the South China Sea. The only way across it was a rotting board that connected to the other side. One at a time, the platoon carefully walked on the board and crossed to the other bank. The weight of our bodies and our loaded packs bowed the plank to its limits.

When Rodriguez stepped onto the plank and got about halfway across, his 220-pound body and heavy pack cracked the rotting plank. He fell straight down into the muddy water about five feet below and sunk up to his chest, keeping his rifle above his head. He couldn't move anything but his arms and head and cursed up a storm as the rest of us laughed hysterically, breaking the silence of our movement.

Someone found a long tree branch to help Rod, but it broke during the attempt to extract him. Then we tossed a thin rope to him, but it snapped under the strain. We had to radio a chopper for help. A crew member lowered a thick rope through the burned trees. Rod grabbed the rope, tied it to his upper body, and the chopper plucked him out like a giant turnip. When he was free, two troopers grabbed Rod and pulled him to dry ground.

A few men searched for and found a safer crossing over the ditch. After everyone made it across, we continued our trek to the South China Sea. None of us had any idea how far away it was. As the platoon spread out into a tactical sweeping formation, we entered another village that was still smoking from the napalm drop. The air was filled with the smell of fuel and burning debris. My throat and lungs burned from inhaling smoke, so I drank some water.

Suddenly, the front of the platoon came under attack by automatic weapon fire. We hit the dirt and returned fire. Being close to the rear with the prisoners, I wasn't in a position to fire my weapon. Bob and Kenny covered the rear of the platoon with the M60 machine gun. Enemy bullets cracked over our heads. After a brief exchange, we continued firing and maneuvered to the right and away from the incoming attack.

Several VC tried to flank the platoon on the left front as each squad maneuvered right. We had little protection and it was a miracle that none of us was hit. A small clearing on the right led to a group of trees that had a straw hut on the other side. We crouched, ran in that direction, but stopped short of entering the clearing.

Rod led the first assault squad. He directed a team of three riflemen to provide a base of fire while he and two others crouched and darted into the open clearing, stopped, got down and fired as the next three men charged behind them for support. The maneuver was a textbook leapfrog technique commonly used by the infantry to advance on an enemy position.

Charlie kept the pressure on our left side. As the first squad entered and secured the other side of the clearing, the rest of us quickly moved across in small groups of four or five troops. Bullets cracked the air very close to me. I figured that Charlie had spotted the prisoners. Kenny pointed out a huge water buffalo frantically exiting a water hole where Rod stood. Its horns appeared to scrape against Rod as he desperately tried to get out of its path. The water buffalo ran through the middle of the platoon into the clearing behind us.

When I reached the trees, I saw a fellow soldier lying on his back in the open with his helmet off. Blood gushed in spurts from his throat. His face was full of dirt and sweat. A continuous stream of blood ran down the side of his mouth. His eyes bulged as he bled and gasped for air. I stopped and knelt down beside him to see what I could do.

Sergeant Dorman screamed, "Get your ass and those prisoners under cover before you get shot."

Doc Bell came out of nowhere and began to assist the wounded soldier. I held the rope that tied the prisoners and pulled them behind me as I rushed into the trees and jumped into the same water hole the water buffalo had left moments before. The dry water pit was about chest-deep at the edge of a row of banana and palm trees. About ten feet to my right, Kenny and Bob lay flat behind a banana tree, savagely firing the M60 machine gun. On my left, a soldier named Knutson fired his M79 grenade launcher at targets across the rice paddy to his front.

From a hasty defensive perimeter around a small clump of trees with a straw hut in its center, the platoon made a stand and fought off Charlie's onslaught. The heaviest action was on our left flank.

Engles yelled to me from the left, "There they are! There they are!" as he fired his M60 machine gun.

VC, clad in khaki uniforms, fired back and darted from place to place across the front. Many enemy soldiers fell dead from a hail of our bullets and grenades.

For the first time since I'd arrived in Vietnam, I aimed my M16 at enemy soldiers and fired. The VC bobbed up and down and fired back from behind a dike fifty yards in front of me. I carefully aimed and fired a slew of magazines above the dike. I tried to hit the VC as they stood up to fire back. I thought I'd silenced some of them, but others held their positions and fought back hard.

On my right, Kenny loaded another 100-round belt of

ammunition into the M60 while Bob maintained his aim behind the gun. Their M60 kicked up dirt and debris all over the area. Lifeless bodies of VC, some no more than fifty yards out, littered the ground around us.

American voices called for a medic. The platoon had taken heavy casualties. Deadly enemy machine gun fire had strafed our small perimeter. Everyone kept reloading and firing back. I noticed that less shooting and fewer explosions came from the right side of the perimeter.

Someone screamed, "There they are on the left! On the left!" This was the direction of the village the platoon had vacated minutes earlier.

Gunships swarmed overhead, firing rockets that exploded almost on top of our platoon. I flinched as shrapnel whizzed through the air, splintering trees and kicking up the dirt around me. The noise was intense. Charlie fought from well-fortified defensive positions in the rice paddies' dikes. He kept shooting back fast and furiously after each rocket exploded. We were all in a reaction mode and I wasn't thinking about what could happen to us.

The extra ammunition I'd decided to carry now came in handy. I'd already used about two 150-rounds by firing on semi-automatic setting.

Kenny's machine gun jammed with a bullet still in its chamber. If it cooked off, the bullet would explode inside and make the weapon useless. Kenny had little time to fix the problem. He reached back to pull his bayonet out of his pistol belt to pry the jammed bullet out of the chamber. Almost immediately, his arm smacked him in the chest; he fell over onto his side and curled up on the ground beside his gun. Kenny's helmet rolled away from his head.

"I'm hit!"

Bob yelled for a medic and then called, "Johnny, Kenny's hit!"

I looked in Bob's direction and saw Kenny lying still in a curled-up position. I was afraid he'd died. I quickly crawled over to him and left my prisoners unattended.

Kenny's first words were, "You're white as a ghost!"

It was shocking for me to see my best friend lying there moaning in severe pain, with open flesh wounds that made him look as if he were bleeding to death. All I could think was, *Please don't die. Please don't die. This is my best friend. You can't take him away from me like this!*

When the medic arrived, he couldn't work on Kenny in the open with all the lead flying around. Incoming bullets kicked dirt up and whizzed around us. We dragged Kenny a few yards into the water hole. I thought, *Thank God he's still alive!*

Kenny had been hit by a VC thirty-caliber machine gun blast. He was suffering and complained of sharp stomach pains. With his fatigue shirt soaked in blood and one sleeve ripped completely off, a large part of his forearm muscle was missing and the white of the bone was exposed. He bled heavily from his wounds. The bullets had torn his arm apart. Several bullet holes were in his stomach, but he didn't have any exit wounds in his back. I carefully removed Kenny's shoulder harness and backpack to make him more comfortable. After I got his gear off, Kenny doubled up in pain. Doc Bell placed Kenny's good arm under his armpit to try to slow the bleeding. He then dressed the wounds and gave him a shot of morphine to ease the pain. The two prisoners looked scared but remained tied together and lying on the dirt at the bottom of the hole, where I'd left them.

Doc Bell grabbed my shirt and pulled me down into the hole. He told me that if I didn't keep my head down, I'd be killed. As he dressed Kenny's wounds, I rejoined the fighting and tried to keep an eye on him and the prisoners. Bob was still on the right, firing the M60 machine gun; he changed the barrel and continued firing short bursts at enemy targets. I tossed him another 100-round belt of ammunition from Kenny's pack.

Above all the shooting and explosions, Sergeant Dorman yelled, "Grab the wounded and dead and get ready to move out!"

The enemy had surrounded our platoon on three sides and was closing in fast. We were about to be overrun, captured, or killed. As fast as I could, I untied Kenny's poncho from his pack, rolled it out, and put it under him. Charlie continued to pour it on with AK-47 rifles, machine gun fire, and grenades. The grenades all fell short and exploded outside our perimeter.

Sergeant Dorman yelled, "Hurry up! We got to go!"

I couldn't lift and carry Kenny by myself. Bob was loaded down with equipment, the M60 machine gun, and ammunition. I cut the two prisoners loose and ordered them, at gunpoint, to each grab a corner of the poncho. Bob and I held on to the other two corners. The four of us lifted Kenny and rushed in a crouched position to the far right side of the perimeter away from the enemy. Our platoon carried out six or seven men who were lying in ponchos.

Sergeant Dorman took a quick count of his men and said, "The rest of our company is waiting for us in the graveyard on the other side of this rice paddy. We have to move one hundred yards in the open exposed to enemy fire. Stay close to the dike on the left of the paddy for cover."

Every able-bodied man helped to carry the wounded in ponchos. It took only a few minutes from the time Sergeant Dorman gave the order for us to grab up the wounded and dead and move into position to cross the rice paddy.

The next thing I heard was, "Let's go!"

Almost at once, we started running in a crouched position as fast as our legs could go. Firing continued in front and behind us. No one stopped running even for a short breather. As our ragged platoon came closer to the other side of the rice paddy, men from our parent company waved us on while covering our advance with a base of fire. When we finally reached the American lines, we were exhausted and breathing heavily. I turned over the two prisoners to a couple of soldiers who hurried them away at gunpoint.

Inside the American lines, other soldiers helped us to move the 2nd Platoon's wounded and dead comrades to a collection point inside the Vietnamese graveyard. The Vietnamese build their graveyards on high dry ground above the rice paddies. Each grave was a mound of dirt about three feet high. The graves were lined up in rows much like any cemetery. The mounds of graves provided a great defensive position and security for our wounded and dead.

Medics began to assist more than fifty wounded men who lay scattered on the ground in ponchos. Not far from the wounded, the bodies of ten or twelve lifeless young men were completely covered in green plastic ponchos and lined up in rows. Only their boots were exposed. I stared at them and thought how sad it was to see these men, lying in the hot sun, side by side in the dirt, underneath pieces of plastic.

When I saw Kenny again, I looked at him and said, "We made it! How do you feel?"

It was difficult for Kenny to talk, but he said he was fine and that the morphine was helping to relieve much of his pain. Kenny strained to speak and said, "Thanks for helping me, Johnny. Don't forget to tell my folks that I'm okay." I assured him that I'd keep my word and write to his folks to tell them what had happened.

The fighting seemed to have stopped. Charlie apparently had broken contact or had been wiped out by our reinforcements.

Sergeant Dorman, Rod, Bob, Engles, and the other survivors of the 2nd Platoon came by to pay their respects to the dead and wounded. I stayed with Kenny until the medics assisted him onto a stretcher and carried my friend to the designated liftoff area.

Several medevac helicopters landed and the wounded were loaded aboard. I watched as Kenny and the others lifted off safely into the sky until the chopper disappeared. After Kenny was gone, I felt relieved that he'd be okay, but desolate at the thought of not having his company.

Would I ever see my friend again? I wondered as I walked along the perimeter.

I found Bob sitting behind his M60 and staring vigilantly across the rice paddy. I took Kenny's place as Bob's assistant gunner. It was quiet except for the medevacs and supply ships flying in and out of the graveyard.

The day was getting late and darkness settled in. Bob and I talked about how the events of the day had unfolded. Sergeant

Dorman came for a visit. He told us that the platoon had five killed-in-action (KIA) and seven wounded-in-action (WIA). The figure included the men who had been wounded by our own troops' "friendly" mortar fire.

I thought, *Hell, we left An Khe with twenty-five men in our platoon, and two days later only thirteen of us are left.*

Sergeant Dorman informed us that our sister company had made a sweep of the area and counted about fifty dead enemy soldiers around the positions our platoon had defended. Sergeant Dorman told us how proud of us he was for being brave and fighting like hell. After Sergeant Dorman left, it started to rain.

I felt empty inside and alone for the first time since I'd arrived in Vietnam. Today, I'd lost my brother. I didn't know if Kenny was going to live or die before they got him to a hospital. What would I say to Kenny's family? What does anyone say to the families of the men who were wounded and those who died for their country?

I realized how quickly death can come and tried to hold my tears back as they streamed down my face. Bob put his arm around me and assured me that it was okay to cry.

I pulled my poncho over my head and stared into the dark night, feeling sad and angry. I couldn't stop thinking about every detail that had happened that day, but these memories only pushed me deeper into depression. I promised myself that I'd never forget the men who had lost their lives that day. I hadn't known most of them, but they were Americans. That was all I cared about. Now I wanted to kill every VC for what they'd done to Kenny and the others.

Later that night, the rain stopped and the clouds cleared. Bob and I stayed alert all night, waiting for a counterattack that never came. We took turns catnapping. The fighting appeared to be over and my first combat experience had finally ended.

The next morning I ate my C rations, shaved, and prepared to move out. I felt better but I was ready to get the hell out of that place. The platoon was resupplied with more ammunition, water, and food for the rest of our journey to the South China Sea. Because we'd been reduced to a squad and a half, we were now being attached to another platoon.

No one talked much as we joined a sister platoon. My squad, led by Sergeant Dorman and his radio/telephone operator (RTO), was positioned as rear guard for the lead platoon. Two radios supported us as we passed through a few more burned-out villages that showed no signs of inhabitants. We didn't even see a chicken, dog, or water buffalo. Small bomb and rocket craters pitted the ground. Charlie was nowhere in sight.

To my amazement, we were within only a mile of the ocean. I figured that the platoon must have covered several miles since we'd started moving a few days earlier. Finally, I could see the ocean straight ahead.

When the platoon arrived at the beach, hundreds of American soldiers were already in the water. Men spread out and relaxed in the sand all along the shoreline. I appreciated the peaceful setting even though I wasn't in the best of spirits. It was great to see the soldiers splashing in the water and having fun. I stopped for a moment and stood on the white sand listening to the waves splashing against the shore. In the distance, I spotted large gray navy ships. I wondered if they were the ones I'd seen from the mountain, firing into the valley.

The platoon stopped in an area where we had room to spread out and set up positions. After Bob and I put our equipment down, Sergeant Dorman came by and told us to enjoy ourselves for the rest of the day. As Sergeant Dorman promised, we had hot food, relaxation, and time to go swimming.

I kept thinking about Kenny and knew that this beach time would have been something he would have enjoyed. I started to feel much better. I propped my back against a palm tree and rested in the shade and wrote a letter to Kenny's parents explaining what had happened to their second son. Another battalion pulled perimeter security guard while I slept on the beach and awoke the next morning to the sounds of seagulls and ocean waves.

A bunch of slicks landed on a road to take us back to An Khe. It was now May 8th as I climbed aboard a chopper and lifted off into the high altitude of cool air and headed home. I sat on the floor of the chopper and peered out the open doors. I tried to locate the positions we'd fought with Charlie, but everything below looked the same. The Bong Son plains appeared peaceful from several thousand feet up. I don't remember how long it took for us to fly home, but it was a very long ride over the mountain range.

When the base camp became visible in the distance, the

choppers began their descent. As we flew closer to the huge perimeter of Camp Radcliff, I could see the road we'd traveled on when we were in the back of a truck going to Bong Son. The choppers made a sharp left turn and landed single file on the road behind the green canvas tents of our company's living quarters. As we exited the choppers, I couldn't believe my eyes and ears. The division band stood on the side of the road and began to play. The sound of the music, mixed with the noise of helicopters, made me feel patriotic. *A nice welcome home touch,* I thought, *Kenny would have liked it, too.*

I slowly walked past the band and headed to my tent. When I got to my cot, I took my steel pot off and laid down my gear. I unpacked the empty magazines, ammunition, claymore mines, grenades, and trip flares. I had to check over everything for serviceability and possible replacement. My first priority was to clean and oil my weapon, which was full of carbon buildup and sand.

Sergeant Dorman walked into the tent and came over to my cot. He asked me to pack Kenny's gear and take it to the company supply tent. So I stuffed all of Kenny's belongings into his duffel bag, which was lying on his cot. Kenny had spent only a handful of nights sleeping in that cot. His wounds were so severe that Sergeant Dorman suspected Kenny would be evacuated to a major army field hospital in Qui Nhom near Bong Son.

It looked as if Kenny wouldn't be reporting back for duty. Neither would the soldiers who had been killed in action. Our platoon's dead would be sent home in caskets to their families. I learned that some of those who had died had been scheduled to serve only a few more months in Vietnam, while others had recently arrived. I felt terrible about the whole situation. I watched several soldiers quietly packing the personal effects of their fallen comrades.

Kenny had spent sixty-five days in South Vietnam. Most of that time, he'd marched long distances through the heat in the jungles and rice paddies, hunting for a fight, eating C rations, digging foxholes, carrying a sixty-pound pack, pulling guard duty every night, and catnapping in the dirt, rain, and mud. I was beginning to learn and understand the true meaning of the nickname *grunt*. Kenny Mook had definitely earned a Combat Infantry Badge and a Purple Heart. He and all the others were the real heroes of our platoon. As darkness fell, I prayed for Kenny and all those who hadn't made it back with us.

I got a liberty pass to go to An Khe—*Sin City*—the small Vietnamese town outside base camp. I went with Sergeant Dorman and Bob Dunn. We had a great time. I bought a small mirror with a frame that was handmade from a metal beer can. The back of the mirror was a cardboard C ration box. The Vietnamese always seemed to find uses for American's discarded trash and sold back to us what we'd originally gotten for free.

Several weeks had passed when Sergeant Dorman called me into his tent. He asked if I'd written to Kenny's parents to tell them what had happened to their son in Bong Son. I told him that I had. He said that my letter had gotten to Kenny's folks before the army's official telegram of notification and that the army brass was embarrassed that they hadn't gotten to his parents first. I told Sergeant Dorman that before we went to Bong Son,

Kenny and I had promised each other that we'd write to the other person's parents if anything should happen to us. I thought that others must have made the same promises. I was told to consider myself warned not to do it again. I'd been in the army for eight very long months and didn't know much about protocol. This was another lesson on how the army's official channels worked.

My next lesson in Vietnam would involve learning how an innocent bamboo stick could be turned into a deadly weapon.

Wounded in Action

On the morning of May 17, 1966, I ate a quick breakfast at the mess hall and returned to the platoon area for an operations order. Sergeant Dorman had directed the platoon to pack
a basic load of ammunition and food for one day. He showed us
his field map and pointed to several mountains for a combat mission he called *hill jumping*.

After studying the map, it was determined that several moun-
taintops had small clearings large enough to land a few helicopters where S-2 (Battalion Intelligence) had reported enemy
sightings. Charlie had been operating in small and highly mobile
squads equipped with mortars and shoulder-mounted rocket
launchers. They had been harassing our airfield, and retaliatory
artillery strikes were not silencing the problem.

Our platoon was given the order to search on foot and destroy
Charlie's hit-and-run squads that were trying to destroy our aircraft on the runways, our ammunition dumps, and communications towers and bunkers.

My platoon was to air-assault by helicopter onto each hilltop
LZ and probe into the surrounding woods and jungle in an
effort to make contact with the enemy and take him out. If the
LZ was hot, we were to secure it and radio for gunships and field
artillery support.

If we did not make contact with the enemy, we were to radio

for liftoff and air-assault into the next LZ marked on the map. The operation was to continue until dark or until all selected targets were checked out. Each team leader had a radio/telephone operator assigned.

I was assigned as the assistant to Van Wilson's M60. Van had provided security for the 3rd Brigade commander, Colonel Hal Moore, before joining the 2nd Platoon. Van was from Arkansas and six feet tall—much bigger than me. He had joined the army in May 1965. After he had completed basic training, advanced infantry training, and graduated from paratrooper school, he arrived in Vietnam in December 1965, four months before me.

Van told me that the reason he had joined the army was because a North Vietnamese soldier had shot his brother in the rear end. He quipped, "I couldn't let the enemy get away with shooting a Wilson in the ass, so I joined up." Van had a cheerful personality and we got along great. One day Van had challenged me to a wrestling match while we were in the field. It didn't last long. I quickly took him down to the dirt and pinned him in seconds. He couldn't understand how a little guy like me could have pinned him that easily.

I joined the service in September 1965, right after graduating from Littleton High School and taking the summer off. I was not ready for college, even though I had a potential wrestling scholarship to attend Trinidad Junior College in Colorado. I was more interested in leaving home and being on my own than pursuing a college education.

I saw a large poster of a soldier wearing a green beret in the window of the U.S. Army Recruiting Station. I got excited and decided to inquire about joining the special forces. Next thing I knew, a sergeant in a snappy army uniform had my complete attention. The recruiter told me that the army offered a great way to travel to foreign lands and visit exotic cities and cultures that I'd otherwise have to pay a lot of money to experience on a vacation. I was young, trusting, had no money, no job, no girl-friend; I was eager to make a positive change in my life, so I signed on the dotted line.

The army shipped me by train from Denver to Fort Leonard, Missouri, for basic training, then to Fort Ord, California, for advanced infantry training, and finally to Fort Benning, Georgia, for paratrooper training. After graduating from paratrooper school in February 1966, I was ordered to Vietnam with no spe-cific unit of assignment listed on my paperwork. I was shocked, as I had no idea there was a war going on in Vietnam or where that country was located on the globe. I asked lots of questions, but learned little to satisfy my curiosity and understanding. I would not have enlisted had I known I'd be sent off to fight in a war, but it was too late. I was now a soldier and I belonged to Uncle Sam.

In preparation for the mission, Van cleaned and oiled his M60 and packed several 100-round belts of ammunition, while I checked the spare parts bag for the M60 and packed it with two 100-round belts of ammunition. I also packed two hundred rounds of M16 ammunition into magazines and slipped them into the pockets of my shoulder-sling bandoliers. I hung several grenades on the webbing of my shoulder harness. It was the lightest load I had ever packed for a mission, one day's worth of supplies.

Three squads were alerted, packed, and ready to go in less then an hour. Sergeant Dorman led one of the three ten-man squads. Each squad consisted of a grenadier with an M79 grenade launcher, a man armed with a twelve-gauge shotgun, four M16 riflemen, a medic, and an M60 machine gunner and assistant gunner. Each squad had enough diversified firepower to handle any small group of VC they might run into.

The time came to saddle up and assemble at the pickup point on the road not far from our living quarters. This would be my first mission without Kenny Mook since Bong Son. Kenny had been like a brother to me, and we'd been inseparable from the day we'd met in Saigon at the replacement center. It felt strange not to have him at my side. I didn't trust anyone as I trusted Kenny. I missed him terribly and wondered now that my best friend was gone, who would protect me like he did?

While we waited for the choppers to arrive, I sat on the ground and leaned against my backpack like the other seasoned combat veterans. Now I knew what to do and how to fight when I made contact with the enemy. I didn't simply fear the possibility of seeing combat. This time, I expected it.

The noisy choppers kicked up dust in our faces as we made our way to their open doors and climbed aboard. I was positioned in the first chopper with Van and several other soldiers. When we lifted off the ground, I noticed there were only three troopships in our airborne formation carting my entire squad. As we flew over the perimeter of our base camp, a gunship joined the group at low altitude.

The morning sun felt good with fresh air circulating inside the ship. The lush jungle canopy covering the ground below looked peaceful. The choppers climbed toward a small range of hills. Before long, they began their descent into a clearing on the first hilltop. As the ships got closer to touchdown, I scooted to the open door and prepared to jump out. The choppers didn't land in the clearing. Instead, they hovered a few feet off the ground only long enough for us to jump.

I jumped to the ground, ran a few feet, and crouched on one knee facing the trees ahead. I didn't look back but heard the sounds of choppers drifting away. When I finally turned around, they were gone. Our entire squad was alone on the ground and it was quiet. The drop-off had taken place in less than a minute. The squad leader lifted his arm and pointed to where he wanted us to move. I heard birds chirping in the trees ahead as we cautiously moved forward in crouched positions with our weapons on the ready. The silence was broken by the noise of a chopper nearby, but I didn't look up. I focused on looking for danger signs.

After we were inside the vegetation beyond the skirt of the small clearing, Sergeant Dorman sent two riflemen to probe deeper into the surrounding area. When they returned and reported that they'd seen nothing suspicious, he moved the squad clockwise to a different spot and repeated the probing tactic around that entire LZ until we ended up where we had started. We found nothing to indicate Charlie had set up mortars or rocket positions near that hilltop.

After about an hour of reconnoitering, Sergeant Dorman reported our squad's situation by radio. Minutes later, three choppers landed. The door gunners on each side pointed their M60s at the trees, ready to fire. We quickly boarded and off we flew to another hilltop without incident.

A gunship escorted our squadron of choppers to our next drop-off point. During the short ride, I scooted on my butt to the open doors to get ready for my second jump. Tall elephant grass covered the entire clearing below. All of a sudden, bullets popped through the air and hit the metal skin of the ship. The door gunner immediately returned fire with his M60 machine gun. I quickly moved into the open door and realized I was about twelve feet above the bending and weaving elephant grass below. I lowered my feet onto the landing skid and stood up. With my right hand, I held on to the side of the ship. With its nose up, the ship moved forward slowly, but didn't land. I was fully exposed and not feeling very safe. Incoming bullets kept slamming into the chopper's side as I hung on getting ready to jump out.

The door gunner tapped my hand as he looked down. I jumped into the tall elephant grass below and hit the ground hard. Suddenly, a sharp pain ripped through my right knee and I fell, twisting onto my stomach. I tried to get up, but the pain in my right knee quickly drove the idea out of my head. When I looked down, I saw a yellow bamboo *punji* stake sticking straight through my knee. It had entered under my kneecap and exited the other side. The rest of the *punji* stake splintered below my leg.

I tried again to move, but was in severe pain and anchored to the ground.

I knew that the VC carved these small bamboo spears and planted them into the natural vegetation. They were placed in the ground at forty-five-degree angles with their sharp points at about thigh level. When anyone walked into or fell on one of the spears, he was immediately incapacitated. Worse yet, the VC dipped the sharp end of the spear into human waste to add infection to the wound. The VC also placed those sharp sticks in man-size holes and covered them with natural vegetation. The more weight pressing against the point, the deeper the *punji* stake penetrated. I couldn't believe I'd been wounded by one of those primitive yet debilitating bamboo spears. I had always thought I'd be shot, not speared.

Although I was in pain, I prepared to defend myself. With my M16 rifle loaded with a round in the chamber, my finger rested on the trigger with the safety off and the selector switch on full automatic. A lot of shooting and tremendous explosions shook the ground all around me. The tall elephant grass surrounded me and blocked my ability to see anything except the sky above. Over the noise, I heard Van's M60 firing, but I wasn't able to move in his direction.

As I tried to prop myself into a better position to shoot, I heard American voices screaming for a medic. Unable to move, I lay in agony and tried to remain calm. Soon, I heard movement in the grass nearby. Since I didn't know the source of the sound, I decided not to take any chances by calling out. I remained silent and my heart began pounding a fast and steady rhythm. The noise in the grass moved closer and the adrenaline started to rush through my body. I pointed my M16 nervously toward the sound with my finger on the trigger. A voice cried out, "Are you okay?" An American helmet broke through the grass near my feet. It was Doc Bell. He crawled to me on his belly as the intensity of the shooting and explosions increased around us. I breathed a sigh of relief as I eased my finger off the trigger and dropped the barrel of the rifle to the ground beside me.

I felt safe with Doc Bell. He encouraged me to lie still as he checked me over. He gave me a shot of painkiller and a drink of water. When Doc Bell moved my knee and snipped away the splintered pieces of bamboo around my wound, I gnashed my teeth and my eyes squirted tears of excruciating pain as the blood gushed out. With one hand Doc Bell quickly pulled the large piece of bamboo from under my kneecap. I cried out in pain. It was difficult to lie still while he bandaged the wound. I grew very dizzy, hot, and weak all at once.

Doc Bell talked to me the whole time, telling me that Van had pointed to where I was and that was how he'd located me. Doc Bell asked me to stay calm while he went to help the others. I watched him crawl away into the grass and out of sight.

The whole time I lay there, I could hear VC voices through the grass but I couldn't see anyone. An hour must have passed, but I didn't fire a single shot. I couldn't believe I'd been stuck by a damn *punji* stake. While lying in the tall grass, I didn't fear being captured or overrun, but I did wonder if I'd ever be able to use my right leg again. All sorts of thoughts passed through my mind: *Hell, I was the first-string linebacker on the varsity football team and won all those wrestling championship medals at Littleton High School. How could this have happened to my leg now? Am I going to ever walk right again?*

The firing and explosions eventually trickled to a stop and then there was a long period of silence. I began to hear other Americans moving through the tall grass, saying, "Watch out for the *punji* stakes." Then I saw Van Wilson. He stood over me and asked if I was okay. Van said he saw me go down before he jumped and that he was lucky not to get stuck too. He told me that fresh *punji* stakes were all over the place.

I asked Van about the rest of the squad. He told me that they had suffered four casualties—two from *punji* stakes and two from enemy fire. There was one American KIA who had died of multiple *punji* wounds. I felt fortunate to have been stuck by only one spear.

Helicopters soon flew low overhead like a swarm of bees. The enemy was gone. God only knows how many of them had died during the firefight. Van helped me take off my heavy pack and stand on one foot, but I felt lightheaded and dizzy. I grabbed Van's shoulder as he pulled me up by my belt. I hobbled on one leg to the awaiting helicopter.

Van fetched my gear and put it beside me in the chopper that held two other wounded soldiers. Before long, we were airborne and on our way to a field hospital in Qui Nhom. After being examined there, I was evacuated to a hospital that had better facilities for reconstructive knee surgery.

My only recurring thought was, *Would I survive this knee wound and walk normal again?*

106 General Hospital

In June 1966, I arrived at the 106 U.S. Army General Hospital in Kashini Barracks, Yokohama, Japan. I felt relieved to be in a country that wasn't at war.

The hospital was situated in a former WWII Japanese army installation. A tall barbed-wire fence surrounded the entire compound. Armed U.S. Army military policemen, dressed in heavily starched khaki uniforms and sporting highly polished black boots, were stationed at the entrance and exit to the base.

I was assigned to Orthopedic Ward D on the second floor of one of the old buildings. At least thirty other men occupied hospital beds lined up in rows against the beige walls of a large room. The place was clean and tidy, and the air smelled of medicine. Large fans at each end of the ward circulated the warm summer air.

Ward D buzzed with the indistinguishable chattering voices of bedridden broken soldiers and nurses moving about carrying medicine trays. My bed was near the entrance to the nurse's station. The soldier on my left had to lie on his stomach because of the wound in his back. The man on my right had an L-shaped cast that ran from his neck to his fingers. Other men were covered with bandages on their arms and legs.

After I got comfortable, a nurse and doctor came by to give me a complete examination. They introduced themselves as

Dr. George Bogumill and Nurse Nancy Jones. Dr. Bogumill had a gentle disposition and a kind bedside manner. He told me that I was too young to be sent to war and he thought I was younger than nineteen years old. The doctor joked by asking if my mother had signed my enlistment papers that got me into the army.

Nurse Jones, a pretty woman in her middle twenties, had a comforting smile and a great figure. I liked the idea that she'd been assigned to take care of me. The medical staff asked many questions about when I was injured, how it happened, and what type of treatment I'd received before arriving. I appreciated their patience and care, especially when they removed the bandages to examine my wound, then cleaned it and redressed it from upper thigh to ankle. None of the medical staff had a clue as to what combat was like or the pain of being wounded in action. But there was no doubt that they could have filled a small library of short stories from what they learned at the bedsides of the wounded soldiers they nursed to health over the course of their tour in Japan.

———————

As the days turned into weeks, I became friendly with patients in the beds around me. Almost everyone I spoke to came from a different infantry unit. We talked about our Vietnam War experiences. Each man told his story of how he'd been wounded.

The man on my right, Robert Lang, had been shot in the arm while on patrol near the Mekong Delta. That was 250 miles south of where I'd been wounded. Charlie had waited for

Robert's squad as they moved on foot parallel to a trail. Robert happened to be a flank guard when Charlie spotted him first. He said Charlie had been a little faster on the trigger than he was. Several bullets from an AK-47 rifle shattered the bone in Robert's forearm and ripped a hole in his biceps. The impact had spun him completely around and onto the ground, where he passed out. Robert hadn't fired one round, and the last thing he remembered was seeing the face of the enemy soldier who had shot him. Robert said that he often would wake up in the night seeing that enemy face that wouldn't let him rest.

Robert had been healing in the hospital for several months. The doctor had told him that he'd soon get his cast off and start physical therapy. Robert was one of several men on the ward able to get out of bed, eat in the dining hall, and walk around the ward.

Gary Morton was the man on my left. His platoon had been ambushed in the jungle while checking out what appeared to be a deserted VC base camp. As his patrol was leaving, the VC took them by surprise. Gary remembered getting down and eluding the first volley of small arms fire. He fired back by emptying an entire magazine of twenty rounds. While he was changing magazines, an enemy machine gun opened fire in front of him. Something slammed into his upper back and rolled him from his stomach to his back. He had felt dazed but thought he was okay. When he tried to roll back to his stomach, he realized that he had no feeling in his arms and then lost consciousness. By the time Gary regained his senses, he was lying in a cot in an army field hospital.

Gary's back was still in terrible shape, and he could lie only on his stomach. A web of silver metal wires was sewn over the open wound, keeping it from tearing open. The bullets had missed his spine but had ripped about eight square inches of flesh and muscle from his back and shoulder. Although the wound was clean, I could actually see his left shoulder blade surrounded by raw flesh. Every so often, the nurse and doctor would bring small patches of skin they'd cut from his leg to graft to the hole in his back. During my stay in the hospital, I watched Gary's skin grafts take hold and grow without much infection, and the hole in his shoulder decreased. I wondered if Gary would ever again have the full use of his left shoulder or the left side of his back.

Even though the men in my ward had suffered wounds as a result of combat in Vietnam, their morale was high. Many of the wounded knew that after they recovered they'd be medically discharged from the army and sent home. Most were young like me and had been in the army for less than a year. Now they would have scars for the rest of their lives.

Finally, the day came when I was prepped and wheeled away for a surgery that lasted several hours. When I returned to consciousness, I was in my bed again, feeling dry-mouthed and drowsy. I really needed to take a leak but I couldn't move because of the pain, so I called for Nurse Jones to bring me a bedpan. She placed the bedpan under the covers between my legs and stood beside me until I used it. Talk about performance anxiety!

The operation was a success. Dr. Bogumill said that I would be able to walk normally again, but I'd have to work hard at physical therapy. A few days later, a physical therapist came to my bedside. He helped and encouraged me to start lifting my leg. The pain was excruciating. The guys in the beds beside me kept joking and calling me a *pussy*. This was typical verbal harassment—a way for us to help each other to persist in our healing efforts. Even though it was painful, I lifted my right knee slowly up and down.

After I'd had some success, the therapist draped socks full of sand over my ankles. If I were going to get better, I'd have to ignore the pain and concentrate on strengthening the muscles in my leg. As my leg strengthened with increased numbers of repetitions, the therapist added more weight and encouraged me to keep going. The guys in the beds next to me continued chanting, "More weight! More weight!" Eventually, I could sit on the edge of the bed and bend my leg slightly at the knee.

Oh, man, what a different level of pain that was when the blood rushed down my leg, and my eyes squinted with tears. Each time I tried to sit up and hang my legs over the edge of the bed, it was the same old thing. I eventually learned to expect the pain of therapy.

After a month, I was able to use crutches to move around the ward, eat in the dining hall, and pee standing up. I'd gotten cocky a few times and let go of the crutches. After one unaided step, I'd fallen flat on my face, but that didn't stop me from trying to walk on my own. I wasn't going to be a cripple and that was that.

My wound seemed to be healing faster than Dr. Bogumill had expected. Maybe because I was only nineteen years old, I joked to him. The sixty stitches were removed from both sides of my knee and I had two ugly ten-inch scars. My shaved knee had tiny hair stubs and was swollen to twice the size of my left knee. Blood oozed from the puffy stitched holes. I had the knee of Frankenstein's monster. Not a pretty sight.

————————

By the end of July 1966, my hospital stay was getting to be a bore. I saw men in the ward get well and go home. I thought about going home too. I missed riding my motorcycle, going on dates, seeing a scary movie at the drive-in theater, eating a juicy cheeseburger with hot French fries, and hanging around with my family and friends. I craved drinking a cold bottle of Coors beer. Most of the guys I knew had never heard of the Coors beer slogan, "Brewed with pure Rocky Mountain spring water." I hadn't met any other soldiers from Colorado, so no one really understood the special things I missed about my home state.

I had a patient take a picture of me while I was propped up on my elbows in bed. I sent that picture to my friend Van Wilson, who was still humping the boonies with the 7th Cavalry in Vietnam.

As soon as one bed was emptied, it was filled almost immediately with another wounded soldier from Vietnam. It was as if there was a line of wounded soldiers outside the door waiting with a reservation for the next available bed. The cycle of men coming in and leaving Ward D was neverending. Every night, I'd hear screams from soldiers having nightmares, which constantly reminded me of the war in Vietnam, but I'm sure they heard my own sleepless nights too. No one ever talked much about what went on at night unless it was an emergency. Thank God no one died in Ward D while I was there.

Eventually, I'd recovered well enough not to require crutches or a cane and got a liberty pass to go to Yokohama, the city right outside our military compound. The rules stated that I'd have to return to the hospital before dark. Civilian clothes weren't authorized for patients, so I was issued a khaki military uniform, a hat, and a pair of shoes. I signed a partial-pay voucher for fifty dollars and suddenly felt rich.

No hospital patient was authorized to go off the base alone; we had to use the buddy system. So I teamed up with another patient and off we went to Yokohama. We caught a cab outside the gate. The Japanese cab driver spoke enough English to ask, "Where to?"

We replied, "Downtown."

He nodded and drove us to what looked like a main street near a pier full of boats and ships and a fish market.

The streets of Yokohama were crowded with people going about their usual business. The Japanese women wore colorful kimonos and the men were in street clothes and suits. This contrasted with the attire of the Vietnamese, who almost all wore black pajamas and straw hats. We took our time, slowly walking the sidewalks and resting as much as possible. The Japanese acted as though we weren't there. They must have been used to seeing American servicemen on their streets. I felt quite comfortable even though we couldn't understand a word anybody said. There was a sense of freedom all around us—something I hadn't experienced in a long time.

We stopped in a bar and ordered a few Japanese beers but we didn't eat anything. Japanese music played on a radio. We sat, talked, and sipped our beer. After a while, we left that bar and roamed the streets and marketplace. I wasn't much of a fish-eater, so I was repulsed by the awful smell of the fish market as we passed by. Not long after our walk, we found a cab to that took us back to Kashini Barracks.

The day finally came when Dr. Bogumill and Nurse Jones informed me that my prognosis was good enough for discharge from the hospital. My knee didn't hurt much. The muscles in my right thigh were strong again as a result of physical therapy. I had strengthened my upper body by using weights and exercising and I even jogged a little now.

Dr. Bogumill shocked me when he said that I was healthy enough to return to active duty. This wasn't what I wanted to hear.

"How about a one-way trip to Littleton, Colorado, doctor?" I asked, even though my wound wasn't severe enough for me to have a medical discharge from service.

I sensed from Dr. Bogumill's mannerisms that he really cared about his patients. His kind advice to me was to get the hell out of the infantry and find a safer job, and then get out of the army and go to college.

Since I'd joined the army, it seemed that I was always being disappointed. First, I didn't get to go to Special Forces school but was sent to Vietnam instead. When I got to Vietnam, I had almost killed several of my own squad by accidentally forgetting to secure my gun's safety. My best friend, Kenny, after only two months' service, had almost been killed. Less than one month after Kenny left Vietnam, I'd been wounded. Now I couldn't get discharged from Uncle Sam's army because I'd healed too well. I was beginning to think that it was my lot in life to be the star of an absurd tragedy; almost making it to safety, only to get pulled back into the soup again.

While I was in the hospital, I'd written many letters home mentioning the possibility that I might be discharged. I'd told people to start planning my coming-home party. Now I had to write home and tell everyone to put away the party hats. The army was going to keep me on active duty in the Pacific.

Even if I wasn't going home, the news that I'd soon be leaving the hospital made me extremely happy. I'd soon leave Japan for an assignment in Okinawa. What I didn't know was that my new assignment would change my life in a totally unexpected way.

I'd soon be meeting my first war dog.

Sentry Dog Platoon

It was January 1967 when the U.S. Army released me
from the 106 Army General Hospital in Yokohama, Japan, and
reassigned me to the island of Okinawa to serve out my
remaining tour in Southeast Asia.

Okinawa was a huge military supply depot that serviced the
war effort in Vietnam. There were no infantry units there, so I
was reassigned to the 267th Chemical Company because they
needed sentry dog handlers. I guess the personnel assignment
clerk felt that an infantryman could perform the duties of a
sentry dog handler. He must have keyed on the words "Infantry"
and "Sentry" as a close enough occupational match.

But I liked the idea of having a dog of my own, though it
really belonged to Uncle Sam. Training with a sentry dog would
involve quite a learning process for me, but it would prove challenging and exciting. And though they could bark, they wouldn't
be barking orders at me like the sergeants. The idea of having a
dog to pal around with sounded too good to be true.

When I reported for work at the 267th Company, I met with
the first sergeant in his office. I stood at attention in front of his
desk. He looked up and saw that I wore a Combat Infantryman
Badge. He said in a soft voice, "At ease, soldier." As I relaxed my
position of attention, he commented, "A CIB on such a young
boy!" I immediately thought, *Here is that "boy" comment again*, but

somehow coming from a salty old veteran it didn't upset me, so I didn't snap back. He smiled and then offered me a cup of coffee. Top, as we commonly called the first sergeant, was a veteran who had served in the infantry and fought against the Nazis in Europe and against the North Koreans and Chinese during the Korean War. Okinawa was probably his last assignment before retirement.

After trading a few war stories, Top told me that I was the only Vietnam combat infantry veteran in the outfit wearing a CIB and a Purple Heart, which made him proud to have me aboard.

When Top briefed me on the mission of the 267th, he explained that the unit provided security for and managed the contents of the army's ammunition supply storage buildings in a controlled area of the island. The job called for a number of sentry dog teams—a German shepherd dog and its handler—to guard the buildings. He explained the sensitive nature of the mission and how important it was not to discuss my work with anyone outside official channels. That restriction included not taking pictures or writing anything about my work in letters home.

Top advised me to be careful about strangers who offered free drinks in downtown bars. "There are spies out there," he said. "They want classified information about what we do. Don't talk or try to figure them out; they are professionals. Report everything immediately to our security officer. Do you understand, soldier?"

I immediately replied, "Yes, sir!"

He barked back, "And don't call me 'sir,' I work for a living!"

It all sounded mysterious, but what the hell did I know about that type of army business. Top instructed me to read and sign an official military document validating that our briefing had taken place. I supposed that if I were suspected of talking with a Communist, the army would have been able to use that document against me, lock my young ass up, and throw away the key.

I thought, *Hell, the army doesn't have to worry about me, man! I'm a true red-white-and-blue-American, who would never sell my country out to any Communist bastard.*

Top got up from behind the desk, shook my hand, and told his clerk sitting outside his office to add my name to the roster of sentry dog handlers. I sat beside the company clerk's desk and filled out a long personal history form so I could get security clearance. My next stop was to meet the men of the sentry dog platoon.

A sentry dog handler named Fred escorted me to my new living quarters on the third floor above the company offices. Fred was about my size in height and build, with straight black hair, brown eyes, a square jaw, and a neatly trimmed mustache. His uniform was starched stiff and his boots spit-shined. Fred had joined the army two years earlier than me and held the enlisted rank of Specialist-4 (SP4), one rank above my private first class ranking.

I picked an empty bunk bed and stored my personals. I was issued a set of white sheets, a blanket, a pillow, and a pillowcase. I felt relieved to finally have a new home. I had slept in about ten different places after leaving my tent in Vietnam.

I thought about the members of my old combat platoon. Was Sergeant Dorman still alive? What about my friend, Kenny, or Van Wilson, our M60 machine gunner who helped to carry me out of harm's way on that hilltop? Van had a November rotation date and must have gone back to Arkansas, I thought. I closed my eyes and was lost in thought about the men I had left in Vietnam. The sound of Sergeant Dorman yelling, "Saddle up!" and the rat-tat-tat of Van's M60 machine gun blasting away on that hilltop remained fresh in my memory.

Fred was anxious for me to meet the rest of the members of the sentry dog platoon, who were out at the kennel or on guard duty. I asked Fred about the small, one-inch-square patch he wore above his name tag. It had the head of a German shepherd dog sewn in black against a yellow background. Fred told me that all the army sentry dog handlers wore that patch. I would have to earn my patch through on-the-job dog training. Fred wanted to know what I knew about sentry dogs. The only sentry dogs I'd encountered were in Vietnam or behind fences guarding junkyards back home.

I was the first Vietnam veteran Fred had met. With excitement in his eyes, he asked me a lot of questions about my combat experiences. I answered him only in very general terms, not comfortable enough yet with Fred or my new surroundings to tell my stories. I felt more comfortable trading stories with the first sergeant even though we were generations apart in age and stations in life. But my CIB was something that seemed to immediately bond us in an unspoken kind of respect.

No one I had met since I left the hospital in Japan had served a day in Vietnam or the infantry. They all had noncombatant, rear-area support jobs, and it wasn't easy to have a one-sided conversation about combat. Most of them told me that they were glad they had been assigned to units outside the fighting in

Vietnam. They stared and hung on every word I said, treating me like I was something unusual, and I felt awkward in their company. I must say, it was kind of odd not being around a bunch of grunts carrying weapons. I just wanted to fit in and see those German shepherd sentry dogs everyone was talking about.

Fred informed me that sentry dog handlers worked the night shifts guarding the compound. Days off varied and I would eventually enter the rotation. Each morning the sentry dog handlers would load up into vehicles and head off to the kennel to work with the dogs.

I had no idea what to expect the first time I arrived at the kennel in the back of a troop truck greeted by the sounds of a bunch of dogs barking. The dog handlers quickly dismounted the truck and entered the kennels. I lagged back a little to observe. Inside the kennels, handlers yelled the names of their dogs—Wolf, Mike, Rex, and Lucky.

After the handlers exited the kennel with their dogs attached to leather leashes, I slowly entered. The fresh smell of dog shit and urine on the concrete floor permeated the air. Several German shepherd dogs were housed behind thick wired fencing. Each dog's name was written on a piece of plywood and attached above his kennel door. A metal choke chain hung on a nail outside each kennel door along with a leather leash and muzzle. Metal water and food bowls sat inside each dog run.

As I walked by the caged German shepherds, they growled and lunged at me. If one of those gates accidentally popped open, I'd have been dog meat, literally. It was a horrifying thought. The dogs probably sensed that I was scared shitless. Not one dog allowed me to get close without growling and showing how big and sharp his teeth were. *Maybe I don't want to be a sentry dog handler after all,* I thought.

At both ends of the kennel were walls of wooden bins labeled with the names of each dog. Each bin neatly stored grooming equipment, long leashes, leather collars, and leather body harnesses. Large boxes of dog food were stacked high alongside several large metal wall lockers. Water hoses were connected to pipes at each end of the kennel. Two of the dog handlers turned the hoses on and washed the waste on the floor through the back of the fenced runs. The handlers laughed as they squirted some of the dogs just to piss them off.

Outside, the handlers groomed their dogs on small wooden tables with posts to which the animals were tied. The dog handlers talked to their dogs while they brushed them, cleaned their teeth, clipped their nails, and checked them for health problems. As I watched, I was impressed by how muscular and fit the animals appeared, not a bit of fat on any of them. The platoon sergeant approached and instructed me to observe and help around the kennels for the next few days.

The platoon sergeant was responsible for matching dogs to new handlers. Usually a handler was assigned the healthiest dog that had spent the most time without a handler. Each dog was already trained on basic obedience, but if a dog didn't work on a regular basis, he became lazy. This meant that training with the dogs was an extremely important part of the handlers' routine. Sentry dogs were trained with the primary function of guarding and attacking on command. Dogs learn through repetition and consistency and are taught to react to the commands of only one master. I would soon learn an essential rule for working with sentry dogs—don't befriend any other animal except for your assigned dog.

Rex held the distinction of being the most ferocious sentry dog. His handler, SP4 Aldridge, was a tall husky man with scars on his arms where Rex had bitten him several times.

The platoon sergeant decided to assign me to Hans—the biggest but not the meanest-looking German shepherd in the kennel. In fact, none of the dogs were friendly to me. They all charged at me, barking and growling and showing me their big teeth as I passed by the runs. So it really didn't matter which dog I got assigned, because they all wanted to eat me. But I really think that the platoon sergeant figured if I could handle Hans, I could handle any dog. I felt that he was testing the level of my fear factor. Right then, I feared every one of those dogs and they sensed it.

The platoon sergeant said, "Come on, Burnam! Before you know it, you'll have Hans eating out of your hand. The hardest part is overcoming your fear. Besides, this job's a piece of cake compared to what you've been through in Vietnam."

I replied, "Yeah, right!"

My first task was to spend quality time with Hans—feeding him, cleaning his cage, and talking to him. During that initial "let's get acquainted" period, I didn't dare go into his run or try to touch Hans through the wire fencing. Physical distance was okay with me. I figured I had plenty of time and was in no hurry to put my hands on that big dog. This was so much different than I had thought. When I arrived in Vietnam, I was eager to fit in and do my job, even though I was a "greenhorn." But this dog job was becoming a different kind of challenge.

Someone remarked, "Just remember, if Hans bites a chunk out of your ass, you'll be getting a tetanus shot instead of a Purple Heart."

Those who heard that comment burst into laughter. I stood there in silence, realizing that I was going through an acceptance process just like in Vietnam.

Every time I visited Hans, he'd growl and try to eat through the wire fence that separated us. The platoon sergeant said Hans growled because it was his way of testing my control and fear. He told me to show no fear if I was ever going to have a chance at commanding an army sentry dog.

Over time, Hans stopped growling and became accustomed to seeing me. I was also getting used to him. As each day passed, my fear slowly diminished, and the day finally came when the platoon sergeant told me to take Hans out of his kennel run.

I asked, "Do you think I'm ready, Sarge?"

The platoon sergeant replied, "It's now or never, Burnam!"

Both the dog and the platoon sergeant were testing me. I had to take Hans out of the kennel and deal with him face-to-face.

I kept thinking, *Well, I can't be a chicken shit about it or let that dog control me. I've got to take control of him and just do it!*

I took a deep breath, cleared my mind, grabbed the leather leash, and connected a choke chain to it. All the while, Hans paced back and forth like a hungry lion in a cage. He knew he was getting out. I tried not to think of what could happen after I opened that door.

The platoon sergeant watched me as I kept delaying the inevitable. I spread the choke chain as far as possible so that the dog's head could pass through quickly and easily. Then I took another long breath and opened the door. Now there was nothing to keep that dog from eating me alive. To my surprise, Hans quickly put his nose and head through the loop of the choke chain and charged past me through the open door, pulling me behind him. Hans headed for the exit and into the open area behind the kennel with me in tow.

The platoon sergeant running behind kept yelling at me, "Yank back on the leash! Command the dog to heel!" I pulled back as hard as I could on the leash and yelled, "Heel! Heel! Heel!" Hans ignored me and pulled away even harder. Finally, Hans must have gotten tired, because he just stopped pulling and started walking and sniffing the ground. Then he lifted his leg and took a leak on a fence pole. After he finished, I pulled on the leash and gave the command to heel. To my surprise, Hans moved to my left side and sat.

The platoon sergeant instructed me to praise Hans by saying, "Good dog! Good dog!" Verbal praise was fine; I just hoped the sergeant wouldn't ask me to give Hans a hug yet. While we marched around the training yard, Hans stayed at my pace. I had a huge smile across my face and felt as if I had won a blue ribbon in a basic obedience contest. My fear had been temporarily replaced with brief joy.

There was a lot more to learn if I was going to become a respected sentry dog handler. The platoon sergeant told me I'd have to master the commands for basic obedience and learn to control Hans under all circumstances. Hans already knew what to do but needed a master to make him do it. I had to remain consistent with how I handled him. I learned that discipline was extremely important. It could be achieved only by practicing every day with Hans. Through effective training, Hans could become my companion and maybe we would make a great sentry dog team.

Several days passed as Hans and I got better acquainted. It reached the point that when I dangled the leash in front of his cage, Hans would go crazy with excitement. When Hans stood on his hind legs he was taller than me, one of the biggest German shepherds the platoon sergeant had ever been around. All the sentry dogs were healthy and lean because of their diet and rigorous daily training. There wasn't one fat dog handler either. Every man was in excellent health and physical condition.

I was issued a military dog-training manual and expected to learn and practice what it preached. The manual contained illustrations of tools and procedures for grooming, voice commands, hand and arm signals, deployment, and first aid. The other dog handlers were already versed in the commands and advanced dog-training techniques. Most had graduated from a formal twelve-week military dog-training school in the States. So I watched the other soldiers work their animals. Everything they did appeared to be simple and smooth and showed a genuine loving bond between dog and handler, even though each dog was trained to be a lethal weapon.

The platoon sergeant assigned Fred to be my tutor in the finer arts of basic dog obedience training. Fred's happy-go-lucky personality was quickly rubbing off on me. He always talked about the pretty Okinawa barmaids working at Club

Lucky, a downtown bar not far from the base that the dog handlers frequented and considered their special hangout.

Fred taught me that positive reinforcement was critical throughout the training exercises. My first lesson included the voice commands: *sit, heel, come, down, stay, no,* and rules on when to praise the dog. Fred taught me how to use inflection in my voice when calling out commands to Hans. I practiced for hours each day until I could voice the commands with the precision of a drill sergeant.

At first, Hans was slow to commit to the action when commanded. When I commanded him to sit, he took his time. When I voiced the command "Down," Hans would get down only partway and then get up and sit. But after several training sessions, Hans became more responsive in obeying my basic voice commands. The dog that had scared the crap out me before was slowly becoming my partner.

———————

Eventually, I was ready to join the rest of the platoon for our regular group training sessions. Uniformity was the key. Each dog handler carried the same equipment attached to specific places on his pistol belt. Each pistol belt held a canteen of water, an eight-foot leather leash, a leather collar, a choke chain, a twenty-five-foot nylon leash, a leather muzzle, a first aid bandage, and a .45-caliber pistol in a black leather holster.

Outside the kennel, the platoon sergeant, positioned several feet front and center, would assemble the twenty dog handlers with their dogs in a formation of four ranks. When he'd call the platoon to attention, everyone assumed the standing position of attention—feet together, shoulders back, head and eyes forward. The position of attention for the dog was a full and proper sitting position on the left side of the handler.

Dogs weren't allowed to slouch or sit leaning on one hind leg. Standing little more than an arm's length from his dog, each handler gripped near the end of the choke chain with his left hand close to the dog's neck. That way he could easily control the dog if it decided to attack a nearby dog or handler. After all, the dogs were trained to attack and kill.

One of the handlers commented, "When an infiltrator enters my guard post, it's bite, bang, halt!"

We would make our way to the training area across the road from the kennel and surrounded by a chain-link fence. We'd all assemble in a platoon formation in the center of the yard and below a tall wooden platform. The platoon sergeant stood on top of the platform to command and dog-drill the platoon.

When the platoon sergeant commanded, "Sit dog command," the dog handlers would simultaneously repeat the command, "Sit!" When all the dogs sat the platoon sergeant would command, "Down dog command." Again, everyone followed in chorus, "Down!" The platoon sergeant would yell at us if we didn't execute the command in unison. Rhythm and precision were both key to the training exercise.

The sergeant would call the platoon to the position of attention and command, "Move to the end of the leash." To carry out this command, the handlers would order his dog to "Stay," then march to the end of the leash, turn and face his dog. Sometimes the dog would disobey and follow behind the handler. When this happened, the platoon sergeant would get pissed off at the handler and yell at him. I got yelled at a lot during those exercises, because Hans would lie down when I turned my back on him. After we were all standing at attention at the end of the leash and facing our dogs, the platoon sergeant would bark, "Down dog command!"

We practiced many other basic obedience drills like *sit, stay, right face, left face, about face, down, heel,* and *march*. We weren't allowed to praise our dogs until we successfully completed a movement and the platoon sergeant gave the command, "Okay." When the dogs were warmed up, we performed three or four successful movements in sequence and the platoon sergeant again commanded, "Okay."

I soon graduated to voice commands with simultaneous hand signals. Hand signals were generally taught with the handler facing the dog at the end of the leash. To get Hans to sit, I'd signal him with my arm and hand and simultaneously voice the command, "Sit." We'd practice hand and voice signals for all the movements of advanced basic obedience, including the *Dead Dog, Roll Over,* and *Crawl*.

If there was one command I wore out, it was, NO! But after many weeks of training, Hans would respond with precision when I used hand signals only. It fascinated me that a dog could learn to do so many tricks on command. I often thought while training Hans that he'd have made a great patrol dog for Vietnam. He was so big that the Viet Cong would run when they saw him.

After about a month, I was ready for another phase of my education: learning how to get Hans to attack and stop on command. This would be the most frightening part of my sentry dog training experience. The platoon sergeant marched us into the fenced training yard. He selected one handler and directed him to put on a heavy burlap attack suit. The rest of us removed our dog's choke chain, quickly attached it to our pistol belt, and buckled the leather collar around the dog's neck. The leather collar was used only when a dog was on official guard duty.

We formed a single line, facing away from the person in the attack suit. The platoon sergeant instructed us to turn around and face away from the platform and the man in the burlap suit. Once the leather collars were on our dogs, they knew what was coming next. The handlers had a difficult time keeping their dogs in a sitting position and facing away from the action.

The soldier outfitted in the burlap suit protected his face with a steel mask that looked like a baseball catcher mask. The dogs growled but stayed at their masters' sides. Hans sat and stared at the man in the burlap suit. We were instructed to hold our dogs still. Each sentry dog team would be given the opportunity to perform an attack. There were three commands to the attack phase, "Watch Him," "Get Him," and "Out." The command "Get Him" meant that the handler wanted his dog to attack the target. The command "Out" meant that the handler wanted the dog to stop attacking and release from the target.

The platoon sergeant called one of the handlers by name and said, "Attack dog command!" The man in the burlap suit assumed a crouched position about thirty feet in front of the dog. The handler commanded, "Watch Him!" The dog watched the target and moved slowly toward the burlap-suited man, who was raising his arms up and down and growling. When the dog was about twenty feet away from the target, the handler commanded, "Get Him!" The handler let go of the leash that remained attached to the dog's leather collar. In a flash the dog charged and lunged at the crouched man's throat and then at his groin.

I had never witnessed a big dog move so fast. Each time the dog lunged, the man in the burlap suit moved backward from the force of the hit. The dog bit down on the arm of the suit, backed off, and lunged again. At one point, the force of the dog's lunge knocked the man onto his back. Relentlessly attacking the man's throat area, the dog bit down and thrashed his head from side to side like a shark in an eating frenzy.

The platoon sergeant gave the command, "Out dog command." The handler responded, "Out!" The dog released his bite and backed off the man who was lying on the ground. The handler commanded, "Heel!" and the dog returned to his side. The handler praised his dog by hugging him and saying, "Good boy! Good boy!"

During the attack, the dog is so agitated that it bites down on the burlap so hard that his teeth sink up to his gums. The dog maintains a strong grip and thrashes back and forth with his head, trying to rip a chunk out with his teeth. The friction between the burlap and the dog's teeth and gums causes the gums to bleed.

The man in the burlap suit got up and took a short breather before preparing for the next dog attack. After four attacks, the platoon sergeant ordered a different man into the burlap suit. After all the dog attacks, the burlap suit was saturated with bloodstains.

Soon it was my turn. I was nervous, unsure how I'd handle Hans throughout the attack process. The platoon sergeant gave me the signal. The man in the burlap suit began to kick up dirt and wave his arms. From about twenty feet away, I commanded, "Get Him!" When Hans reached the end of the leash, the force of his charge pulled it out of my right hand. In a flash Hans was all over the guy in the burlap suit. I ran behind Hans and grabbed the leash while he had the man on the ground biting and twisting his entire body trying to rip off the man's leg.

The hair on the back of Hans's neck stood straight up and his teeth buried deep into the burlap. The guy in the suit screamed, "Call him off! Call him off!" I frantically yelled, "Out! Out! Out!" as I pulled back on the leash. Finally, Hans let go. It took every bit of strength I had to keep Hans back and away from the man on the ground. I was exhausted, even though the action lasted less than a minute. The platoon sergeant told me in what was surely an understatement—that I'd have to learn to control my dog better.

After the attack, Hans's gums were bleeding and the muscles in his shoulders and legs were twitching tensely and hot to the touch. I praised Hans as he sat with his ears pointed high and forward alerted to the man. It was a scary thought knowing that Hans was fully capable of killing a man.

Later, the soldier who had worn the attack suit told me that he could feel the powerful jaw pressure of Hans's teeth clamped on his leg near his groin area. He said Hans had the most crushing bite of all the animals that had attacked him.

Back in the barracks, several of the dog handlers commented on how well my training was coming along. Fred invited me to go to town for drinks at Club Lucky. I didn't make very much money as a private first class, but being overseas, I didn't have to pay taxes either. A few bucks at the Club Lucky went a long way.

Outside the main gate of the base, *skoshi* cabs (small cabs) were parked alongside the fence. Fred instructed the driver to take us to Club Lucky. The streets were crowded with people walking, riding bicycles, and driving funny little cars.

The signs above the bars were in English—Club BC Night, Club California, Club Texas, and so on. Japanese men dressed in black slacks and white shirts stood in the doorways hawking to people to come inside the bars. The streets were crowded with American servicemen—sailors, marines, soldiers, and airmen.

My new friends and I entered Club Lucky as a short and stocky Japanese male hawker bowed and opened the door. I was warned not to mess with the bar hawkers. Although they were little guys, bar hawkers were also club bouncers, many of them karate and judo experts.

I said to Fred, "You mean these little shits can fight?"

Fred replied, "You bet your ass! I've seen the little fellows take down some big boys." That was enough to convince me. I'd never been one to pick a fight, though I did enjoy fast one-on-one competition. I still had that wrestling fever I caught in high school. My friends and I had referred to wrestling as the fastest six minutes in sports. The sport required talent, strength, speed, endurance, training, and a driving desire to win. Since I hadn't heard of any wrestlers from Okinawa, I wondered if I could teach these bar hawkers a few tricks. I thought, *I'd love to take on one of them in a wrestling match.*

During my brief tour in Vietnam, I'd learned that winning in combat, in contrast to wrestling, was a *team* activity with human lives at stake. The prize for winning in that war was to go home in one piece after twelve months. The prize for losing was to get wounded or sent home in a body bag.

The war in Vietnam was a deadly game of cat and mouse, played inside a giant labyrinth of treacherous terrain and weather conditions. The enemy, unlike a wrestler, wasn't easy to identify, find, or engage. The rules of fighting in Vietnam weren't as clear as they had been on the wrestling mats. There was no referee to call a foul in the heat of an exchange or award the opponent points for a takedown. Dead body counts seemed to be all that mattered to American military commanders on the battlefields of Vietnam. These were hard lessons to learn for a teenage boy.

From behind the bar, an older Japanese woman greeted our crowd. She gave us a big friendly smile as if we were all old friends. Everyone called her Mama San. Small groups of Asian women dressed in long, colorfully flowered, silk dresses sat at the bar and tables talking and giggling at one another.

Fred ordered a round of Japanese beer and we moved to an empty table to sit down. The jukebox filled the air with the sound of American rock 'n roll. One of the barmaids came over and asked for money to put into the jukebox. Someone gave her change and off she went. Soon, several other young and attractive barmaids came to our table. Everyone except me knew them by name.

When the drinks came, we ordered a round for the girls. I was introduced to each of the barmaids, who smiled and talked in broken English. Gradually, I learned that some of the guys considered certain girls as their girlfriends, which meant they were off-limits to everyone else. Fred pointed out the women not taken. I wasn't interested in what was left over, and besides, I was having too much fun watching everyone else.

I quickly learned that if I didn't buy a barmaid a drink, she'd leave and sit with someone who did. It was their job to rotate to all the customers. That was how they made their tips. The locals were considered by the guys as poor people, who survived on the money Americans poured into their economy. The bars created big business. Fred told me that none of the women at the Club Lucky were prostitutes, but I found that hard to believe.

Meeting decent girls in a foreign country as an American serviceman wasn't as easy as it was back home. Many of the young women on the island were simply looking for a way to get to the United States. The best method was to marry an American serviceman. That would insure them of a ticket to the States, a home on a military base, money, and medical benefits. Many of the high-ranking soldiers paid for their girlfriends' apartments in town so they'd have a place to shack up after duty and on weekends. Apparently, that was a common practice among those who could afford it. As soon as a soldier got reassigned off the island, another soldier was in line to rent his woman and apartment. I never got in line; I couldn't afford it.

Some American servicemen fathered children and abandoned them when they left the island. It really bothered me when I'd see kids of mixed heritage on the streets begging for money. Most of those kids appeared to be shunned by the people within their own culture.

The Japanese beer gave me a good buzz by the end of the evening, which was midnight due to the curfew set for all military personnel. MPs from all the military services roamed the streets and checked the bars for soldiers who caused problems or violated curfew. The native island police force also patrolled the streets on foot to enforce local law and order. We left the bar at about eleven-thirty, flagged a *skoshi* cab, and were back on base before midnight. Everyone understood the negative consequences of missing curfew or being picked up by the MPs. I wasn't one to get into trouble with MPs or to become involved in a military court-martial for drunk and disorderly conduct. Besides, we all had a great time and I planned to do it again real soon, because there were other bars I hadn't had a chance to check out.

———————

By February 1967, my secret clearance had been approved. I could now patrol the classified military sites with Hans. I couldn't wait to work with a sentry dog in a live situation. For the first four-hour tour of night-shift guard duty, I was driven by truck to the kennel at around ten o'clock. With the dogs barking in the background, I got my gear together and filled two canteens of water for Hans and one for me.

Hans had been fed a strict diet of Purina Dog Chow and water. The dogs were not given any treats. They weren't family pets. Fred said that the only praise I should give a dog is to hug him and tell him that he's a good dog.

I had two seven-round clips of ammunition for my .45-caliber pistol, which I wasn't supposed to insert until I was at the work-site. I attached my poncho to the pistol belt in case it rained. My gear weighed about four pounds, which seemed light compared to the sixty pounds I used to carry on my back in Vietnam. I buckled on my pistol belt and strapped the leather collar on Hans.

My right knee was feeling stronger than ever, and I experienced little pain when I jumped down from the back of the truck or stood for extended periods of time. Dr. Bogumill had done a terrific job patching me up. Even the hair around my knee had fully grown back except along the ugly scar tissue.

There were six sentry dog teams in back of the troop truck headed for guard duty. Like the rest of the dogs, Hans was muzzled and sat between my legs for control, safety, and protection. I took up the slack in the leash and held Hans by his collar during the entire ride. I had already learned what Hans could do to a man in a burlap suit, so I felt safe and relieved to see him and the other dogs wearing muzzles.

We arrived at the entrance gate of a fully lighted and fenced area. The guard checked us over, opened the gate, and waved us into the classified compound. Armed guards patrolled in jeeps between two electric fences that encircled the compound perimeter. Sentry dogs patrolled the inner fenced perimeter, where the munitions buildings were located.

The inner perimeter contained many munitions bunkers covered with dirt and grass. The bunkers were called *igloos* because of their rounded shape. The igloos were well-spaced and lined up in rows. Each igloo had huge steel double doors surrounded by windowless concrete walls. The entire igloo was buried under dirt with grass. The only exposed areas were the steel doors and the air vents on top. From the sky, the area must have appeared to be a flat grassy field with a grid of roads.

My guard post included five igloos. Fred instructed me to check each door to insure that each igloo was secure. When on duty, I was to have my .45-caliber pistol loaded with one round in the chamber, but holstered until I needed to use it. If a perpetrator entered my guard post area, my orders were to use the dog to attack and shoot to kill.

I carried two black rubber gas masks, one for me and the other for Hans. I asked Fred what was inside the igloos. He told me that that was classified information. I informed him that I had secret clearance and needed to know just what in hell I was responsible to guard. Fred gave in and told me that the military had a stockpile of chemical warfare weapons inside the igloos. He warned me that I now had a classified secret to protect and not to discuss it with him again.

I was to frequently check the cages that were near the vents on top of each igloo and quietly observe the behavior of the rabbits housed inside. I also had to do the same thing with the goats that would roam freely into my guard post from time to time during my shift. I thought, *Holy shit!* Well, it didn't take my young ass but one brain fart to figure out why the army put animals in there with us. If those chemicals weapons sprung a leak, the rabbits would be the first to get the airborne scent, since they were near the vent. Hans and the goats had no shoes to protect them from contamination if chemicals seeped through the concrete walls and into the soil.

Whoa! If I smelled or tasted anything foul in the air, I was basically fucked. I remembered the tear gas drill during my infantry training. We were escorted into an empty wooden building out in the woods. They closed the doors and forced us to breathe tear gas. I remember coming out of that damn building with my eyes and throat on fire, but it was not tear gas we stored in those igloos. We were talking about the killer stuff I had learned about during basic infantry training on the use and deployment of chemical warfare like nerve gas, choking agents, and blood agents. That was the type of shit that quickly gave you an upset stomach, followed by vomiting and convulsions, and then a slow agonizing death in the fetal position. Even if I was quick enough to get my rubber protective mask on in seconds, I'd still buy the farm. What about Hans? He had absolutely no idea that he was a guinea pig, too.

I must have practiced putting on that protective mask ten times that night. Hans was getting annoyed with the exercise, so I stopped when he started growling at me. *Hans, if you only knew, if you only knew!* I thought.

By the time my first shift ended, I was thankful that all the rabbits and goats were still alive and not doing the shimmy-shimmy-shake. As I sat in the back of that troop truck heading back to the kennels, I contemplated how long I'd last doing that job with Hans. I thought I'd rather take my chances fighting the North Vietnamese Army rather than guard a village of igloos full of rabbits, goats, and killer chemical weapons.

Hans and I had gotten along fine thus far and I really loved him. For many nights over the course of a month or so, we guarded those igloos and never reported an unusual incident. Even though my fear factor never subsided, I was growing bored with the whole routine. During those long night hours on guard, I had plenty of time to become homesick. I missed the majestic Rocky Mountains towering over Denver from the west. I remembered how I'd drive fifty miles to Lookout Point, high above the city, and felt as if I could see forever. I recalled how especially beautiful Denver was all lit up at night in the crystal clear air, and how brightly the stars shone from a mountaintop view.

My house in Littleton had been about forty-five minutes away from the tranquility of mountain wilderness. I longed to again listen to the whispering aspen tree leaves, to watch water rapidly rushing over the boulders of a rocky mountain stream, and to breathe fresh cool air.

During the greater part of 1966 and early 1967, I lived in Vietnam, Japan, and Okinawa and never got used to the climates. Okinawa was a small island sixty miles long and twenty miles wide and heavily populated by every branch of the United States military. All of my friends wore military uniforms and I didn't have one civilian buddy. The local people, culture, food, language, and natural surroundings didn't appeal to me. Even if I'd been a civilian, I wouldn't have wanted to live in Vietnam, Japan, or Okinawa.

———————

I had met a local barmaid, Kiko, who worked at Club Texas. She was the most beautiful Japanese girl I'd ever seen. Kiko looked like a calendar model. It seemed like every time I entered the Club Texas, soldiers surrounded Kiko and sat at her table. During my nights off, I'd be found at the Club Texas, vying for time with her. But I rarely had to buy her drinks to keep her at my table. It wasn't long before I was taking her to the local Japanese theater and dining at her favorite Japanese restaurants off the main bar strip. We seemed to enjoy each other's company.

Kiko had never traveled outside the island of Okinawa, but learned to speak and write in English from all the American servicemen she had met working in bars. Kiko was eighteen years old and wanted to have children and make a home with me in the United States. I thought about it many times and even checked into the military administrative procedures.

There was a lot of legal paperwork involved, but deep down I knew I wasn't ready for marriage. The only girl I had ever had a crush on before was Tena. She had attended Littleton High School with me. She was beautiful. From the letters I had received, Tena was finishing her freshman year at the University of Colorado. I wondered if she'd found a steady boyfriend in college or would ever date me when I came back home.

The more I thought about marrying a shy, petite Japanese girl, the more I realized that I didn't want to take home a girl from a different culture and have to face the problems of prejudice and huge cultural transition. Like most guys my age, I was lonely for female companionship, but I had concluded that marriage would be too big a step for me at nineteen years of age. The relationship had become way too much for me to deal with. My need to break it off gave me another reason for trying to leave the island of Okinawa.

The army wasn't going to let me off the island for another year, so I pondered the idea of volunteering to go back to Vietnam. After Vietnam, I could return home to Littleton and attend a state college. That, I thought, was the perfect remedy for my current depressing predicament.

I had assumed that being an infantryman was all I was capable of doing at the time and convinced myself that fighting in Vietnam wasn't such a bad job after all. Although I was troubled with the idea of leaving Hans, I felt that requesting reassignment to Vietnam was my only way out of Okinawa. I thought that I might even get to select an assignment with an elite paratrooper outfit. With all that information stirring in my mind, I made an appointment with the personnel office to volunteer for a return trip to Vietnam.

My friends thought that I had gone completely out of my mind. Returning to Vietnam as an infantryman was the worst thing any one of them could possibly imagine to free me from Okinawa. I was told time and time again, "You'll be killed if you go back there."

I tried to justify my reasons, but I couldn't convince my friends that I wasn't insane. Their words—*dead, killed, blown away, dying, pine box, body bag,* and *POW*—failed to trigger any sense that tragedy could befall me. I had confidence in my decisions and in myself and I didn't fear their cries of danger.

I thought about what I needed to buy in Okinawa that I could add to my standard issue of combat gear in South Vietnam. Many crazy ideas went through my head. Something I regretted about my first tour in Vietnam with the 1st Air Cavalry Division was that I had not one photo to document my experience. Now I had a chance to go back and record what I would want to remember.

I bought my first camera, a Canon 35mm half-frame small enough to carry in an ammo pouch. Then I bought a shiny pair of handmade black patent leather paratrooper boots. I'd wear them in base camp when I wasn't wearing my army-issue green canvas jungle boots. The last item I bought was a bone-handled hunting knife with a six-inch blade. With those items, I started preparing for my planned return trip to Vietnam.

When I went to see the personnel clerk, he told me that I had two options. The first option was to fill out a request for transfer for duty in Vietnam. That option would get me to Vietnam and the army would assign me according to their needs after I got there. The paperwork process, however, could take several months, which didn't appeal to me in the least. I wanted control over where I was going in Vietnam, and I wanted to get there first—especially if I was volunteering to return.

The second option was to reenlist in the army for an additional year and get assigned to the outfit of my choice. The paperwork process would only take a week or so, and I could be on my way within a month. I didn't think twice about giving the army another year of my life if they could work that fast for me.

So, I reenlisted to join the 173rd Airborne Brigade, an elite paratrooper outfit operating in the southern jungles of South Vietnam. A week later, my unit of choice was granted and I received official orders to report to the Republic of South Vietnam in March 1967. Jump school had finally paid off.

Don Vestal was a good friend at the time and former infantryman. He had a job operating a forklift at the warehouse loading docks. We met while shopping at the post exchange (PX). When I saw he was wearing a CIB, I introduced myself. We had become friends and started hanging out together after work. Don told me that I had the balls of a real American fighting soldier. He said, "To go back to that hellhole after being wounded is a choice only you can understand. No matter what happens to you in life, John, I will always respect your decision." Don had been wounded in Vietnam and had received the Army Commendation Medal for valor in combat. He was counting the days until he went home to Texas. I spent my last days in Okinawa hanging around with Don until I boarded a C-130 cargo plane at Kadena Air Force Base heading for Vietnam.

What I couldn't have foreseen was how my sentry dog training would make a huge difference in why I survived my second combat tour in South Vietnam.

Return to Vietnam

I arrived in South Vietnam for my second tour of duty in March 1967, a few days after I turned twenty years of age. I flew in on a C-130 cargo plane loaded with new recruits getting their first glimpse of Saigon and Ton Son Nhut Air Force Base. Their innocence and fear of the unknown contrasted with my eagerness to get in-processed and be on my way to the elite 173rd Airborne Brigade.

The airfield was busy with the sounds of equipment moving about and the deafening roar of fighter jets speeding down runways. On the ground I rode in an olive drab bus like I had ridden on before with steel mesh covering the windows. The climate was hot and humid with that familiar smell of stale fish permeating the air. Military officers had been separated from the enlisted troops and rode a separate bus.

The vehicles cruised through the airfield passing armed guards and manned bunkers. I noticed that everything looked much as it had one year earlier. Saigon was still an extremely crowded city of people, bicycles, rickshaws, strange-looking foreign buses, and tiny cars everywhere. There was no sign of a war going on, but I knew it was a different story outside the city limits and deep into the remote jungles.

Soon I entered the gates of Camp Alpha. As I stepped off the bus, I glanced at my surroundings and realized that the camp hadn't changed either. In a familiar drill we were quickly shuffled into a large reception building. Personnel clerks greeted us with comments like, "Give me a copy of your orders, soldier. Wait right here and don't move. We'll get you processed as soon as possible." I was accustomed to the hurry-up-and-wait routine. Whatever those folks did was never fast enough for me. My main objective was to get to the 173rd Airborne Brigade, and I didn't like the idea of hanging around a deadbeat replacement camp with a bunch of bewildered FNGs (Fucking New Guys) fresh from the States sporting bald heads, new fatigues, and farmer tans.

I heard my name called over a loudspeaker, so I reported to a wooden building where a sergeant sat behind a gray metal desk. He asked me to sit while he prepared my assignment. When he finished, he told me I was going to be assigned to the 3rd Brigade, 4th Infantry Division in Dau Tieng.

I couldn't believe what I was hearing. "What do you mean?" I asked. "Didn't you read my orders? There has to be some kind of mistake here, Sarge. Are you sure you have the right guy? Look, Sarge, I have orders guaranteeing my assignment to the 173rd Airborne Brigade."

The sergeant looked at me with a complete lack of interest and sternly stated, "Look, soldier, I process hundreds of men through here each day. You're not so special because you were here before or because you have orders to the 173rd. Remember, you are in a combat zone, and Uncle Sam reserves the right to change your orders anytime he desires. Got it?"

I replied in heated anger, "Well, I'm not going to accept this. I was guaranteed an assignment to the 173rd Airborne Brigade. That's the only reason I came back to Vietnam."

The personnel sergeant didn't respond. He just sat there with his head down and stuffed my papers back into the file folder on his desk.

I shouted, "Are you listening to me? Look, Sarge! I want to talk to the officer in charge here!"

The personnel sergeant pointed to an officer who was sitting behind a desk and reading documents. I marched over to him. The personnel sergeant was right behind me carrying a brown folder containing my military personnel file.

The major looked up from his desk and asked, "Can I help you, soldier?"

I blurted out, "Sir, I have a guaranteed assignment to the 173rd Airborne Brigade and this sergeant just changed my orders and I want to know why, sir!"

The sergeant handed the major my file. The major asked me to sit down as he dismissed the personnel sergeant. After reading through the papers in my file, he explained that under normal circumstances it would be no problem to process me for assignment to the 173rd. However, the camp commander had directed that the 3rd Brigade, 4th Infantry Division be given the highest priority for infantry replacements. He indicated that I had just happened to arrive while that order was in full effect. The 3rd Brigade of the 4th Infantry Division had recently suffered numerous casualties, and the major was under direct orders to process all available infantrymen into that unit.

Again, I couldn't believe what I was hearing. I said, "This is my second tour. I should be given priority since I reenlisted to come back to Vietnam as an infantryman."

The major patiently listened, but kept telling me that there was nothing he could do to help. I was starting to comprehend that I was being screwed out of my promised assignment, and I got more enraged. I told the major that if I'd known such a thing could happen, I would never have volunteered to come back to Vietnam.

The officer sympathized with me. He told me that I was a brave man for going back into the infantry after having been wounded in action, but there was absolutely nothing he could do to change my assignment. He pointed out that he'd processed only a few soldiers who had returned as infantrymen.

"Sir, is there anyone else I can talk to?"

"No! And seeking counsel with the base camp commander is also out of the question," he barked.

The major assured me that he'd give my new assignment top priority for out-processing. I picked up my orders from his desk and stomped out of the building. There was nowhere I could go and no one else I could talk to. The army had me in a straitjacket and completely neutralized my entire plan. I paced around the replacement camp like a wounded tiger, getting more furious by the minute.

After passing the camp chapel for a third time, I decided to step inside. It was quiet and dimly lit with candles. I sat at the end of a pew and stared at a wooden cross above the altar. An older soldier sat nearby. He turned and smiled at me. I immediately recognized that he was an officer wearing the rank of captain. I also saw a small cross that was sewn to his collar signifying that he was a chaplain.

The chaplain saw that I was shook up and came over to me, shook my hand, and welcomed me to the place of the Lord. I explained my situation and how unfair I thought it was for the army to treat me in such a manner. The chaplain patiently listened without interruption. Then he told me that he'd talk to the personnel officer and see what he could do.

I waited in the chapel and said a few prayers. When the chaplain returned, he told me that he was sorry and that there was nothing he could do to help my situation. I was visibly distraught, thanked him, got up, and walked out of the chapel.

The next morning, I heard my name called over the loudspeaker, so I reported to the personnel officer. When I got there, the major told me that my out-processing was complete and a jeep had been dispatched to transport me to the airfield. We shook hands, exchanged salutes, and the major wished me luck. I grabbed my gear and climbed into the jeep for the short ride to the airfield. I still couldn't quite believe it. I was going to the 3rd Brigade, 4th Infantry Division. My new assignment was located at the U.S. Army base camp of Dau Tieng, sixty miles west of Saigon and not far from the Cambodian border.

When I arrived at the airfield, I didn't have to wait long before boarding a Chinook resupply helicopter. It felt like old times flying over the rice paddies, villages, and jungle terrain. Not knowing any of the other soldiers riding along with me, I sat quietly as my mind drifted back in time. I thought of Kenny Mook and our first helicopter ride with the 7th Cavalry. It had been almost a year to the day that Kenny and I were brand-spanking-new guys from the States. A few months later, we were in deep shit in Bong Son. And now Kenny was back home in Pennsylvania recovering from his wounds and I was back in Vietnam as an infantryman.

I had a lot of concerns and questions and concerns on my mind, like what kind of hell had the 3rd Brigade run into to that caused it to lose so many infantrymen? What would my fellow veteran infantrymen think of my volunteering to return? What platoon and squad would I end up joining? What was I getting myself into?

The second I had set foot back in this crazy place called "Nam," my entire plan had taken a sharp turn off-target. I had begun to question my ability to make sound decisions based on what the army had told me. And now I was on my way to a remote outpost almost in Cambodia.

I had no idea that this strange twist of fate meant that my work with military working dogs was not over. I was about to discover that teaming with a German shepherd scout dog in a combat situation was safer than teaming with a two-legged soldier.

Dau Tieng Base Camp

The Chinook helicopter began its descent to the dirt runway of a small base camp located in the middle of a huge Michelin rubber tree plantation. Raised in the inner city and suburbs of Denver, I'd never seen such a huge orchard of tall trees. From the air, the base camp appeared small, remote, dusty, and temporary. The edge of the Vietnamese village of Dau Tieng lay just outside several rings of connecting barbed wire and a stone's throw from the nearest parked chopper. A low range of mountains bordered the north side of the camp and within mortar range of the airstrip.

The two rotary blades of the huge Chinook kicked up dust as it landed on its four wheels. The airstrip was constructed with interconnecting perforated steel plating (PSP) that overlaid the packed dirt. I grabbed my duffel bag and walked down the ramp.

So this is Dau Tieng, I thought.

A buck sergeant (three stripes) in dusty jungle fatigues waved us replacements over to him. We handed him copies of our assignment orders, climbed into the back of a small utility truck, and headed to the replacement facility. We traveled along the camp's main dirt road, passing by a small field hospital, an armored squadron of tanks, a squadron of armored personnel carriers, a few infantry encampments, and a small motor pool of jeeps and trucks. The utility truck finally squeaked to a stop at the entrance of the replacement center. Barbed-wire fencing enclosed its perimeter.

I asked, "Are they trying to keep the replacements from running away, or what?"

No one answered me.

After we jumped out of the truck and grabbed our gear, we moved inside the main wooden building surrounded by sandbags piled waist-high. As we sat in a small classroom, the noncommissioned officer in charge, a master sergeant (six stripes), stood before us. He was a husky, towering figure with the presence of an old drill sergeant.

In a deep penetrating voice, he welcomed us and emphasized the importance of the 3rd Brigade, 4th Infantry Division's mission. He explained that the base camp was strategically located as a buffer between Cambodia and Saigon and called the area *III Corps* and *War Zone C,* according to the nomenclature dictated by high-level military commanders who decided how South Vietnam would be strategically divided for military operations.

The master sergeant explained that the entire area surrounding Dau Tieng had a high concentration of enemy troops that regularly waged mortar attacks on the airstrip. He stated that if the VC tried to overrun our camp, we'd be issued weapons and ammunition stored in bunkers inside the replacement compound.

He also explained that on March 21, the 3rd Brigade's 2nd Battalion, 12th Infantry had fought a victorious battle with the North Vietnamese Army (NVA) in a place called LZ Gold, which was not far from Dau Tieng. The battle was initiated by the NVA by reacting to a *mad minute.*

A mad minute was an operation designed to discard a unit's old and possibly faulty ammunition by shooting it up at a predetermined time. At LZ Gold, the enemy had several hidden regiments preparing to attack the unsuspecting infantry battalion. When the Americans initiated the mad minute, the enemy had assumed that the Americans were engaging with them and launched their attack, which was a complete surprise to the Americans. In the end, the NVA had lost the battle. Bulldozers were airlifted in to dig mass graves for the hundreds of enemy dead. Although the number of American casualties was low in comparison, the 2nd Battalion of the 12th Infantry and the 2nd Battalion of the 22nd Infantry were in desperate need of replacements.

The Vietnamese town of Dau Tieng was hostile and off-limits to soldiers. Even with a pass, we were required to carry our weapons at all times when leaving the confines of the base camp and entering any of the surrounding villages within the rubber tree plantations. At night, the military police patrolled the village of Dau Tieng because of its close proximity to the perimeter of the base camp. The Army Republic of Vietnam (ARVN), our allies, occupied a command post inside the village of Dau Tieng that didn't seem to deter enemy presence. That didn't seem to surprise us, since we knew that the Americans were doing most of the fighting and knew the capabilities of the ARVN were less than stellar.

Before my release from the replacement center and assignment to an infantry combat unit for duty, I had to put up with some training. The training consisted of orientation on the use and maintenance of the M16 rifle, hearing the history of the 3rd

Brigade, memorizing various Vietnamese phrases of simple communication, recognizing the different enemy uniforms and equipment, and learning about the weaponry used to kill and maim Americans. It was similar to the indoctrination I got when I joined the 1st Air Cavalry Division up north in the central highlands.

The master sergeant used a pointer and a large military map, thumb-tacked to the wall, to provide a geographical overview. He pointed out the base camp location in relation to other military camps scattered throughout South Vietnam. The 3rd Brigade's encampment split the district town of Dau Tieng into two parts. A dirt road running straight through the base camp connected the east and west ends of Dau Tieng.

Dau Tieng was large enough to contain a brigade-size unit of three battalions of infantry and an assortment of small unit attachments. Each battalion of infantry was strategically placed around the perimeter. The Saigon River snaked its way north and south, less than a mile west of the perimeter. The Ben Cui rubber tree plantation was situated west and south of the Saigon River.

Tay Ninh, the next largest populated province, was several miles northwest of Dau Tieng. Southwest lay Cu Chi, home of the U.S. Army 25th Infantry Division, nicknamed *Tropical Lightning* with its American home base on the Hawaiian island of Oahu. Cu Chi was big enough to fit five Dau Tieng inside its perimeter. The three base camps (Dau Tieng, Tay Ninh, and Cu Chi) formed a large triangle on the map.

After the briefing, I walked up to the master sergeant and boldly stated, "I've been through all this shit before. Can I skip the training and join a unit right away?"

The master sergeant replied, "No! You will be treated like everyone else with no exceptions for past experience. Besides, you can be of value to me by helping the others learn from your combat experience."

I impatiently replied, "I didn't come back to train replacements."

The master sergeant got pissed and said, "You, soldier, have a bad attitude. If you don't back the fuck off, I'll put your ass in a sling!"

I got the message and quickly backed off. My only ambition was to get to a unit. Besides, I didn't want any trouble or to get my name on his shit list and be labeled a troublemaker. The master sergeant looked as if he could kick my ass into the following week. In those days, it wasn't uncommon for a sergeant like him to take a young trooper like me to the shed of physical discipline. I had no choice but to go along with the situation.

The next day, everyone formed up for training outside the wooden hooch. The training area had mock booby traps, mines, bamboo *punji* pits, and a huge ball of dried mud with bamboo spikes sticking out all over it. A vine attached to a large branch of a tree suspended it. In reality, the trap would work like this: The spiked ball rigged by a trip wire or vine was camouflaged and suspended above a trail in the jungle. When tripped by a passerby, the spiked ball would swing down with all its momentum and hit the soldier about chest-high. There was little chance surviving several spears through the chest.

The enemy was very clever at creating all kinds of nasty booby traps for their American foes. I already knew what it felt like to be penetrated by a bamboo *punji* stake. Strangely, I wasn't afraid that I'd be wounded again, and dying was something I did not think about with a fresh twelve month-tour as an infantryman. Perhaps the fears I might have had were drowned out by my anger at going through this damn training again.

————————

To my surprise, as part of our training, two scout dog handlers with two leashed German shepherd dogs showed up to give us a presentation on their mission in Vietnam. They were members of the 44th Infantry Platoon Scout Dogs (IPSD). Their presentation was directed at trying to recruit dog handlers. I was excited to hear what they had to say. Oliver Whetstone, a dog handler whom everyone called Ollie, was from Kenosha, Wisconsin. Ollie was a tall, skinny, blond-haired, blue-eyed, friendly guy with a Midwestern accent. Ollie explained the mission of a scout dog team and how the dog provided an early silent warning for the troops of the 3rd Brigade infantry units.

Scout dogs used their natural instincts and training to alert their handler of a smell, sight, or sound. It was up to the handler to signal an alert to the rest of the patrol and provide an explanation of the dog's signal. Ollie explained that their dogs alerted on things like booby traps, enemy foxholes, ambushes, and even other animals. I was completely fascinated by what scout dog teams could achieve in a combat zone. I immediately started mentally comparing the scout dogs' duties with the experiences I had with my sentry dog, Hans.

The handlers provided a short demonstration of basic obedience. When they gave their dogs the command "Sit," the dogs sat and stayed. When the handlers commanded the dogs to lie down, the dogs obeyed. Each time they gave the dogs a command, the dogs obeyed immediately. The discipline between the handlers and their dogs thoroughly impressed me. The handlers demonstrated the dogs' ability to attack on command. This reminded me again of Hans.

At the end of their presentation, the scout dog handlers asked, "Is anyone interested in joining the 44th Scout Dogs?" They assured us that we'd be trained before we went out on a mission. All we had to do was to show a genuine interest in working with dogs. If we didn't love animals, Ollie said, then we shouldn't consider handling a military war dog.

As I listened to the scout dog handlers describe their job, I knew I'd be joining them soon. I had dog handling experience and loved animals of all kinds—even Hans, who scared the shit out of me at first. I missed Hans and wanted another chance to work with a German shepherd.

As the handlers talked with the group of replacements, I was getting more anxious to volunteer to work with them. Then someone popped a question that was probably on many minds. He asked, "Where is the scout dog team positioned in a tactical formation?"

The handlers looked at one another as if to say, "We were hoping no one would ask that question."

After a short pause, Ollie answered it. He told the soldier that the scout dog and handler always walked point. In other words, they led the way. Handlers and scout dogs were first in a combat formation, first in the jungle, first across clearings, first down roads and trails, and, it was hoped, first to find the enemy before the enemy found them. He went on to explain that after the dog alerted and enemy contact had been made, the dog and handler pulled back inside the safety net of the perimeter.

"Our job is done after we make contact with the enemy. Remember, we're only the early warning system, but we fight the enemy when we have to."

Ollie explained that dogs must have the best possible conditions to use their natural senses and instincts. That meant working them up front and on point, where the air is fresh and the scent is unobstructed. Ollie concluded that walking point was the most effective way of deploying a scout dog team and that they saved lives.

Another fellow asked, "How many dogs and handlers have you guys lost?"

Ollie replied, "A few have been wounded, but no one has been killed."

Everyone in that small training area was quiet. Ollie broke the silence by asking if any of us had experience working with dogs. I stood up and stated that I'd had some sentry dog training in Okinawa. Each dog handler asked me several questions. Apparently, I answered to their satisfaction.

They finally asked me if I wanted to join the 44th IPSD. Without hesitation, I said, "Yes!"

Out of the entire group of replacements, I was the only one to volunteer to join the K-9 platoon, the only one in the group with any experience handling a military dog, and I guess, the only replacement who would accept the job of being a point man in Vietnam. The other replacements thought I was crazy for coming back to Vietnam, and now they thought I was doubly crazy for wanting to be a point man. Maybe I was a little different in the head, but I wasn't crazy. I figured that I'd rather take my chances having a well-trained dog lead the way than trying to survive with my own experience and instincts.

The next day, the master sergeant told me that if I wanted to go to the 44th IPSD, he'd let me leave earlier than the others since I had so much experience with dogs. He called the 44th on the landline to confirm my assignment. I felt relieved to be on my way to doing something that I believed I could do successfully.

I told the master sergeant, "This isn't the 173rd Airborne Brigade, but it's the next best thing for me."

Man, was I glad to get the hell out of that replacement center.

44th Scout Dog Platoon

The 44th IPSD was the last war dog platoon to be activated and sent overseas during WWII. They served along with the 811th Military Police Company on the island of Saipan. Japanese soldiers, some in small groups but mostly individuals, hid in the vast number of caves and bunkers throughout the island. The scout dogs helped to locate and eliminate those enemy troops who resisted capture. The 44th remained on the island of Saipan until the war was over and returned to the United States on January 6, 1946, and deactivated.

The 44th Scout Dog Platoon was reactivated in 1966 at Fort Benning, Georgia. The unit was given new life with fresh young soldiers teamed with spry German shepherd dogs. Those new dance partners trained and prepared for the war in Vietnam.

The 44th arrived in Vietnam in January 1967 and built their first home in the Michelin rubber tree plantation of Dau Tieng.

I walked to the K-9 compound in the company of Ollie Whetstone and his German shepherd scout dog, Erik. As we neared the K-9 compound, I could hear the dogs barking in the kennel just beyond the entrance. The smell of dogs filled the air, reminding me of the sentry dog kennel in Okinawa.

After stowing my gear in my quarters, I was introduced to the platoon leader, Lieutenant Robert Fenner. He was a thin man about five-feet-seven with short blond hair. He informed me that the entire platoon had graduated together from a twelve-week scout dog training course at Fort Benning, Georgia. The platoon had arrived in Vietnam three months earlier in January 1967. There were about fifteen scout dog handlers and twice as many dogs. They were shorthanded for the number of missions they had to support.

Most of the dog handlers had attended college and some were college graduates. The majority failed to finish the U.S. Army Officer Candidate School (OCS) at Fort Benning, Georgia, and subsequently reassigned to the local Scout Dog Training Center.

Lieutenant Fenner briefed me on the dog platoon's tactical mission and deployment. The dog handlers were assigned to support the scouting needs of the 3rd Brigade, 25th Infantry Division. The combat units of the 3rd Brigade used the scout dog teams extensively. Some of the scout dog teams had participated in the battle for LZ Gold.

A scout dog team could be assigned to support a squad (10 men), platoon (25 men), company (100 men), mechanized armored units, and the local military police detachment. Lieutenant Fenner coordinated the scheduling of assignments when higher headquarters requested the use of the teams. The assignment policy was simple; one scout dog team per tactical mission. A schedule was developed as a matter of policy to ensure equitable rotations, so that no one hander would do more than his share of missions.

The German shepherd dog was the only breed assigned to the 44th. The only other dog breed deployed by the military was the Labrador retriever. That breed worked exclusively as a tracker dog within a Combat Tracker Team (CTT). Dau Tieng had no CTTs assigned to support the 3rd Brigade's combat missions.

All the military services—army, air force, navy, and marine corps—used military working dogs in Vietnam. There were several thousand dogs serving throughout South Vietnam performing a variety of jobs such as scout, sentry, mine and booby trap detection, tunnel detection, and tracking. The primary breed was the German shepherd dog.

As I listened to Lieutenant Fenner describe the work I'd be doing, I knew my new assignment of relying on a dog to save lives in combat was far beyond what I'd imagined I'd be doing during my second tour in Vietnam. I realized that the sentry dog training I'd experienced with Hans in Okinawa would prove very useful in preparing me for the job of a scout dog handler.

Lieutenant Fenner explained that over time an infantryman could acclimate to his surroundings and develop animal-like instincts, but he could never match the natural instincts of a dog. When a scout dog acclimates to working in the jungle, open terrain, woods, and dry and wet weather, his natural senses and instincts become unbelievably keen.

A dog's eyes can detect movement at greater distances than any foot solder, even at night. A dog is capable of hearing sounds at much greater distances than a soldier can. A dog's sense of smell and touch is far greater then any human. A dog's natural senses, coupled with his loyalty and desire to serve a master, make him invaluable as a scout. The relationship and bond that develops between a dog and handler is remarkable. The more frequent the handler and dog train, the more experienced they become as a combat scouting team.

A single mission for a scout dog team in the 44th could last anywhere from one day to a week. The K-9 platoon had compiled a record of highly successful combat missions, where no one had been killed in action. They earned the respect of the patrols they had supported based upon successful performance and saving lives.

The platoon had its own veterinarian technician specialist, Robert Glydon. He lived by himself in a hooch that was fully equipped with medical supplies. Aside from his general medical duties, Doc Glydon was also qualified to perform minor surgery on the animals.

During my orientation with Lieutenant Fenner, he had noticed my Combat Infantry Badge. He'd tried to talk with me about my prior Vietnam experiences, but the stories wouldn't come. I didn't feel comfortable discussing the specific details about what it was like to face the enemy. Lieutenant Fenner didn't ask me why I'd returned to Vietnam. My new platoon leader was soft-spoken, quiet, and easygoing. He never pushed his rank around like some of the officers I'd met in the past. I wasn't sure if I completely liked him, but he was my new boss and I had no problem following his orders. I knew that I had to pay attention to everything and learn all I could as I settled into my new job.

The Army Corps of Engineers had built the dog kennels between rows of rubber trees with floors that were long slabs of concrete. Wood and metal fence sidings and a tin roof formed the rest of the structure. The kennel had a capacity to house forty dogs. The engineers had wired the kennel for electricity and installed overhead lights. Several empty runs were used for food, supplies, dog crates, and equipment. A metal fence separated each dog's run. Sandbags were filled and stacked waist-high around one side of the kennel to provide the dogs with protection against deadly shrapnel and small arms fire.

Shortly before my arrival, the platoon had employed local Vietnamese laborers to fill and stack the sandbags around the kennel. One day, several hours after the Vietnamese departed the kennel area, one of the sandbags exploded. No one was hurt, but after that incident, Lieutenant Fenner decided not to allow Vietnamese laborers inside the K-9 compound. The dog handlers now had the job of completing the job of filling and stacking sandbags.

The dogs were kept inside the kennel after dark and the handlers slept in their own quarters. During the day, each dog was taken out of his run and leashed to his own rubber tree and next to his water bucket. The dogs were fed once in the morning and once in the afternoon.

I soon learned that if a dog handler wanted any comfort in his life, he had to trade something for it. I enjoyed hearing stories the handlers told about how they'd improved on the original design of our base camp.

One day, a few dog handlers had seen a supply sergeant from another unit preparing equipment for transport by Chinooks and C-130s on the Dau Tieng airstrip. There were prefab hooch kits and corrugated sheets of tin for roofing, neatly stacked on the ground. The dog handlers had decided to offer the supply sergeant a fifty-kilowatt generator in trade for some hooch kits and roofing materials. After making sure that the generator worked, the supply sergeant smiled, and the trade was negotiated.

The dog handlers had confiscated that air force generator while in Saigon. Such action was known as an *emergency requisition*. Most of us grunts learned to never leave equipment and supplies unattended. That air force generator had remained hidden behind the kennel until that opportunity for trading it to that supply sergeant.

Everyone had participated in cutting the planks of timber and hammering nails to assemble new hooches between the rows of the rubber trees. The "K-9 Klub" was the final construction, and it turned out to be the most popular building on the compound. We even had a volleyball court and a basketball hoop. The playground helped morale and kill time while waiting on our next mission rotation.

Two huge metal water barrels were suspended on a wood frame for showering under the trees near the hooches. A wood pallet was used as a floor. A water truck came by every few days to fill the containers. Actually, some of these rear-area-type jobs like the water delivery service were given to short-timers. Those were the lucky infantrymen with thirty days or less before going home. Having a job that didn't involve enemy contact was one of those unwritten short-timer benefits commonly practiced throughout the infantry. During wartime, I guess the army made up these benefits as they went along.

A typical day as a dog handler in base camp was different from a typical day in the jungle. In base camp, we got up at six or seven in the morning. We shaved, put on jungle fatigues, and ate some chow. After breakfast, we went to the kennel to feed the dogs, refresh their water, and clean the runs. A few handlers were assigned other cleanup chores, such as burning the shit in the outhouse. A rather patriotic crew, one of the handlers painted our outhouse red, white, and blue, but it wasn't long before Lieutenant Fenner got a call from higher headquarters to have us repaint it olive drab.

Other chores included cleaning the K-9 Klub, getting supplies, filling sandbags, and repairing hooches. The dog handlers worked at a leisurely pace. No one busted butt to get any chore done.

The bond between the handler and his dog grew so strong that many times the handler treated his dog like a human companion. So it wasn't unusual to see a handler talking to his dog like he'd talk to a human, or notice a handler sitting under a tree reading a book or letter to his dog.

After the dogs had been put into the kennel for the night, many of the handlers gathered at the K-9 Klub, where they got to know one another a little better. They played poker; read books; drank beer, soda pop, and Kool-Aid; and talked about girls, family, and friends back home.

The handlers had brought a tiny mixed-breed dog from the States to serve as their pet and mascot. Her name was 44. She had a shiny black, short-hair coat, a long snout, floppy ears, and a skinny, long black tail. The little dog ran all over the compound and hung around like one of the guys. One day, she ran into the road and was killed by a truck. We gave 44 a proper burial in a secluded place under a rubber tree.

Not long after 44 died, one of the dog handlers showed up with a tiny Vietnamese puppy he'd found on a mission. The puppy was about the size of a large squirrel with short white hair and a few black spots and floppy little ears. We named him

Hardcore because he was high-spirited and chewed on every-thing. If we found tiny teeth marks in our boots, we knew that Hardcore had been there. Hardcore spent a considerable amount of time roaming in and out of our hooches and chewing on whatever he found. He was killed when he played too close to one of the more aggressive scout dogs.

Even though Hardcore met an early demise, he fared better with us than being left in the jungle, where he'd probably become a meal for some hungry Vietnamese soldier. Dog was a delicacy in the Vietnamese culture. They raised dogs for food just like we raise cattle for food. There were no large Vietnamese dogs, only scrawny and undernourished small ones. I enjoyed seeing the bewildered looks on the faces of Vietnamese villagers when they saw a full-grown, muscular German shepherd. They had no idea what a military working dog could do.

Timber and Ambush

My first German shepherd Scout Dog was named Timber. He was about two years old and had a beautiful tan-and-black mane and perfectly shaped ears that always stood at attention. Timber was a little on the thin side and smaller in height than the other dogs. His temperament was high-spirited, aggressive, and he didn't like to be disciplined. Ollie told me that Timber would settle down after he got used to my handling. It seemed that Timber was cut from the same stone as my old friend Hans the sentry dog. I wondered why I always got the mean ones.

Base camp training was essential in preparing me to lead combat patrols with a dog. The handlers of the 44th had built an infantry-blue obstacle course behind the kennel to train the dogs. Among the obstacles were a five-foot wall with a window opening big enough for a dog to jump through, and a seesaw like the kind you might see on a playground. The dogs learned to walk up one side, balance the board in the center, and then walk down the other side as the board hit the ground. Hurdles were built to teach the dogs to jump on command, and several fifty-gallon drums were welded together to teach the dogs to crawl through tunnels.

We stretched out a twelve-foot section of wire mesh fence, staked it about two feet above the ground, and used it to teach the dogs to crawl in tight spaces. For balance training, we used both a long log without branches for them to walk across and a narrow wooden plank used as a ramp to climb up a horizontal ladder. The ladder was constructed with twenty narrow slats of wood. Each slat was spaced about six inches apart. Since dogs aren't as surefooted as cats, I found it amusing to watch how awkward it was for them to negotiate that horizontal ladder about five feet above the ground.

Basic obedience was the root of training. If the dog listened to and obeyed the handler's commands, then the handler could steer his dog through each obstacle on the course. Initially, Timber was reluctant to obey my commands. I practiced my voice and hand signals constantly and Timber and I learned to work together. I soon discovered that successful scout dog training was all about repetition. I hadn't attended the formal twelve-week scout dog training course at Fort Benning, so I worked furiously to make the best of my on-the-job base camp training.

As Timber and I worked through the obstacle course day after day, his confidence, balance, strength, muscle tone, and obedience grew in leaps and bounds. Scout dogs had to learn to maneuver on command—to go over, around, under, and through whatever terrain, vegetation, or water hazard they might encounter during a combat mission. Timber was soon performing admirably.

His only reward for his performance was the verbal and physical affection I gave him. We never gave treats to our dogs. The dogs were on a basic diet of water and canned and packaged food issued by the military and monitored by Doc Glydon. In combat situations, it was easy to imagine running out of treats and being in deep shit with a disobedient dog and Charlie lurking in the shadows of the of the jungle. Things out there happened too fast to have to bribe or coax a dog into performing. We played on the German shepherd's natural intelligence and love for human companionship to produce split-second obedience.

The breed is known for its adaptability to almost any climate and environmental condition. Their coats are black and brown, which blends well with the terrain and vegetation. Their size is intimidating and they can take a man down quite easily. They can be trained to be aggressive for sentry duty or passive for scouting. They can change from one handler to another over a short period of time. The army had decided wisely that the German shepherd was the best breed for use in Vietnam.

During my training, I learned that you get out of a dog what you put into a dog. Dogs adapt to the personality of their handler. If the handler is lazy, more than likely his dog is going to act accordingly. If a handler is an energetic go-getter, he'll have an A-1 partner.

The scout dog has to learn the scent of his master, the pitch of his voice, what type of physical gestures he uses, the pace he walks, his general mood and disposition, and which commands he gives that are more important than others. The more time the handler and his dog work together, the more responsive they'll be to one another. Consistent training creates understanding, teamwork, and unconditional loyalty.

I found that one of the more difficult parts of being a handler was interpreting what a dog already knows. I learned more about scouting from my fellow handlers, Ollie and Mike (Mac) McClellan, than I did from anyone else. The key, they taught me, was to keep my eyes on the dog at all times. A dog's natural instincts will tell you what he smells, sees, and hears, and when danger is near.

Timber would be the real point man, not me. It would be my job to translate his dog language into English so that I could convey to everyone else what he was telling me. When Timber and I worked together, he was the one in charge and I was relegated as his interpreter. That was a funny revelation, because before joining the dogs, I thought I'd be in charge and make all the decisions; now I was having to follow and take orders from a dog.

Ollie and his dog, Erik, worked with precision as a team. They were something special to watch. Ollie used silent arm and hand signals to Erik at distances well beyond the length of the standard-issue leash. Ollie worked Erik off-leash while in base camp and on missions, and Erik responded quickly to each of his commands. Their movements struck me as an art form. I hoped I could teach Timber to be as well-trained as Erik.

Mac McClellan was considered to be the top off-leash handler in the platoon. Watching Mac and his dog, Archates, work was a learning experience as well as great entertainment. The communication and movement between the handler and dog was like watching dance partners who had been together for a long time. Like the other dog handlers, Mac and Ollie were formally schooled in handling dogs and scouting techniques. However, training was at the discretion of the handler between missions, and they were constantly training. The only hard-and-fast rule was that a handler better be ready to go on a mission when scheduled.

I felt less prepared than my fellow scout dog handlers. Sentry dog training had given me basic knowledge, but it hadn't prepared me for anything like what I was about to face as a scout dog handler in Vietnam. The functional use of sentry dogs was vastly different from that of scout dogs. I preferred the intricacies of deploying scout dogs over those of sentry dogs. A sentry dog was trained primarily to guard and attack. The scout dog was used in more complex and diversified maneuvers. That made my scout dog assignment much more interesting and challenging. Even though the danger was greater in combat, I wasn't apprehensive about learning and performing my new job. Now I looked forward to my first real scouting mission with Timber.

I reported to the commanding officer (CO) of Company B, 2nd Battalion, 22nd Mechanized Infantry (the "Regulars"). The unit dated back to 1866. Their motto was "Deeds Not Words" and they were commonly referred to as the *triple deuce*. Their encampment was within walking distance of the K-9 platoon. Since we worked with a different unit each time we went out on a mission, and the turnover rate in most combat units was a constant, it was my job to brief the new CO or platoon leader on where the scout dog team was best used. When I arrived, the CO was new to the use and deployment of dogs and directed me to brief the platoon leader and platoon sergeant I'd be supporting.

The platoon leader had never had scout dog team support, so I briefed him on what Timber and I could do. He, in turn, briefed me on his unit's next mission by using a map and grid to point out the objective. The brigade's long-range reconnaissance patrol (LRRP) had recently located a large concentration of VC operating several miles west of Dau Tieng. A long column of armored personnel carriers (APCs) had assembled on the main road leading out of Dau Tieng. The first leg of the mission was to travel on several dirt roads until we reached a point near the target area. Riding inside or sitting on top of an APC, I knew, would neutralize Timber's effectiveness, but Timber and I would have to do our best.

After we reached the target area, we were to get off the road and break trail through the jungle for about a half mile until we reached a large clearing where the APCs would form a defensive perimeter. When the perimeter was set up, Timber and I would join foot patrols to search for VC. The area on the map was considered uninhabited and hostile.

I explained that negotiating our way through dense jungle terrain rather than open areas would be difficult, because it shortened the distance of a dog's alert to a target and allowed for little reaction time. One of the objectives of the scout dog team would be to locate and check out the narrow paths that zigzagged through the terrain. These trails were dangerous, but I knew that with a dog we had a better chance of getting an alert than by sending a soldier to check out that treacherous area.

Timber was frisky and eager to go on our first mission. The APCs lined up, one behind the other, on the road. With their engines running and ramps up, most were ready to move out through the main gate. On top of the APCs, several armed grunts wore helmets and thick flack vests that increased body temperature in the hot sun. Fifty-caliber machine guns were manned in their turrets and radios squawked as we prepared to move out. Timber and I followed at a quick step closely behind the platoon leaders.

The smell of diesel fuel filled the air. The platoon leader stopped near the front of the column, turned, looked at me, and pointed to an APC. The APC's ramp was already down, so Timber and I climbed aboard. The driver yanked a hand-lever. A greasy cable slowly pulled the heavy metal ramp door up until it locked in a closed position, eliminating the light from outside. Inside the APC, we had to shout to be heard above the engine noise.

I wasn't fond of APCs. Scout dog teams were useless riding inside any type of vehicle, and large APCs presented an easy target for a VC rocket-propelled grenade (RPG), which was designed to destroy helicopters and other vehicles. RPGs damaged bunkers and buildings, blew up ammunition dumps, and killed. Nonetheless, I had no choice about my assignment. It was my first scouting mission with a mechanized infantry unit, and I would have to make the best of it.

The Russian-made RPGs were lightweight, fired very quickly, and reloaded easily. Like their American counterparts, the lightweight antitank weapon (LAW), the RPGs were deployed by resting them on top of a man's shoulder. One disadvantage to the LAW was that it could fire only one shot, while the RPG could be reused. The elusive VC didn't make as easy targets as Americans did. They didn't ride around in jeeps, trucks, tanks, or helicopters. Their strengths were their knowledge of the terrain, ability to strike without warning, and the quickness with which they could escape.

Inside the APC troop compartment, two other infantrymen accompanied Timber and me. The manually operated hatch over our heads was locked open. If a person didn't mind standing, he could look out over the top of the APC as it motored down the road. Sometimes the rifleman would sit on top of the APC to enjoy cooler air and view the countryside. If the enemy attacked, the men on top could easily and quickly pile inside and return fire from a standing position. For that ride, I sat quietly with the leash on Timber, who was lying down on the cool metal floor.

I thought about many things during that trip, like my unfamiliarity with the crew. I had no idea how Timber and I would work out in a mechanized infantry unit. I didn't feel part of the camaraderie that the others displayed. It was still a question of whether I'd be accepted by the crew, but I'd come to do a job, not to make a bunch of new friends.

Each time one of the crew tried to touch Timber, he growled and showed his teeth. They quickly backed off as I shouted, "No, Timber! No!" Timber stopped showing his teeth as long as the soldiers kept their distance. Since my mission equipment didn't include a muzzle, I held Timber close on a short leash and explained to the others that he was a little aggressive around new people. I assured them that Timber would get used to them over time. I was telling a white lie, though. Timber was an aggressive dog, period. He'd even wanted to bite me many times. I don't think Timber liked his job or Vietnam. He was like a grumpy draftee with a let's-get-this-crap-over-with attitude.

One of the grunts commented, "I have a dog at home. He's a Lab. No way would I send his ass over here to fight this fucking war."

Another grunt said, "Fuck that! I don't know shit about what you and your dog are supposed to do for me. All I know is that he wants to bite my ass."

The crew had never worked with a scout dog team before I arrived on the scene. I did my best to explain how a scout dog team worked in the field. Although the grunts appeared interested, I didn't think I had gained their confidence. They seemed to take a wait-and-see attitude. But what the hell—at least I was getting to know them a little better even if it was their testy side.

I thought, *I hope they aren't like this for the whole mission. If they are, working with this crew is going to be a real bummer.*

While the long column of APCs noisily clattered down the road for several hours, I couldn't hear any war activity. As we came to a long stop, the radio started to squawk with chatter. I gathered from what I could hear that we were to break up the convoy, get off the road, and head into the thicket. I stood up through the open hatch to take a look around. The dust was heavy and irritated my eyes, so I sat back down.

The APCs moved off the road into the jungle and headed for a clearing. Sitting inside as a passenger, I had no way of knowing which clearing was our destination or how far we'd traveled without looking at the field map. The tracks under the APC slowly cranked and ground their way through thick brush. Leaves and small branches, along with bugs and fire ants, began to fall through the open hatch and land on us, so we buttoned it down. Then we had to quickly kill the fire ants that had fallen inside, because those little predators hurt like hell when they bit.

The APC moved forward, bulldozing everything in its way. It left a wide path of mashed brush in its wake and created a new trail behind it. The engine roared and the exhaust pipe spewed plumes of black smoke. The brush crackled underneath the APC's heavy metal plates. It was slow and bumpy. The tracks struggled to get over rocks, stumps, stubborn trees, and bushes.

There was no doubt in my mind that if Charlie was in the area, he was tracking us and knew where we were heading. The lead track was responsible for setting our direction and breaking the trail for the others to follow. Inside my APC, our ride was a little smoother on the path that the leader had created. After about a half hour of blazing a trail through the bush, we entered a huge clearing. I looked out at the surrounding area and saw that the APCs were assembling into a giant defensive perimeter.

The command APC was easy to spot with all its antennas sticking out. I watched it set up by a clump of trees near the center of the perimeter and figured that we must have reached our first objective. We would position ourselves defensively and organize into foot patrols. That's when Timber and I would get our chance to show what we could do.

When my APC finally stopped, the driver lowered the ramp. I got up and Timber followed me outside. I saw APCs strategically spaced on each side of ours. The gunners on top of the APCs manned their guns to the front. I introduced myself to the track commander, a sergeant, and asked him about the next phase. He said that we would set up camp for the night, send out some outposts, and deploy foot patrols in the morning. I told the sergeant that I was ready to take the lead when the patrol assembled. The sergeant nodded and told me that I'd get my chance the next morning.

It was midafternoon and hot as hell. Crews milled around

talking, assembling their gear, checking their weapons and ammunition, and setting up defensive positions. I tied Timber to the track and poured water into my steel pot for him to drink. I'd brought four canteens of water—three for Timber and one for me.

My weapon was the latest model of the M16—a CAR15—and had a metal retractable stock. When extended it served as a rifle, yet fired the same 5.56-caliber steel-jacket bullets as the M16. Internally, it had the same mechanism of functional parts as the M16. However, the CAR15 was much shorter, lighter, and easier to carry. I could hang it from my shoulder by a sling and fire it from my hip with one hand. The rifle had little or no kickback when I fired it that way. That feature allowed me to simultaneously manage Timber on the leash and shoot.

Most of the grunts carried the standard M16 rifle. Some carried the M79 grenade launcher, M60 machine gun, or 12-gauge shotguns. I was the only one sporting the new CAR15. I felt like hot shit because my weapon got second looks from the grunts who hung around the track. I had backpacked twenty clips of ammunition, which amounted to two hundred rounds, along with two grenades, a hunting knife, food, water, poncho, and a poncho liner for wrapping up in at night.

My backpack held enough food for three days, but if I had thought ahead, I could have lightened my load to dog food and two canteens of water because I was working with a mechanized infantry unit. Inside the APCs, the grunts stored all the food and water they needed, using the vehicles as pack mules. I learned that the men who rode in APCs carried only one canteen of water and a few meals of C rations when they went on patrols, because they never ventured far from their supply on the track.

When it rained, the mechanized infantrymen usually slept inside the cover of the APC. I was learning new things all the time on this trip. I thought, *Leave it to grunts. If there was a way not to have to carry their shit, they would capitalize on it.* I could understand why they were so proud of those luxuries that I didn't have when I worked with the regular infantry.

I was getting hungry, but I fed Timber first. I checked his food package for bugs before I gave it to him. Bugs were everywhere in Vietnam, and they'd get into anything except a metal can of C rations. There were probably even some that could eat through cans. Timber ate the semimoist packaged food as fast as I put it down and slurped up the water I poured for him.

I took a can of beefsteak and potatoes from my stash and soon realized that I hadn't packed a can opener. Most of the time, I had a P38 attached to the dog tags chained around my neck, but now the damn thing was missing. I felt embarrassed to ask for one from grunts I didn't know very well. I was a new face to those guys, and forgetting to pack my P38 might make them think of me as a greenhorn. I was a veteran, but they didn't know that or anything about my first tour as an infantryman without a dog.

I thought, *Ah, what the hell—I gotta eat, don't I?* So I asked a guy from New York if I could borrow his P38. He was about five-feet-seven, weighed a husky 175 pounds, and had jet-black hair and a crusty black mustache. He spoke with a heavy New York accent and was quite friendly but had an inner-city, tough-guy attitude.

He loudly said, "My P38? Sure, you can borrow it, but I'll have to kill you if you don't give it back," then immediately burst into laughter and told me to keep it as a souvenir of the 2nd Squad. I was relieved when he asked me to join him for chow. As we ate our C rations, we talked about where we were from. Timber lay quietly on the ground beside the APC, sheltered from the hot late-afternoon sun.

Suddenly, activity on the radio picked up. Troops quickly moved around the two tracks on each side of me. My track commander yelled, "Saddle up! Hurry! Let's go! Come on! Let's go! Go! Go!"

I hustled to gather Timber and my gear, leaving my half-eaten can of C rations on the ground. Clutching my backpack in one hand and Timber's leash in the other, I scrambled up the ramp into the track, then sat down with Timber between my legs on the bench seat close to the hinged ramp. The other guys quickly loaded their gear and sat facing Timber and me.

Within seconds the driver had the engine going, raised the ramp, and moved forward. The sergeant was on the radio. I leaned over to ask him what was going on. He told me that a bunch of armed NVA troops had been spotted from the air, heading away from the perimeter. His squad was closest to them, so he'd been ordered to close in and engage the enemy. The sergeant laid his compass on the map and pointed to a strategic area that wasn't too far from where the enemy was heading.

During the pursuit, Timber and I were in the lead APC. It was moving as fast as it could go. We bounced around and hung on. Small trees and bushes splintered as the APC crashed into the brush. When the terrain became rougher, the APC slowed down and mashed whatever was in its way. The APC dipped down with a jolt when the tracks hit something solid. It felt as if we were stuck in a ditch. The tracks kept grinding underneath us. The APC tried to climb up and over the sides of the depression. There was a thick smell of diesel fuel and stagnant smoke filling the air as the engine revved and the metal tracks spun in place. The driver repeatedly backed up and then slammed forward trying to break free. We rocked back and forth inside. Finally, the APC climbed up over the bank and into more jungle growth.

The machine gunner on top ducked under tree limbs. Looking up, I couldn't see the sky. Green vegetation was falling in on top of us. It felt as if we were inside a blender. Then a deafening BANG! rang out. The APC stopped in its tracks. I swore I was inside a metal drum that someone had hit with a sledgehammer. The explosion's force ripped through the thin panel that covered the engine. Black smoke streamed from the driver's compartment and filled the inside of the cabin. I noticed that the driver was wounded in the right leg as he quickly scrambled up through his hatch and out of the APC. Simultaneously, the .50-caliber machine gun on top began firing. I looked at the other two soldiers across from me. They looked startled and said nothing. It all took place in a matter of a few seconds.

There was no way to reach the handle to lower the ramp, because it was in the driver's compartment. My survival instincts took over and I grabbed the small emergency door handle and yanked it open. With my boot, I pushed the heavy metal door as hard as I could. It swung out on its hinges and latched itself open.

With Timber's leash in one hand, I grabbed my CAR15 and a bandolier of magazines. I dove through the open door and lay flat on my belly in the dirt behind the smoking track. I pulled on Timber's leash as I tried to crawl away, but was stopped cold. The end of his leash had gotten trapped between the ramp and the door. It must have happened when the ramp door had closed behind me as I'd rushed inside, leaving my food in the dirt.

The other two grunts had already jumped out of the APC and were crawling away. I frantically pulled and yanked to free the leash. It wouldn't budge, so I cut it with the hunting knife that I'd bought in Okinawa. Only about ten inches of leash remained to connect me with Timber. My dog panicked and jumped up and down as he tried to free himself from my grip. The shooting and explosions increased to my front and on the left.

I crouched on my knees, leaned against the back of the APC, and attempted to control Timber's panic. I quickly looked around and realized that the APC was sitting perpendicular on a narrow dirt road. Its back provided some protection from the incoming bullets. The front of the APC was on fire. Nothing but a flat and narrow dirt road spread out to my right. I didn't detect any shots coming from that direction. I couldn't see the left side of the road. Another stationary APC stood directly behind me in the path we had made in the jungle. The rest of the column was somewhere behind it.

The shooting increased. The VC fired on the APC column from its front and left sides. I saw my track commander lying on top of the burning APC and firing directly to his front with the .50-caliber machine gun. The vegetation on both sides of the dirt road was thick and dark. I couldn't see the enemy through it but could feel his bullets hammering the APC close to my position.

I aimed to the front of the APC into the thick jungle and fired several rounds on semiautomatic. Charlie returned fire immediately. I still couldn't see the enemy but could feel his presence. I realized that I'd become a sitting duck behind the track in the middle of the road. I decided to seek better cover. I got on my stomach and crawled away, dragging Timber from the inflamed track. We made it into the jungle about fifty feet behind the APC. Timber continued to growl and jerk away from my grasp. I was determined not to let him run. If Timber ran away, I would never forgive myself. He'd surely be killed. I thought, *We are in this together and we'll stay together.*

I scanned the jungle for signs of enemy movement. Charlie was still invisible. The column of APCs was to my left. I could hear American weapons firing and the turret-mounted heavy machine guns blasting away. Small arms fire from the Americans and VC filled the air with constant cracking noises. I heard another loud explosion nearby. Through the thick vegetation, I saw black smoke and red flames coming from a second APC. I hung on to Timber and hugged the jungle floor.

Two APCs, pinned down by enemy fire from the left and front of the column, had definitely been knocked out of action during the first few minutes of that attack. Charlie had hit my APC first, which probably meant that the ambush had sprung along the left side of our column.

Bullets zinged through the air around my position, chopping jungle foliage everywhere. Nothing was coming from my right side. That led me to believe that we were in an *L*-shaped ambush. The small part of the *L* was the direction my APCs had been heading. The large part of the *L* was the left side of the column of our four APCs. The VC we had chased had maneuvered us into their trap.

Timber was going crazy. I crawled around looking for a better fighting position. I discovered a wounded American soldier and Timber growled at him, but I kept my dog at bay. Timber was scared and didn't want to be in that situation any more than I did. The soldier sat on his knees and stared blindly into nothingness. He didn't have his weapon or a helmet on his head. I recognized him as one of the crew who had been in my APC. A chunk of shrapnel stuck out from his forehead, and his eyes were glazed over. I pulled the wounded soldier to the ground and tried to comfort him. I had no first aid bandages—only my CAR15, Timber, and a bandolier of ammunition. With my free hand, I ripped a strip of cloth from my fatigue jacket and used it to soak up the blood dripping down the soldier's face. I helped him to crawl to a nearby tree.

Timber still struggled desperately to get away and tried to bite me several times. I was getting pissed off, so I slapped Timber hard across the mouth with my free hand. That only upset him more. I quickly realized that I'd lost my composure. I shouldn't have struck my dog. There was too much confusion. I had too many things to concentrate on at once. The whole situation was out of control. For the first time, I began to wonder if I'd survive.

The constant rifle fire, exploding grenades, and chatter of machine guns was deafening. I fired into the jungle in front of the track that still burned in the road. Although the shooting was to my left, I didn't want to shoot over the heads of the Americans positioned around the APCs. I was fortunate to have a good firing position from behind the thick base of a tropical tree. It had large roots growing a few feet above the ground and connecting to its base. For protection, I wedged between the tree's roots with Timber and the wounded soldier. Even if the wounded soldier had his weapon, he was in too much shock to defend himself.

There was another APC on fire to my left behind the one I vacated on the road. It bothered me not to have both hands free, but I kept returning fire into the thick jungle to my front, aware that I needed to conserve my ammunition.

I figured Charlie would eventually surround and trap us all. I had no idea how large a force we were up against. The nonstop firing was brutal. I thought that there must be more than a platoon of VC for them to be putting out so much firepower. Maybe there were fifty enemy soldiers attacking us. I couldn't be certain.

We had started out with four APCs. Now I could only hear two of them firing their .50-caliber machine guns, a distinct American sound as Charlie didn't have fifties. Now I was certain that we were trapped in an *L*-shaped ambush. That allowed for interlocking fire and maximized the killing zone without causing friendly-fire casualties on the enemy's side. Charlie had pulled off the attack very well.

I thought, *Charlie is going to be coming around on my side at any time now. I'm not prepared to hold off an all-out assault. He's definitely got the advantage to overrun me.*

I was on the right side of the burning APC and receiving intense fire from across the road to my front. I could see from where the bullets were landing that Charlie knew my location exactly. I couldn't see the VC through the jungle but I knew they were there. I had no idea if I was hitting any of them when I returned their fire. Charlie appeared to have been dug in and seemed to know where all the Americans were positioned.

I kept reloading and fired on the semiautomatic setting. Trying to maintain my confidence, I thought that Charlie probably suspected American reinforcements would be here soon. On the downside, I also knew that the enemy's bullets and rocket-propelled grenades would take less than a second to kill us all. I kept thinking, *Reinforcements won't be here in time. We're all going to die.*

The attack wasn't typical of how Charlie operated. Usually, he would hit the Americans fast and run like hell before we could regroup and reinforce. This time, Charlie wasn't running. I figured he was preparing to move in for the kill.

Timber kept on fighting to get free. I refused to let him go and tried talking softly, hoping he'd calm down. The wounded soldier was still alive and lying quietly on the ground between the roots of a tree. If Charlie charged across the road, I decided that I'd switch to full automatic and take out as many of them as I could before they took me out.

I didn't see any other Americans near me, so I assumed that I was the only one to defend our right flank. My mind raced with frantic thoughts: *If Charlie realizes I'm the only man defending this side, he'll overrun my position. Why hasn't he attacked already? Maybe he's getting ready to. Maybe he knows I'm low on ammunition. I must make every shot count. Reinforcements have to get to us soon. I can't hold out much longer. My grenades are in the burning APC. Going back there to get them would be suicide. Timber has gone mad.*

All these thoughts were driving me out of my mind. For the first time while serving in Vietnam, I felt completely isolated and vulnerable.

BOOM! The noise of a tremendous explosion filled the air. The ground shook, and so did I. The APC I had escaped from had blown sky high. Timber let out a painful cry and went down on his side. At the same instant, I felt the heat of sharp stings burning into my face and left hand. I could feel small cuts on my face. Blood trickled down my cheeks. My hands and arms had small cuts, too. My muscles were tense. Timber was bleeding badly from his right rear flank. I had no bandages, so there wasn't much I could do to cover my dog's wound. Timber lay on his side in pain and panted quietly. I'd been lucky once more; I was still alive. The tree had taken the brunt of the explosive shrapnel. Afterward, I looked to my left front, where the explosion had occurred. The APC had been reduced to a smoking slab of metal resting on its tracks in the middle of the dirt road.

Then it became strangely quiet for a few moments. My eyes anxiously darted around the area looking for any kind of movement. I saw nothing, but I heard groans nearby. The shooting started again on the left side of the column of APCs. A soldier lying on top of the burning APC had fired his .50-caliber machine gun and then had disappeared with the explosion. I knew there was no way that he had survived the explosion. Several brass casings of .50-caliber machine gun bullets, hot to the touch and split wide open from the exploding powder, were scattered near my feet. Their black metal links still connected the brass casings.

The other APCs on my left were too close for comfort. One of them was still smoking, and I figured that it was only a matter of time before it blew up. Soldiers moved around on the ground using the protection of the APCs to defend themselves. I decided to help another wounded soldier nearby, so I left Timber and crawled over to him. Timber didn't follow me. He was too hurt to move. I recognized the soldier as the fellow from New York who had given me his P38 to open my C rations. Then I saw the most penetrating, mind-boggling scene I'd ever witnessed in combat.

That poor soldier, suffering from severe wounds, crawled on his hands and knees aimlessly. The sleeves of his shirt were torn away, exposing nothing but the remains of his arms—white bones and joints. Most of the flesh was gone. Chunks of flesh had ripped away from his thighs and back. I couldn't understand how that man could still be alive and crawl around in such a condition.

The wounded soldier grabbed my shoulder and stopped crawling. He looked as if he recognized me. Then slowly, he rolled over on his back. His eyes stared up at me. He moved his mouth and tried to talk, but I couldn't understand a word he said. I couldn't stop staring at him, either.

Then something happened that I would never forget for as long as I lived. The wounded soldier stared at me and muttered sounds I couldn't understand. His body began to glow a soft white, as if a light fog were slowly covering him. That only lasted a few seconds. When it disappeared, the soldier stopped breathing. I knew that he was dead. I closed his eyes and slowly moved away. I had seen my share of men die in Vietnam, but I'd never witnessed anything like that before. Had I watched that man's spirit leave his body? I didn't really know.

Then I thought about the tragedy of the situation. Here was a man I'd barely known and now he was dead. His face had burned into my memory. I knew that I would never be able to recall that experience without feeling the deep sadness and senselessness of that moment.

I felt helpless and hopeless. The shooting seemed to never stop.

I returned to the tree to check on Timber and the other wounded man. Their conditions hadn't changed. Timber wasn't moving anymore but he still breathed. I told Timber that he was going to be okay. I assured him that I'd get him out of there. I don't know if Timber understood a word I said, but he didn't move.

The other wounded soldier was alive but still in shock. Small arms fire poured in on us. I spotted movement in the jungle across the road. I fired on semiautomatic. The movement stopped. I might have silenced one VC, but I wasn't going out to confirm the kill.

I kept firing single shots at invisible enemies wherever I heard something. I looked around and spotted more wounded Americans huddled in the vegetation and behind nearby trees. Some were curled up on the ground crying in pain and unable to continue to fight.

I left the safety of my position again to try to help. I found the platoon leader I had met at the start of the mission. Badly burned, he sat with his back propped up against a tree. His smoking fatigue jacket had welded to his flesh. His right arm was mangled.

With the numbness of a man in shock, the lieutenant asked, "Do I look okay?"

"You look fine, sir. Everything's going to be all right," I said, trying to give him some shred of hope to hang on to.

The lieutenant said, "Before we abandoned the burning APC, I radioed for air strikes on our position."

There was nothing I could do for the lieutenant, so I returned to the tree to check on my dog and the other wounded man.

American artillery and air strikes zeroed in on our positions and dropped their loads. Nothing is more frightening than the incredible cracking sounds of exploding artillery shells and bombs within a rock's throw of a soldier's position. Those jets couldn't possibly see where we were under the jungle's canopy. I hugged the jungle floor near a tree, kept my head down, and held Timber to the ground. Even though Timber had lost some blood, he came to life when the artillery shells and bombs exploded, but he quickly wore himself out struggling to get away from me and finally gave up and lay still.

The fighting seemed to last forever, and I was absorbing too much that was happening. It was hard to believe anyone was going to make it out of there alive. I knew it was only a matter of time before I'd be hit. I tried to keep my wits about me and to stay focused on the VC who were still out there.

I began to feel a strange numbness coming over me. I'd never experienced such a feeling. I'd been in combat before, but for some reason I now felt mentally and physically strange. I felt exhausted and thirsty. Numbness spread quickly throughout my entire body. Something weird was happening. I couldn't shake it off.

Suddenly, I heard commotion in the brush to my right. It was the first time there had been noise on that side of the jungle. My numbness intensified. *This is it!* I thought. *The Gooks are coming for me now. It's all over! Charlie is at my doorstep. Charlie won't be taking prisoners. I will fucking kill myself before I let those fuckers get me.*

The noise grew closer. My adrenaline spiked. Nervously, I aimed my CAR15. I shook as I listened and waited with my eyes wide open for something to happen. Then I heard English-speaking voices calling out from the brush, "Don't shoot! We're

Americans!" I dropped my weapon in my lap and sat there staring aimlessly as American soldiers poured into the surroundings. I had been saved. Now they were going to prevent us all from being wiped out.

I was still in a daze when one of the soldiers came over. He stooped and brushed the ants and dirt from my naked arms and offered me water from his canteen. I couldn't speak or stand up. I still couldn't shake that strange numb feeling. The soldier told me to stay where I was and that he'd be back. Another soldier tended to the wounded man lying next to me. Several fresh troops moved all around the area.

I could hear the leaders giving instructions, "Let's get these wounded men some help over here! Check out those APCs for survivors! Help that man over there! Set up a firing position! Oh, my God, we have some dead Americans over there! Cover them with ponchos!"

The shooting and explosions had stopped. The only noise was the sound of American voices. I sat silently clutching the short leash still attached to Timber. I watched helplessly as American troops helped the wounded and covered our dead. It was a complete mess.

Why is this happening to me? Why can't I get up? I thought.

A huge armored wrecker drove past the tree where I sat. Right in front of me, without warning, it ran over a land mine that exploded. Everyone nearby instantly hit the ground. I didn't even flinch. Dirt and debris flew everywhere. I only sat there and watched without responding or talking. It was as if I were deep inside myself, looking out.

Our rescuers loaded the dead and wounded into APCs idling

on the road. Two soldiers came over to me. I recognized Mac McClellan, my fellow scout dog handler from the 44th Scout Dog Platoon.

Mac said, "John, I'm going to take care of Timber. You need to let these guys get you into the APC and to a hospital."

I shook my head and yelled, "No! No! No!"

Mac pried my hand open to take Timber's leash. He picked up my wounded dog and carried him away. Two soldiers helped me to my feet and into an APC. As we rode away, I sat without saying a word and not moving a muscle. I felt completely withdrawn and useless. When the APC stopped, the soldiers helped me get up and put me on a stretcher. I lay very still, staring up at the darkening sky. I heard and saw choppers everywhere.

A face appeared and looked down at me. His eyes were fixed on mine. I glanced at his collar and noticed a chaplain's white cross. My eyes welled up with tears, blurring my vision. The chaplain hugged and blessed me. He told me that the Lord was with me now and not to worry. He said that I was safe. The chaplain walked beside the stretcher while two soldiers carried me to the awaiting medical evacuation chopper. The medevac lifted off and I was on my way to a field hospital. My body felt paralyzed, but my mind was clear and active.

When the chopper landed, I was carried into a tent that smelled like medicine. I realized I was inside a field hospital as I looked up at the bright lights overhead. Wounded men on stretchers and tables were all over the place. A nurse with a mask over her mouth asked me where I hurt. I couldn't speak. I lay there on my back and stared at her, unable to respond. The nurse pointed a bright light into my eyes. I didn't even blink. She cut away my fatigue jacket and trousers and checked over my entire body. The nurse cleaned the cuts on my face and arms and then stuck me with a needle. I soon passed out.

The next morning, I awoke in a recovery tent. I sat up on my cot and looked around the room, feeling a little sore but otherwise perfectly fine. I no longer felt the strange feeling and numbness. *What the hell happened to me out there?* I thought.

The room was filled with soldiers all bandaged up and lying on cots. A doctor came over and told me to lie back down. I tried to explain that I felt fine and wanted to check on Timber. The doctor said they didn't have a patient by that name. He said that I had no serious wounds and would soon be released. I had suffered a bout of traumatic combat shock and battle fatigue. I told the doctor that nothing like that had ever happened to me before and that I'd been on many missions and seen plenty of combat prior to that incident. I asked, "Why this time?"

The doctor believed that this type of medical condition occurred when a soldier's resilience to violent combat wears down and his system has had enough. He explained that the consequences of combat could linger for a while, but that I should recover soon. He told me to take it easy for a few weeks before heading out on another mission. The doctor said that he'd release me from medical care on the next day.

When I arrived back at the 44th scout dog compound, Mac welcomed me and said that Doc Glydon had patched up Timber. Most of my gear had burned up in the APC, but Mac had put my weapon on my cot. I went to my hooch to rest. It was hard to believe, but I had only been gone for a few days.

I pondered the events that had led to the ambush and all those casualties. I thought about Timber jumping all around and how difficult he'd been to control. I was still pissed off that he'd tried to run away and even more upset that I'd struck him. I most certainly didn't want to ride in another APC for as long as I lived.

I looked at the P38 attached to my dog tags and instantly flashed back to that poor soul from New York who had given it to me as a souvenir. That young man had died in the middle of nowhere, and there had been nothing I could do but watch it happen. I played that battle over and over in my mind. All the faces of the nameless men I'd fought beside flashed through my head. *God rest their souls,* I prayed.

I briefed the mission to Lieutenant Fenner, commander of the 44th Scout Dog Platoon. He listened intently and was happy to see that I was okay. That was about it. Lieutenant Fenner wasn't one to dwell on the details of what had happened. I guess that as a leader, he wanted me to recover and try to forget.

Doc Glydon told me that Timber had been a frightened animal when he was brought to him. Timber's right rear flank had been badly chewed up by shrapnel. The dog had lost some blood but he'd recover.

I went to the kennel and found Timber lying on his concrete run. He didn't respond much when I called his name, so I went inside and sat next to him, talking to him and petting his head and back. I apologized to Timber for striking him and asked for his forgiveness.

Timber didn't show any excitement or spunk the whole time I was there with him. It was too early to expect much healing from him. Timber was obviously having a hard time dealing with all that had happened to him. I could certainly understand. Hell,

The entrance to the 44th Scout Dog Platoon compound. The sign depicts the coveted Combat Infantry Badge (CIB) and the shoulder patch (Tropical Lightning) of the 25th Infantry Division. Photo courtesy of author's collection.

The 44th Scout Dog Platoon kennel with repaired roof after mortar attack of November 9, 1967. Our dogs were so successful that the Viet Cong high command put a price on their heads. Photo courtesy of author's collection.

Members of the 44th Scout Dog Platoon (left to right) Mike Phillips,
Wiggins, "Mac" McClellan (sitting), Sergeant Shelton, Cecil Davis,
Dan Barnett, Lieutenant Robert Fenner, Unknown, Unknown, Walters
(kneeling), Bill Zantos, John Burnam, and Ollie Whetstone. Photo
courtesy of author's collection.

Sergeant Way and American Red Cross volunteer "Donut Dolly" enter
the K-9 Klub. The K-9 Klub was the dog handlers' hangout, where we
picked up our mail, played card games, discussed the stories in
Stars and Stripes, sucked down beer and soda, talked about home,
and honored fallen handlers and dogs. Photo courtesy of author's
collection.

Sergeant Dan Barnett and scout dog, Johnny. Dan was heart-
broken when he had to put down Dan Scott's dog, Shadow, after the
mortar attack on the kennel in November 1967. Photo courtesy of
author's collection.

Wade Evans and Robert Glydon, veterinarian technician (vet tech),
giving Buckshot an injection of medication outside the 44th
Scout Dog kennel area in Dau Tieng. Photo courtesy of author's
collection.

Sergeant Barnett and Ringo after Ringo returned to Dau Tieng from
surgery in Saigon. Note that part of Ringo's tongue is missing.
He was seriously wounded while on patrol, separated from his handler, considered missing in action, and found hiding in the
jungle by a passing American unit. Photo courtesy of Dan Barnett.

The author with his scout dog, Clipper. Many dog handlers took a
lot of what we called "kennel shots" to send home. Clipper was a
ham. Photo courtesy of author's collection.

Members of the 44th Scout Dog Platoon sitting with their scout dogs in the back of the platoon's truck. This photo was taken when the 44th first arrived at Dau Tieng in January 1967. Photo courtesy of "Mac" MacClellan.

Clipper gets ready for a ride on a helicopter waiting to take off from Dau Tieng airfield. Clipper loved helicopter rides because of the open-door natural air conditioning produced by a chopper's 100-plus miles per hour velocity. Photo courtesy of author's collection.

Ollie Whetstone and his scout dog, Erik, posing in the field. Erik
was killed during the mortar attack on the kennel one month
before Ollie was scheduled to leave Vietnam. They had worked
countless combat missions without serious injury for 11 months.
Photo courtesy of Ollie Whetstone.

A dead scout dog believed to be Prince. We never left our dead
behind on the battlefield and honored them with a proper burial
in our base camp. Photo courtesy of Dan Barnett.

Shadow (left) and Clipper. The 44th consisted of about fifteen scout dog handlers and twice as many dogs. Photo courtesy of author's collection.

Clipper taking a well-earned nap in the jungle. The sad truth is that most of the military dogs in Vietnam were left behind as expendable "equipment". When the author left Clipper in March 1968, he was a healthy, happy dog. Clipper is believed to have died in combat, but there is no final status posted on his archived record at Lackland Air Force Base, Texas. Photo courtesy of author's collection.

Army Staff Sergeant Robert W. Hartsock earned the Congressional Medal of Honor, posthumously, for extraordinary heroism while defending the Dau Tieng base camp on February 23, 1969. He is pictured wearing the coveted Black Beret of the 44th Scout Dog Platoon. Hartsock was the only handler to receive the nation's highest award for heroism during the Vietnam War. He was born on January 24, 1945 in Cumberland, Maryland. Photo courtesy of his fiancée, Norma E. Packard.

I knew how he felt. I wondered if Timber and I would ever get over what we had gone through in that jungle. Would he ever be the same dog as before? I knew I would go on other missions, but would I be okay? Time would tell.

A week had passed. I continued feeding and caring for Timber. His wounds appeared to be healing. I took him out of his run several times and tried some basic obedience exercises. Timber didn't respond to commands as he had before. He had no snap and lacked his usual aggressiveness. My instincts told me that Timber wasn't going to be ready for any missions in the near future. I wasn't sure what I wanted to do. I felt sorry for my dog.

As much as I loved Timber, I decided that the best thing for both of us was to ask Lieutenant Fenner for a different scout dog. The lieutenant agreed. If I didn't feel comfortable handling Timber anymore, I could replace him with another available dog.

Over the course of the next several days, I thought about that APC mission many times. I never had the chance to work Timber the way we'd trained to work. Regardless of my title as a scout dog handler, in reality I was an infantryman. We had entered that ambush with four APCs. Each had at least four to six men. Charlie's *L*-shaped ambush had surprised, trapped, and picked us off one by one. Enemy RPGs, grenades, rifle and machine gun fire had kicked our American butts that day, but the final VC death blow, which I had been so sure would come, never did.

I didn't know how many enemy troops paid with their lives. I thought I'd killed a few of them, but I never saw their bodies. No doubt Charlie had drawn us into that spot on the map to kick our asses, and the Americans fell right into the trap. Only a handful survived the attack. Without the timely rescue, I'd have gone home in a coffin.

Mac McClellan, the 44th's poet, had expressed so well what it had been like to ride in an APC and become an easy target for the enemy.

Kaiser Coffin

Aluminum-hulled hearse, carrier of cattle.
Made by Detroit to take men to battle.
Gas tank high on the left-hand side.
Charlie found out, and a lot of men died.
Gasoline tanks in the floor and wall,
One rocket hit, and you're in a fiery ball.
Beer can aluminum, two inches thick,
A browning fifty will go through slick.
Can it stop anything except a trifle?
You're safe as can be from a Daisy air rifle.
—*Michael (Mac) McClellan, 44th Scout Dogs, 1967*

Now, with all my strength, I had to put that traumatic experience behind me and heal. My task would be to prepare for my next mission. I would have to serve with all the uncertainties of learning how to handle a new scout dog. My life and the lives of others would depend on my succeeding.

Clipper

It took several days for me to decide which of the available dogs I wanted as my next partner. I selected a fine-looking dog named Clipper. I was excited from the first time I saw that dog, and he took to me as if we'd worked together before.

The military permanently marked Clipper as theirs when they tattooed the serial number 12X3 on the inside of his left ear. We both wore dog tags. Mine were simply metal ones worn around my neck.

Clipper had an official military medical record as did each scout dog in the 44th Scout Dog Platoon. It contained information such as who donated or sold him to the military, date and place of entry into military service, age, weight, height, training record, and a picture of his profile. Doc Glydon maintained a record of all the medical treatment provided to each scout dog assigned.

Clipper was docile and very smart. He had a healthy black-and-brown coat, big brown eyes, and great-looking ears. He was a handsome dog of about eighty pounds of toned muscles. Clipper walked with a sense of pride, intelligence, confidence, and control. In my opinion, he was a perfect specimen of a German shepherd, even though he was not a pure breed by show dog standards. He'd let any American soldier pet him, no matter where we were.

Whenever Clipper was around the local Vietnamese people, friendly or not, he became agitated and aggressive. One reason was that the native Vietnamese looked, talked, smelled, walked, and ate differently from Americans. Secondly, all the scout dogs were trained to hunt for those characteristics and rewarded with love and affection when they encountered them.

Between missions, Ollie and I decided to do some dog training together. We found a perfect place within the base camp's outer defensive perimeter in the tall rubber tree rows behind the kennel. The trees offered the added advantage of providing shade from the hot and humid Vietnam climate.

One of the things I wanted to teach Clipper was how to recognize and alert me to the presence of trip wires. I also needed to learn how to clearly recognize when and how Clipper alerted so I could quickly relay the alert to the other soldiers when on a mission. For instance, I had to know what Clipper would do when he sensed different kinds of danger. How would he alert me when he suspected that there were enemy hiding in foxholes, behind or up in trees, or standing in full view? At what distance from the stimulus could Clipper alert when he detected movement, noise, or smell? Did he alert the same way on a man as he would on an animal or a booby trap? For me to learn the answers, I had to work with Clipper on every possible situation.

During my training sessions, we set up a different mock situation each time. Many times, we would use captured enemy clothing, equipment, and weapons to prepare our dogs for particular sounds and scents. In this one specific training scenario, we would send a fellow dog handler out into the woods far enough so that I wouldn't know exactly where the decoy was. While the decoy hid behind a tree or some other form of cover, I'd keep Clipper distracted from what was going on by walking and playing with him in another area. I'd allow several minutes to pass before we'd begin the hunt. When enough time had passed, I would command Clipper by slapping my hand against the side of my left leg. That would be Clipper's signal to heel and sit.

When it was time to go, I would work Clipper on a six-foot leather leash. I'd tug the leash to signal Clipper to move to the end of it and give the command, "Search!" I'd keep the pace slow as if we were walking point on a live patrol. I would walk behind Clipper, keeping my eyes on the back of his head and ears at all times, monitoring any physical reactions other than ordinary behavior.

As we headed toward the hidden target this time, I observed Clipper's neck and head rising sharply and his ears popping straight up and forward. Clipper stopped, stood erect with his mouth closed and stared straight ahead, just for a moment. Then the alert was relaxed. If I didn't have my eyes on him at all times, I would have missed that first quick signal that he had heard or sighted something. Clipper turned and gave me a quick glance. I interpreted his reactions to be a strong alert. I quickly got to one knee, as I was taught, and looked in the direction Clipper's head had pointed. Clipper sat quietly and waited for his next command. I put my weapon on the ready and scanned to our front. I had seen and heard nothing. We moved only twenty or thirty yards toward where I'd assumed the target decoy was hiding.

I got up slowly and tugged Clipper to move out again. Clipper obeyed, moved a few more feet and again gave the same strong alert. I knew that he'd spotted something to the front, but I couldn't tell how far away the target was, only the direction.

There were hundreds of trees in every direction. The question was, which one hid the decoy? I decided to continue to move forward. Clipper continued in the same direction, and when he was within thirty yards of one particular tree, he stood erect with his ears up and refused to go any farther. Then the decoy came out from behind the tree. I grabbed Clipper around the neck and hugged and praised him for doing a great job at finding the target.

As it turned out, Clipper's first alert had been about one hundred yards from the decoy. Using these training techniques helped me to learn how Clipper alerted on a human hiding behind a tree. I began to repeat the training exercise over and over, even in the rain. I learned that weather conditions such as wind, heat, humidity, density of vegetation and terrain, surrounding noises, and the movement of others all played an important role in how far and strong a scout dog could alert. During our sessions, Ollie was a terrific tutor, always patient and understanding as he thoroughly explained and demonstrated the training techniques.

Sometimes when we trained, we dug foxholes and had men hide in them, or we'd hide military equipment in the woods and in foxholes to see how the dog could alert on a scent carried by the wind or saturated in the air without a wind factor, or after a heavy rain. Over time, I learned to read Clipper's reactions by concentrating on his head and ear movements. I was gaining confidence in what Clipper could do and was totally amazed at the consistent accuracy.

We couldn't conduct training missions outside the Dau Tieng base camp. Everything beyond the barbed-wire fences was considered hostile. We had to be on an actual mission for me to learn if Clipper's alerts during our training sessions would be the same in the various terrain conditions outside our base camp. I wondered how Clipper would work when fatigued by the heat. How would he handle marching long distances through the jungle, or moving across a lot of open terrain? After all, Clipper was not a machine; he was a dog and before he was inducted into the army, he had been a family pet.

Walking point was one of the most dangerous jobs in South Vietnam. Since that is what a dog handler did, he had to constantly stay focused. The enemy usually had the advantage of spotting the American point men first. With a scout dog team though, the tables were turned. The Americans had gained the advantage because a dog's sense of smell, hearing, sight, and instinct was hundreds of times greater then a human's. Clipper was like a walking radar beam.

Even though we were expected to go on missions and always situated as the lead element of a patrol, it was normal for a scout dog handler to be a little apprehensive.

On missions with Clipper, I carried my own ammunition and equipment and his water and food supply. Clipper relied on me to recognize when he was thirsty, hungry, tired, hurt, or sick. We bonded as a team, because we always took care of one another. Over time our bond would only get stronger.

When Clipper alerted, my job was to drop down on one knee immediately, determine what the alert meant, and as quickly and quietly as possible, relay the information to the men behind me. The platoon leader would then assess the situation and determine if the patrol should act on the alert, check it out, ignore it, or proceed with caution. Even though I briefed the platoon leader ahead of time, if the leader had never worked with a scout dog team, it was difficult to figure out how he would react when Clipper alerted.

Most of the patrol leaders trusted the dog's natural instincts and my assessment of the situation. However, some leaders didn't like the idea of a scout dog team making assessments of the situation. Often they'd ignore the scout dog team's warning. Sometimes they'd get away with it, but other times they paid a price. When I worked as point man on a scout team, I insisted that every strong alert my dog gave be checked out. I didn't like the crapshoot of ignoring the dog's signals.

If soldiers checked out Clipper's alert and we didn't make enemy contact, he and I resumed the lead and continued pushing in the mission's direction. If Clipper's alert did result in enemy contact, he and I quickly moved back inside the patrol's main body if the situation allowed.

The scout dog team's job was considered complete after the enemy was engaged. Standard operating procedure for every mission was that when the fighting was over, and if casualties were light, the scout dog team resumed the point position and continued the mission. If casualties were considered heavy, the entire platoon was usually relieved from its mission and replaced by a fresh unit. I had been trained as an infantryman and scout handler to follow that process, but it didn't always work as planned. Sometimes, the scout dog handler and his dog were so far out in front that they got caught during a fight.

Since I'd been in combat before, I took my base camp training with Clipper seriously. I knew that I'd have to rely on him. I had experienced negotiating jungle conditions, open terrain, rivers, creeks, villages, hills, valleys, rice paddies, nighttime operations, and various weather conditions. Now I had to adjust to working with a dog under those same conditions and rely on him more than any human I had worked with before. The patrol behind Clipper and me would watch out for our flanks and rear and depended on Clipper for an early silent warning of danger to their front. I wanted to earn respect and confidence from everyone by doing my job and hopefully save lives in the process.

Death in the Kennel

Fred DeBarros and his scout dog, Tinzer, were original members of the 44th Scout Dog Platoon that trained at Fort Benning and arrived in Vietnam in January 1967.

Fred and Tinzer took one of their turns on the platoon's rotation schedule to scout for an infantry unit on a search and destroy mission in the surrounding jungles of Dau Tieng. After a few days in the bush without making enemy contact, Fred was ordered to join a small detachment of the platoon on a night ambush operation that would set up alongside a narrow dirt road the Viet Cong had been using.

It was dusk when Fred's detachment of ten infantrymen reached a suitable ambush site inside some thick vegetation a few yards off the road. Everyone observed complete silence as they quietly settled into hidden positions for what Fred thought would be a long and boring night, like most ambushes he had supported.

After an hour had passed, it was completely dark and the surrounding jungle came alive with its characteristic nocturnal noises. That was when Tinzer started fidgeting and turning away from the road and toward the rear of the ambush. Fred thought there was probably just an animal moving through the darkness behind them, which was a common alert, so he ignored Tinzer's movements and kept pulling him around to observe the road.

This went on for a while before Fred realized that Tinzer was really indicating that something other than animal may be moving behind them.

As a precaution, Fred quietly passed the word down the line to advise the detachment leader that Tinzer was alerting to the rear and that it could be human scent and movement. The detachment leader was quick to react and passed the word back along the line to quietly change positions and train their weapons to the rear.

Shortly after they were all in a position to defend the rear, all hell broke loose as a force of Viet Cong attacked with small arms fire at close range. The firing was intense from both sides as muzzle flashes and bullet-tracers lit up the night. Fred kept shooting through the darkness in the direction of the muzzle flashes while Tinzer lay by his side without moving or barking.

After a long exchange of concentrated firing, the enemy broke off contact. Everyone stayed vigilant the rest of the night waiting nervously for the enemy to launch a counterattack, but it never happened. By morning's light, the weary detachment found three dead enemy soldiers nearby and some blood trails leading away into the jungle. The Americans had suffered no casualties.

Fred believed that the enemy must have spotted the detachment setting up the ambush and decided to wait until everyone got settled before sneaking up behind them. And everyone knew that if it hadn't been for Tinzer's unwavering attention to the rear and Fred's astute judgment to report it, the detachment easily could have been surprised by the enemy and wiped out that night. Tinzer had saved the lives of the men in that detachment and Fred showered him with praise.

Mission after mission, scout dogs alerted American patrols of snipers, ambushes, and booby traps. Their bravery and courage in inhospitable conditions and often under fire saved many American lives. The enemy counteracted the success of the scout dog teams by rewarding their soldiers who killed the dogs and handlers.

On November 9, 1967, several scout dog teams from the 44th Scout Dog Platoon in Dau Tieng were out on combat missions supporting local infantry units. As it got dark that evening, I walked to the kennel to say good night to Clipper. It was a typical quiet evening in base camp, with all of the dogs sheltered in the kennel for the night. After hanging out in the K-9 Klub until after ten o'clock that night, I hit the sack. Most of the other dog handlers had already turned in for the night.

After midnight, I awoke to the deafening sound of a nearby explosion. I could hear and feel the shrapnel splintering the outside walls of my hooch. I jumped up, grabbed my CAR15, slipped my bare feet into jungle boots, and went flying into the screen door. I tripped and fell to the ground outside. Clad only in my underwear and unlaced boots, I darted to the nearby bunker. It was pitch-black outside except for the blinding flashes of light that were coming from exploding missiles.

Everyone else hurried to one of the two bunkers' entrances outside our sleeping quarters. The bunkers were huge steel containers, once used as shipping crates and buried in the ground under dirt and sandbags. Portholes were cut through the steel on all four sides to provide ventilation and create a 360-degree field of fire. We had no radio communication between bunkers on the K-9 compound.

After I entered the bunker, I couldn't stop shivering. My hands and body were shaking uncontrollably. It was a terrifying experience to wake up at night, in the supposed safety of my base camp, with my life in danger.

While everyone ran for their lives to the safety of the bunkers, I heard at least ten explosions. Dog handlers crammed inside the bunkers and huddled tightly in the small floor space. Although there was no way to account for everyone, it appeared as if by some miracle no one had been wounded while running to the safety of the bunkers. When I looked around, I realized that I wasn't the only one in underwear and unlaced boots. Hell, some guys were barefoot. We were all wide awake and shocked that for the first time, the K-9 compound was taking direct hits from enemy mortars in a surprise attack.

Another volley of shells whistled down and exploded in the trees and on the ground. I shuddered with fear at each metallic sound of shrapnel striking and piercing objects all around us.

The bunkers provided the only safe area to fight from on the K-9 compound. American troops had armed the compound with several mortar tubes to add to our defense. The enemy was somewhere inside the nearby rubber trees and not far from the base camp perimeter. From the sounds of the explosions, Mac McClellan suspected that Charlie, launching his larger 82mm mortars, overpowered the American infantry platoon's portable 61mm mortar tubes.

The K-9 compound was several hundred yards inside the primary defensive perimeter of Dau Tieng. The bunkers were fully stocked with weapons, grenades, and plenty of ammunition.

Between barrages of mortar fire, the dog handlers nervously waited to see the silhouettes of enemy soldiers assaulting the compound. If we spotted the VC, that would mean that they'd breached the perimeter.

We loaded weapons, pointed them out of the portholes, and waited for a target to appear. During the relentless VC barrage, one round hit the top of my bunker and exploded. We all flinched simultaneously. The bunkers had never been tested like that. We didn't know how safe they'd be. But our bunker held up, and made us feel more secure.

The kennel was across an open area from the bunkers. We couldn't see the kennel very well through the dark shadows of the rubber trees that surrounded the compound. Months before the attack, we had filled and stacked sandbags waist-high on the side of the kennel that faced the bunkers. On the night of the attack, the back side of the kennel was still unprotected. No sandbags protected the dogs from shrapnel or the bullets that flew over the ground.

During the bombardment, the war dogs barked in panic. They were used to their handlers being with them during dangerous situations. I knew Clipper felt confused, wondering where I was or when I'd be coming to move him out of harm's way. Because of the frequent volley of explosions inside the compound, it was too dangerous for us to leave the bunkers. As long as the dogs kept barking, the dog handlers assumed they were okay. However, several of the men wanted to get their dogs and bring them inside the bunkers. Lieutenant Fenner directed us to quiet down and stay where we were.

We could hear small arms and machine gun fire in the near

distance. We had assumed Charlie had decided to assault our camp's perimeter of defense, which was well-fortified and manned 24 hours a day, 7 days a week, 365 days a year. If Charlie somehow got through the perimeter, the K-9 compound was the second line of defense. I wondered how long we would be able to hold off an enemy assault.

The scout dogs were the only ones unprotected from an enemy ground attack. Caged inside their runs, they couldn't get out. If Charlie and his sappers got to them, the dogs could be easily killed without having the opportunity to fight back.

Every dog handler's worst fear became a reality when several 82mm mortar rounds hit the tin roof over the kennel and exploded, sending shrapnel in every direction.

"Oh, my God!" one handler screamed.

Another handler yelled, "They hit the kennel! They hit the kennel!"

The scene inside the bunkers was chaotic. We strained to see through the portholes. The tin roof of the kennel had been visibly damaged. We knew that one or more of our dogs had either been wounded or killed. The question was, which dogs? Several of us started to leave the bunkers. Lieutenant Fenner screamed, "Everyone stay in the bunkers! That's an order!"

Indescribable dismay filled the eyes of my fellow dog handlers. We couldn't do anything but wait as more rounds exploded outside. I worried that Clipper had been hit or, worse yet, killed. Several more explosions damaged trees near the entrance to our small compound. I figured that the VC had directed fire using a spotter who was hiding nearby.

To our surprise, a jeep with its lights on and no doors or

canvas top suddenly roared through the compound's entrance. Someone screamed, "That's our jeep! Who the hell is it?"

A man jumped out of the jeep and ran toward the bunkers. Sergeant Dan Barnett was halfway out of his bunker, motioning the man to hurry when a mortar landed and exploded near them. We watched in horror. The impact of the explosion blew the driver to the ground face first. The jeep lurched forward from the blast. Its engine died when it was a few yards from the bunkers. A large piece of flying shrapnel shattered Sergeant Barnett's elbow.

The sergeant Barnett and another man dragged the jeep driver inside the bunker. Someone turned on a flashlight to identify him. It was Kentucky, one of the new men in the platoon. His back side, from head to buttocks, was bleeding and peppered with gray and silver slivers of shrapnel. He looked more frightened than filled with pain. A quick look at his wounds indicated that Kentucky wasn't in a life-threatening situation, but he definitely needed medical attention. A dog handler got some field dressings from the first-aid kit and wrapped up Kentucky's larger shrapnel wounds and Sergeant Barnett's elbow.

Kentucky's pain would have been unbearable if he sat down or rested on his back. Two dog handlers helped him to stand, because that would be less painful. The front of his body and hands were unscathed. He didn't complain and tried to tough it out. Most of the dog handlers had experienced the brutality of combat. It was easy for us to imagine how bad Kentucky must have felt. We knew that when the blood dried from all those splinter wounds, Kentucky had better not try to move or he would experience pure agony.

Lieutenant Fenner asked Kentucky why he'd driven a jeep into the middle of a mortar attack. Kentucky explained that he'd been visiting a friend across the compound when he saw the flashes of light and heard explosions. The area he'd been in wasn't under attack. Kentucky wanted to help us, so he drove the jeep as fast as he could. Kentucky said, "Hey, I almost made it through before that mortar hit me from behind."

A voice in the bunker blurted, "Kentucky, you're fucking nuts! You should have stayed put!"

––––––––––––––

Shortly after we brought Kentucky into the bunker, the mortar shells stopped dropping. The only noises we could still hear were the pitiful sounds of our scout dogs crying out in the kennel. Lieutenant Fenner finally let us check on them. In underwear and boots and carrying our weapons loaded and on the ready, one by one, we darted from the bunkers. We moved quickly over shards of glass from the jeep's blown-out windshield and debris from the trees and kennel.

After a shelling like that, there was always the danger that one of us might step on an unexploded mortar round lying on the ground. We also knew that the enemy could be waiting behind rubber trees or lying in the weeds seeking a target. Even so, we braved the dark unknown to reach our dogs. The closer we came to the kennels, the louder the dogs howled. They knew we were coming and couldn't wait to get out of the runs. I couldn't imagine how they must have felt being trapped and helpless while waiting on their handlers to rescue them.

A few of us stepped inside the open entrances at either end of the kennel. Others checked the surrounding area for signs of the enemy. In the darkness, we could hear the dogs groaning in pain.

A voice cried out in the darkness, "My dog's hit!"

I was only a few feet inside the kennel. I stopped in my tracks, apprehensive about what I might see. Clipper's run was close to the middle. I took a deep breath, and hoped I'd find him alive and unhurt. I moved closer to his run. Unexpectedly, someone flipped on the overhead lights to reveal a sickening sight. Large pools of blood marked the entrances of several dog runs. Splinters of wood and structural debris littered the concrete floor. Gaping holes scarred the tin roof.

By now, most of the dog handlers had made it inside the kennel. Several handlers sobbed as they held their wounded and bleeding companions. Some of the dogs lay in pools of blood inside their runs. Others limped from their wounds.

I hurried to Clipper's run. He was pawing at the door and trying to get out. I opened the door and went inside. Clipper jumped all over me with his bloody paws. I touched and examined every inch of his body. Although Clipper's paws were bloody from clawing at the door, he had no life-threatening injuries or any wounds at all. Clipper was so excited to see me that he couldn't keep still. I sat on the floor, hugged him tightly, and cried like a little kid. I told him how sorry I was that I hadn't been able to protect him. I felt partly responsible that my dog had been helplessly caged during that attack.

The sight of the other suffering dogs completely devastated me. The smell of blood saturated the air, and Doc Glydon was away on R & R, so he wasn't available to tend to the wounded and dying animals.

On that awful night, Ollie, who was scheduled to rotate back to the States in only a few months, found his scout dog, Erik, serial number 36X3, bleeding to death in his kennel run. Erik's body had taken several shrapnel wounds. Both of the dog's lungs were punctured. Ollie held his limp friend in his arms and cried. He was crushed to know that his best friend suffered painfully and was dying slowly.

No one could save Erik's life.

Mac came over to Ollie and sadly offered him his weapon. Ollie told Mac that he couldn't bring himself to use it, even to relieve Erik's pain and suffering. He asked Mac if he would take care of the terrible task. Visibly shaking, and with tears streaming down his face, Ollie stood on unsteady legs. Without looking back, he walked away from Erik and Mac. After Ollie left the kennel, a single shot rang out. Erik was dead.

Ollie had made the hardest decision of his life by releasing Erik. The thought of losing his best friend must have been devastating to him. Ollie had trained with Erik back in the States, and worked with him on countless missions in Vietnam. We considered Ollie and Erik to be one of the best-trained scout dog teams in the platoon.

I'd learned a great deal about scout dogs from Ollie and held him and Erik in the highest respect as soldiers and friends. Ollie and Erik had been through tons of scrapes with the enemy over the past ten months. There was no telling how many lives had been saved as a result of Erik's alerts and courage under fire. On that tragic night, Ollie had to watch helplessly as the kennels were bombed, only to find Erik bleeding to death. The experience was unbelievably painful for him and for the rest of us.

Dan Scott's dog, Shadow, serial number 9X00, was in the run next to Clipper. Barely breathing, Shadow lay in a large pool of blood. Dan was on the other side of base camp during the mortar attack and couldn't get back to the K-9 compound in time to do anything for his dog. So Sergeant Barnett tended to Shadow after making sure his own dog, Sergeant, was okay.

On that tragic night, Doc Glydon's absence was deeply felt. He was used to making medical decisions about the dogs. It became our duty to make tough choices about the injured and dying. Sergeant Barnett stood over Shadow struggling over whether to put him out of his misery or allow the dog to continue suffering in hopes that he'd somehow recover. Barnett assessed Shadow's wounds and decided that he was too badly hurt to be saved. Shadow was slowly dying from a massive loss of blood. In the absence of Shadow's handler, Dan Scott, and the veterinarian, Barnett decided Shadow's final fate. He fired a single bullet into the dog's head. It was one of the hardest calls any dog handler ever had to make. Barnett was visibly shaken, realizing he had made the most difficult call of his life.

When Dan Scott returned later that night to find Shadow in his run, dead from a gunshot wound to the head and covered in a poncho, he went berserk. Several dog handlers had to restrain him from physically attacking Sergeant Barnett. Dan believed that Shadow hadn't been so badly wounded and didn't need to be killed, that with proper medical attention and a blood transfusion, he'd still be alive. He pointed out that another handler's dog had been saved, even though he'd suffered severe face and jaw wounds.

But Sergeant Barnett had done what he thought was best for the dog. He stood his ground and defended his decision. Nevertheless, Dan called Barnett "The Dog Killer." Dan Scott and Shadow had worked together for eight months and had become inseparable. I wondered if Dan would ever recover from Shadow's untimely and unfortunate death.

A medical vehicle took Kentucky and Sergeant Barnett to the Dau Tieng field hospital. We all pitched in to help clean wounds and patch up the dogs that had survived. I washed the blood-stained concrete floor of the kennel. Other dog handlers picked up debris and hunted for unexploded 82mm mortar rounds.

Before long, it was morning and the sun was shining. Even with all we'd gone through, none of us looked tired, probably because we were so keyed up all night. That morning, we paid our respects by giving Erik and Shadow a proper burial. While someone led us in prayer, Dan Scott and Ollie Whetstone buried their friends. We marked the dogs' graves in the scout dog cemetery, which was in a quiet spot away from the kennel and sleeping quarters, under the shade of rubber trees.

Later that morning, someone yelled, "Formation!" We assembled in front of the orderly room next to the K-9 Klub. Lieutenant Fenner made an announcement that Major General Mearns, Commanding General of the 25th Infantry Division, was flying in from his headquarters in Cu Chi. The CG planned to visit the 44th and evaluate the damage to our K-9 compound. Lieutenant Fenner ordered us to clean up, shave, and get into proper uniform.

Soon thereafter, someone spotted a clean jeep heading to the K-9 compound. We were alerted and gathered in the parking area in front of the K-9 Klub. Several jeeps drove under the 44th Scout Dog sign and into our small compound. When the vehicles stopped, Lieutenant Fenner walked to the lead jeep, which sported two white stars on small red flags, and saluted. Major General Mearns returned his salute, stepped out of the vehicle, and shook the lieutenant's hand. It was the first time that a distinguished military officer had visited the K-9 compound since it was built eleven months earlier.

Fifteen dog handlers gathered to greet him. We hung out in a very loose group. Anyone would hesitate to call it a military formation. The dog handlers weren't showing disrespect but we weren't used to showing snappy protocol. At least we were each properly dressed and had baseball caps on our heads.

Major General Mearns addressed us and expressed his sorrow over the scout dogs that had been lost and the handlers and dogs who had been wounded. He explained how important scout dogs were to the mission of infantry in Vietnam. He also described how the 44th had successfully contributed to the mission of the 3rd Brigade, 25th Infantry Division. It was obvious that the CG was well informed of several recent K-9 missions that had saved American lives. The look in his eyes was sincere as he shook each dog handler's hand after his short speech.

The CG took Ollie Whetstone and Dan Scott aside and spoke to them privately. The general asked Ollie how long he had before he rotated back to the States. Ollie told him that his rotation date would be in January, only two months away. Major General Mearns promised Ollie that he'd be home for

Christmas. He asked Dan the same question. Dan said that he was scheduled to rotate in four months. The general told Dan that, regrettably, he had too much time left to justify ordering an earlier rotation date. After talking to Ollie and Dan, Major General Mearns toured the damaged kennels and the rest of our compound. He ordered his attending staff officers to make sure that repairing the kennel would be given top priority.

———————————

The VC were quickly learning the advantage we had by using scout dog teams against them, and now they were doing all they could to eliminate them. I was very grateful that Clipper had lived so that he could help me and others make it through the battles yet to come. With great sorrow for our losses, I prepared for my next mission to hunt down the enemy with extreme prejudice.

Trapped

A few weeks after the demoralizing attack on our K-9 compound, the kennel had been repaired and we were going about our business as usual. Those of us who were healthy continued to support the infantry units of Dau Tieng.

On November 25 Dan Scott, Mike Eply, Ed Hughes, Ollie Whetstone, Mac McClellan, Dan Barnett, and a few others were socializing in the K-9 Klub. A fight broke out between Mike and Ed. During the scuffle, Mike went flying through the screen door and hit the hard ground outside. Ed ran after him to punch him again. Lieutenant Fenner came out of nowhere and stepped between them to end the altercation.

Mike complained to Lieutenant Fenner that his ankle hurt so badly he couldn't go on his assigned mission in the morning. Lieutenant Fenner, clearly angry, ordered Ed to take Mike's place.

Ed turned to Mike and with hostility in his voice said, "Eply, if I get killed out there tomorrow, I'm gonna come back here and kick your fucking ass."

Mike said nothing as he limped away, but I'm sure he thought about the possibility of Ed returning from the dead to exact his revenge.

In spite of the brawl between Ed and Mike, we all liked Ed and nicknamed him "The California Boy." He and I were good friends. Before joining the canines, he explained, he was assigned to the Old

Guard to stand watch over the Tomb of the Unknown Soldier at Arlington National Cemetery in Virginia. Ed boasted that for a soldier to be an honor guard, he had to project the right image of a Hollywood model with a certain height and weight and the right physique. Short and stumpy guys weren't considered for that assignment. The public visited the tomb every day, he said, and the guards had to stand tall, always look clean cut. There were no excuses for failing to strike the right pose.

Well, Ed was tall and had the ideal physique for that job, and I could picture him in a perfectly tailored army dress-blue uniform with shoes and boots spit-shined, although most of us dog handlers had never seen dress blues.

Ed demonstrated how to march properly with stiff and snappy movements as he paraded around like a toy soldier. Ed had learned a marching rhythm that the rest of us had never seen before. We got a kick out of watching him demonstrate Old Guard rifle drills with his M16. Yup, among the scraggly scout dog handlers of Vietnam, he was the California Boy.

The next morning I got up early and greeted Ed in the kennel while he was with his dog, Sergeant. I let Clipper out of his run. As usual, Clipper raced past me and headed to his tree. He'd sit there until I arrived to hook him to the twenty-foot leash and bring a fresh bucket of water.

Each dog had a tree with his name on it. I had nailed a small piece of wood from an ammunition box to Clipper's tree and painted CLIPPER on it in large black letters. Below his name, in smaller letters I wrote, "War is Good Business. Invest Your Dog." At the time, I thought that was a pretty cool slogan.

While I cleaned Clipper's run, I couldn't help noticing the faded stains of blood in Shadow's and Erik's empty runs—a constant reminder of what had happened to them. I wondered if these dogs would be replaced. We'd had no new dogs in the eleven months the platoon had been in Vietnam.

When I returned to Clipper's tree with my field gear, he became excited, wagged his tail, and paced back and forth. It always amazed me how a dog knew when it was time for a mission. He knew he was going somewhere and would soon have freedom from the kennel area.

I met Ed near the entrance of the compound. He and Sergeant were ready to leave. As the sun peeked over the trees, we walked onto the main dirt road leading to our respective units of assignment. Along the way, we talked and agreed to get together to exchange stories after the mission. I didn't ask Ed about the incident with Mike, because it didn't seem like an appropriate issue to discuss at the time.

Ed and I split up when we reached the infantry battalion area so that I could search for the unit sign that read "Company A" while Ed looked for his outfit. They weren't difficult to find. Because pride was such an important part of army life, every unit marked their territory with their name, unit crest, unit patch, and logo. We knew we'd found our mission assignments when we saw soldiers milling around and preparing their field gear.

When I arrived at Headquarters, Company A, I recognized the company commander by the two black bars attached to his helmet. He finished his conversation with several lieutenants, acknowledged my presence, and introduced me to the platoon leader Clipper and I had been assigned to support. We shook hands and the lieutenant knelt to pet Clipper. He seemed pleased to have a scout dog team with his unit.

The platoon leader briefed me on the mission. Choppers would fly the company into a landing zone close to the Cambodian border and west of Dau Tieng. My platoon was to hit the ground first and serve as the company's point platoon with the scout dog team in the lead.

Other platoons were to follow after the first platoon had secured the LZ. Then each platoon would split up and maneuver into tactical sweeping formations. The orders were for us to sweep the South Vietnam side of the Cambodian border for several miles. Battalion reconnaissance teams had reported large numbers of North Vietnam Army regulars and Viet Cong throughout the area. No other American units were operating in that area. It was a remote area and considered a primary NVA infiltration route from Cambodia into South Vietnam. The infamous Ho Chi Minh Trail was just inside Cambodia and stretched all the way into North Vietnam.

The field map showed terrain that appeared to be fairly flat with thick vegetation and jungle. There were also a few large natural clearings running alongside the border. American troops were never to cross into Cambodia to search for or pursue the enemy. I told the lieutenant that while I was working the point position someone needed to direct my forward movement to make sure that I didn't venture into Cambodia. He smiled and assured me that I'd stay advised as long as I didn't get too far ahead of the platoon.

The border between South Vietnam and Cambodia may have been clearly designated on the map, but it wasn't marked on the ground. Where we were going there would be no villages, signs, fences, walls, outposts, roads, or other significant ground markers to identify the boundary separating the two countries. I knew that it would be easy to cross into Cambodia accidentally. Besides, who would have reported us if we accidentally crossed the border?

The area of operation (AO) we were going into was designated as a hostile free-fire zone, which meant that I could lock and load, fire first, and ask questions later. I liked that scenario over the limited-fire zones, where I could only lock and load when the enemy fired at me first. And operating in a "no-fire zone," which was usually in densely populated areas, just plain sucked, like walking around with a target on my chest. The enemy had the upper hand, anyway, because he blended right in with the population. Evidently, in no-fire zones, it was okay for us to have casualties, but we couldn't inflict them for fear of killing innocent noncombatants. I didn't think that the people who made up these rules had ever served as infantrymen.

It was more than frustrating that the American and Vietnamese political leaders were making and controlling the ground rules of war. Even though Vietnam was classified as a conflict and not a war, soldiers were killing each other just the same. The ground rules for fighting the Vietnam *conflict* should have been left up to the men who were fighting it. If Charlie didn't abide by any rules of war, and he didn't, why handicap Americans with restrictions? Vietnam was no gentleman's war. Soldiers on both sides were serious and used every trick possible to hunt and kill each other. I believed that American soldiers put themselves at a disadvantage by fighting within the guidelines of those ridiculous fire-zone rules.

I told the lieutenant, "Get real! It's a bunch of bullshit that we can't pursue Charlie into Cambodia. Those multiple fire-zone restrictions are a crazy idea!"

The lieutenant replied, "Just do your job, soldier!"

I learned that the company was at full strength with four platoons of about 150 fighters. My platoon would be breaking trail when we reached the landing objective. The other platoons would follow not far behind.

Ed and I had both been assigned to the same mission, and not knowing anyone in my platoon, I wondered where he and his dog, Sergeant, were positioned in relation to my company of assignment.

The platoon split up for transport into small chopper-size groups. The morning sun was heating the air. I thought it might hit over 100 degrees. My backpack was jammed full with the usual stuff. I had enough food and water for three days and expected to be resupplied in the field. My gear weighed about fifty pounds. I listened to some guys complaining that they were carrying over sixty pounds of gear on their backs. No one was going to feel sorry for them and offer to carry another man's load. I had at least one hundred rounds of ammunition for my CAR15, but had forgotten to pack any grenades—which could have affected the outcome of the mission. I moved out to the Dau Tieng airstrip with my chopper group and the rest of the platoon. The choppers warmed up and prepared to go. The door gunners' M60s were freshly oiled and loaded with ammunition. I climbed aboard with several infantrymen I didn't know.

When we were airborne, Clipper stood up and leaned forward, sticking his head out the open door. His eyes squinted with his mouth wide open as his tongue dangled out to one side of his mouth. It was his favorite position during a cool chopper ride. Who could blame him? He was a dog, and dogs liked that cool fresh air just as much as the troops in Vietnam.

It was really a comfort for everyone to have that natural air conditioning during a chopper ride. Clipper knew I had a solid grip on his leash as he leaned out the opened door, stretching the leash taut. We'd done this before and seemed confident that I wouldn't let go of him. The lean out the door had become Clipper's typical tactic when he rode in a chopper.

On these helicopter rides, the weight of Clipper leaning forward out the opened door usually tired my arm. After a while, I would use his leash to yank him back inside. When I did that, Clipper would back off and lay down beside me for about a minute. Because the view and cool air felt so good, Clipper would get back up and assume the leaning-out-the-door-position. Again, I would yank him inside. That back-and-forth routine went on for every chopper ride. What was a dog handler to do?

On this particular mission, I thought of a possible solution to

Clipper's habit of stretching the leash taut while leaning forward and poking his head out of the chopper's opened door. I decided to take up a little slack in Clipper's leash and clutch it tightly in my fist. I figured that when Clipper got up and assumed the leaning-out-the-door-position, I'd just let the slack go. Well, I did and Clipper freaked out. He fell forward enough to think that he might be falling out of the chopper. His ears and the hair on the back of his neck stood straight up like a porcupine. When he turned to me, his eyes were as big as baseballs. He dropped to all fours so fast that he scared himself. Clipper hugged the metal floor of the chopper on his belly and scooted backward to get next to me. He gave me that dirty dog look, which I interpreted as, "Hey, John! Are you trying get me killed?" I looked at Clipper and hugged him with affection as I said, "Hey, buddy, are you okay? I just saved you from falling out!" Clipper was really too frightened to be interested in hearing my explanation. My ploy worked and Clipper never leaned out the door on his hind legs and never pulled on the leash again. New techniques of dog training in Vietnam sometimes happened on the fly.

The chopper formation in the air was quite a sight. Gunship escorts flew below the formation. Twenty or thirty ships were clustered in small groups of a large spread-out tactical flying formation. Below, the enemy probably saw us and wondered where the hell we were going to land. Flying into our target area with such a formidable display of force gave me a huge feeling of confidence, one almost of invincibility.

Through the open doors, I saw well-armed soldiers sitting inside the other ships that flew alongside us. The door gunners' M60 machine guns were loaded and pointed downward, but we were flying too high to be in any danger from ground fire. I was delighted that the VC didn't have surface-to-air-missiles. I was pumped with adrenaline watching the huge heavily armed armada in tactical flight all around me. *With a force like that, how could the lesser-armed NVA and VC possibly whip the Americans?* I wondered.

The ships began their descent into a large LZ of flat ground with short vegetation. When we landed, I immediately jumped out and ran in a crouched position with Clipper beside me. We headed to the tree line away from the landing area to provide security for the ships. With the choppers blowing any airborne scent away, the noise and movement made it impossible for Clipper to alert on anything in our immediate area. That was the type of situation when a scout dog team was neutralized and as vulnerable as everyone else.

No enemy fire was drawn when we moved into the trees. The soldiers spread out quickly and crept into the woods. Though we had made no contact with Charlie, the squad leaders directed their men to stay spread apart, keep their eyes open, and have weapons on the ready. We moved into a swift defensive position almost immediately after the entire platoon was on the ground and under the cover of the surrounding woods.

The platoon leader quickly took control, assembling the lead squad that included Clipper and me. Ships kept landing and dropping off troops in the clearing behind us, causing a lot of noise. The platoon leader gave me a hand signal, pointing out where he wanted me to go. I told the two men assigned as my security to stay far enough behind us for Clipper to have full scent capability in the direction of travel. I instructed my security team not to get in front of the dog or me unless I signaled them. I told them that I would turn periodically to check for their signals to direct my forward progress. I didn't want to get too far ahead or off track.

Clipper and I moved out through the short vegetation and lightly wooded terrain. The rest of the platoon followed cautiously and eventually stretched out behind our lead. I stepped forward slowly, keeping my eyes on Clipper's head and ears and body behavior. Occasionally, I'd glance to the rear to check my security net and get directions. Using hand signals, the troops behind me made sure I stayed on the compass azimuth. The farther we moved away from the landing zone, the quieter the surrounding woods and jungle vegetation became.

During that initial penetration into enemy territory, Clipper didn't alert at all. I wondered if his ears were still ringing from all the noise of the helicopters or were distracted by the noise from the movement of troops all around him. Since Clipper kept moving forward with no apparent concern for his surroundings, I had to assume that he wasn't sensing danger at his end of the leash.

It wasn't long before Clipper gave a slight alert by flicking his ears and canting his head ever so slightly. I stopped and knelt on one knee. Everyone behind us stopped, too. I listened closely and heard nothing. I looked at the area where Clipper had alerted and saw nothing. Unsure if Clipper had given a strong enough alert for me to signal for help, I got up and tugged his leash to move out again.

Clipper continued to walk without alerting for another hundred yards, and then his ears shot straight up and forward. I stopped and signaled for one of the security guards behind me to come up. I told the soldier that Clipper had alerted the same way twice and I thought that his warning was worth checking out. I couldn't tell him specifically what Clipper had sensed or how far away it might be. The soldier quietly moved back to deliberate with the platoon leader, who then came forward. He signaled two men to cautiously sweep the front about fifty yards out and report back.

When they returned, the men reported seeing fresh footprints about forty yards directly ahead that didn't resemble a GI's jungle boot. Despite my confidence in Clipper's ability, I was amazed. Clipper had alerted on an airborne scent. A dog's sense of smell could pick up a scent left behind by the enemy long after he was gone. I immediately praised and hugged Clipper for his alert.

The platoon leader hand-signaled me to keep moving forward. As Clipper approached the footprints, he sniffed the ground and moved in the direction of the scent. I followed him for several yards and then aborted. The path of footprints headed away from our direction of travel, and I was getting too far away from the rest of the troops.

Standing in tall grass about fifty yards ahead of the rest of the platoon, I signaled the man behind me to come forward. While we both knelt down and talked about the situation, the platoon leader arrived on the scene. I whispered to him that Clipper was getting a fairly good scent and seemed to want to track the trail of footprints. The platoon leader directed a squad of men to follow the fresh tracks for a short distance and report back. When the squad leader returned, he reported that there were fresh footprints all over the place but nothing else. We stayed halted for a few minutes while the platoon leader got on the radio and made his report. Shortly afterward, we were ordered not to follow the suspected trail of enemy footprints, but to continue the mission in the direction planned.

We moved out of the grassy area and into the woods. We were several hours into our mission, and it was fairly quiet except for the commonplace sounds of birds and insects. Clipper, with his head rising above the vegetation, moved forward into the woods without a problem even though the jungle got thicker with low vegetation and vines. I had clear visibility above the eye level of Clipper. So far, navigating through that part of the jungle wasn't proving very difficult.

In his pursuit of the enemy, Clipper, with mouth closed, paused for a moment and lifted his head high as if he had sensed something directly in front of us. I stopped and dropped to one knee. I scanned and listened for anything unusual. Again I saw and heard nothing out of the ordinary. I motioned the closest man behind me to come up. I told him that Clipper's alert was fairly strong and straight ahead.

The platoon leader assembled a rifle team to search the forward area. They reported a huge clearing about seventy-five yards through the woods, but there were no signs of the enemy. Looking at his map, the platoon leader nodded, and then hand-signaled me to push on. I complimented Clipper for the alert by hugging him and telling him, "Good boy! Good boy!" Clipper had done a great job up to that point.

We moved ahead, but in accordance with standard operating procedure (SOP), we stopped before entering the clearing. No one was supposed to enter a clearing when coming out of the woods unless the platoon leader directed. The platoon leader was responsible to assess the situation and decide how he wanted the platoon to maneuver across a clearing.

Everyone stayed just inside the woods, waiting for orders to cross the clearing. I noticed Clipper sniffing a small pile of bamboo shavings a few feet away from us. I figured it was probably where the enemy had placed a bunch of *punji* stakes. As I pondered over the pile, Clipper alerted sharply to the rear. I quickly turned to find Clipper standing erect and staring at a man. He was tall and wore clean jungle fatigues with only a pistol belt and a holstered .45-caliber pistol side arm. I immediately recognized two black stars sewn into his camouflage-covered helmet. He held a field map inside a plastic sleeve. I couldn't believe my eyes. It was Major General Mearns, the commanding officer of the 25th Infantry Division. He was the same officer who had visited our K-9 compound after the VC mortar attack.

I wondered, *What the hell is he doing out here? Is he trying to earn his combat pay or what? And how the hell did he get here in the first place?*

I quickly rose to a standing position and nervously greeted him without saluting. "Good morning, sir," I said. It was forbidden to stand at attention and render a snappy salute in a combat zone because if Charlie was watching and saw me salute, the CG could get a bullet between the eyes.

The CG was under the cover of vegetation and out of view. He smiled and asked me, "What's the name of your dog, soldier?"

"Clipper, sir!"

The general knelt and said, "He sure is frisky."

He asked me several questions about how scouting worked while he examined his map and peered at the open clearing through the trees. The general's radio operator and several of his staff officers, all wearing clean jungle fatigues, surrounded him. They didn't say a word to me but kept looking and smiling at Clipper. I chatted with MG Mearns for a few minutes before he turned and headed back into the main element of the platoon.

I looked down at Clipper and said, "Clipper, you just met the CG of the 25th Infantry Division! He's the most powerful man in the division."

Clipper didn't appear to be too excited.

Ed Hughes and his scout dog, Sergeant, were working somewhere nearby. During the mission briefing we were told that there would be an entire battalion of several hundred troops working the area. I figured that the CG had landed with us on the choppers and had been beating the bush all morning. It was quite rare for a general officer to show up in the jungle and hump with his troops. Unlike World War II, Vietnam had no front lines, so danger was expected everywhere we traveled outside our base camps. I was impressed to see the commanding general walk with his men in a combat zone. He reminded me of the time I saw Lieutenant Colonel Hal Moore in the Ia Drang valley during my first tour.

After Major General Mearns departed, we were given a short break in place. I poured Clipper some water into my steel pot and hugged him for doing such a terrific job. I was extremely happy with how Clipper and I were working together as a team. Clipper was a source of loyalty, comfort, and satisfaction for me. Even though I'd worked with Clipper many times up to that point, each mission was different and we learned new things every time we went out together. Our bond was very strong.

After about fifteen minutes, I heard some choppers flying overhead just above the treetops. They landed in the clearing we were about to cross, picked up some passengers, and took off. I figured that MG Mearns and his staff were the passengers. Clipper sat facing the clearing watching everything take place. He moved his head back and forth as if he was searching the clearing and sensing clues about what might be out there.

My friend Ed Hughes and his war dog partner, Sergeant, were out somewhere in the same area of operation. I recalled telling Ed that we would trade stories when we got back to the K9 Klub. *Oh, boy,* I thought, *Would I have a tale to tell about how Major General Mearns came up to me and petted Clipper!*

The platoon leader finally gave me the command to move out across the clearing. Clipper and I slowly moved out, exposing ourselves to whatever there was waiting for us on the other side. I was tense looking at the other side of the clearing several hundred yards away. Left and right of us the visibility was clear. As we walked farther into the clearing, I glanced to my rear. My two bodyguards were spread out ten yards to my left and right rear. The rest of the platoon spaced themselves apart and cautiously moved forward. I could feel a light wind, but had confidence that Clipper wouldn't miss a scent of danger.

As we moved deeper into enemy territory, my eyes stayed glued to Clipper's head and ears. All of a sudden, Clipper's neck and head went rigid and his ears popped up. Then he cocked his head slightly to one side and gave his strongest alert of the day. I immediately crouched low on one knee. I kept looking and listening but could not see nor hear anything unusual. I turned around and noticed that everyone behind us had also stopped and had gone down on one knee.

My right knee was beginning to hurt a little from kneeling on the hard ground. A long time had passed since I'd jumped from that chopper and had a *punji* stake sticking out of it. That was a hell of a painful memory indeed. Now I had to keep moving and deal with the lingering and annoying pain from that old injury.

I felt uncomfortable being in the open with vegetation no higher than the top of my boots. Clipper's ears and head remained erect, so I decided not to push our luck by proceeding. I turned and motioned to the man behind him. The platoon leader moved up forty yards to join me at my position. He asked for my thoughts. I told him that I had a bad feeling about going any farther.

The platoon leader didn't waste any time. He motioned for the nearest squad leader, who directed two fire teams of three men each to move forward and sweep the area for danger. After reconnoitering, the two fire teams returned and reported that they saw a long, wide, and recently used trail about fifty yards away. They'd made no contact with the enemy. The platoon leader then hand-signaled for me to lead them to the trail.

When Clipper and I reached the trail, which ran perpendicular to the mission's direction of travel, we saw fresh footprints and tracks of wheeled carts and oxen leading into South Vietnam from Cambodia. These certainly weren't the prints one would expect of peasant farmers moving around, especially when there were no farms or villages around.

The platoon leader figured the Cambodian border must be less than a half mile away. This had to be a branch trail leading off the main Ho Chi Minh Trail. Since the tracks were so fresh, the platoon leader thought that a heavily armed battalion-size NVA or VC force must have moved into South Vietnam from Cambodia within the past day or so. He used a grease pencil to mark the enemy movement on his map.

I took the lead and crossed the trail, heading toward the facing wood line that was less than seventy-five yards out. We were now traveling parallel to the Cambodian border. Before long, Clipper stopped and stood erect with his ears pointed high and forward, and the muscles in his shoulders grew tense and started to twitch.

When I looked back, my security guards motioned for me to keep going. The platoon leader must have decided to ignore Clipper's alert. I was a little puzzled, but got up and tugged on Clipper's leash. Clipper started stepping side to side as if he didn't want to go forward. Then several shots rang out over our heads. In an instant, we dropped quickly to the ground in a prone position. Clipper's head was up and pointed in the direction of the tree line ahead. I hugged Clipper close and told him what a good dog he was. In response, he licked my face.

There was a brief moment of silence as I strained to spot the shooter. I saw nothing but a wall of green ahead. Behind me, everyone was lying in a prone position in the short grass trying to figure out where the shots had come from. Someone decided to fire an M16 over my head into the wall of trees. Almost instantly everyone else started shooting.

I knew that if a sniper was hiding in a tree, the entire platoon was visible to him. From the direction of the shots, I thought that

Clipper may have been Charlie's first target. We were definitely not out of a sniper's range of fire, because the rounds had gone over our heads. Charlie was either a poor shooter, or Clipper and I had been mighty lucky.

The firing stopped after it became apparent that the Americans were doing all the shooting, and then there was another long moment of silence. The platoon leader ordered two squads to fire and maneuver until they reached and secured a position at the edge of the trees ahead of us. As the squads tried to fire and maneuver, several more shots rang out from the woods. Voices behind Clipper and me were giving orders to get up and move out on line. I got to my feet and tugged Clipper to move forward along with everyone else.

Several more shots rang out from the woods ahead. The entire platoon again dropped on their bellies and poured a deadly barrage of bullets into the trees just ahead. I placed several rounds where I thought the shooter was positioned. Clipper didn't move while I fired. I patted him on the back and told him that he was a good boy. Several men flanked us, taking up firing positions.

A voice cried out directly behind me, "Get up and move out on line, soldier!"

Certain that the sniper would zero in on me, I ignored the voice and remained on the ground. When I looked up, I saw a tall man standing over me with two black bars on his helmet. It was the captain, the company commander I'd met that morning. I was startled to see him glaring down at me with a disgusted look on his face. He gazed down at me and shouted, "I said get up and assault the tree line!"

I looked at him as if he were crazy and replied, "Sir, why don't you call for artillery or air strikes before we go into those trees?"

"Soldier, I said get up and assault!"

I finally obeyed and moved forward with everyone else. Charlie didn't fire a single round while I closed in on the tree line with the rest of the troops.

By the time Clipper and I reached the edge of the wall of trees, there was a lot of fussing and shouting going on. Everyone seemed to be in a state of commotion and confusion as to what to do next. Clipper and I stopped among a bunch of troops who were standing around waiting for the next command. There was too much activity and noise for Clipper to be effective. At that point we were useless as scouts.

The platoon leader approached me. He told me that one of his men had spotted a bunker not far from us. He asked me if I would use my dog to check it out.

I told the lieutenant, "Clipper doesn't like going into holes in the ground, but I'll go with you to see if he gets an alert."

On other missions, Clipper avoided going into bunkers, fox-holes, or tunnels. I learned that you never force a dog to do anything he did not want to do, especially in enemy territory.

The lieutenant told me that he would lead the way to the bunker. He moved out at a quick pace with Clipper. I followed him closely. A few yards after I had passed the last man in our platoon, Clipper raised his head and alerted up into the trees. I didn't give it a second thought, because there was too much activity all around us for the alert to be accurate.

It wasn't long before the three of us were by ourselves. The lieutenant snaked a path through the dark jungle, thick with tall vegetation. The closest American was at least twenty yards behind us. At point-blank range, muzzle flashes lit up in my face. The lieutenant's body slammed into my chest like a sack of rocks, knocking me onto my back and causing my helmet to fly off my head. All hell broke loose. Clipper rolled over on top of me as I hung on to his leash.

Directly to my front, Charlie opened up with automatic rifle and machine gun fire. Fortunately, I'd fallen near a small tree. I rolled behind it with Clipper at my side. Rifle and machine gun fire opened up from behind. Clipper and I were caught in the crossfire between the enemy and Americans. With my arm around Clipper, I hugged the ground. Firing became so intense from both sides that it chopped up the vegetation like the blades of a lawn mower. Charlie was dug in and shooting at us from camouflaged bunker positions.

Clipper and I were trapped and unable to move. I knew that the lieutenant had absorbed the initial burst of bullets. He had to be close by, but I couldn't see him through the thick vegetation. The lieutenant wasn't crying for help or calling for a medic. After a few minutes had passed, I assumed that he must be dead.

Charlie and the Americans fired furiously back and forth over our heads. I thought, *Charlie must not see us, or maybe he thinks he's already killed us!* I decided not to make any sudden moves to give Charlie a second chance. I slowly moved my rifle to a firing position. As I got the barrel up by my face, I noticed that the muzzle had a plug of mud jammed inside. I thought, *It must have happened when I fell backward onto the damp jungle floor.* Trying to clear it with my finger only packed it deeper into the muzzle. I thought of using grenades, but then I realized that I hadn't packed any grenades.

It would have been suicidal under those circumstances to break down my weapon and run a cleaning rod through the bore and chamber to clear the plug. Right then, it was more important for me to stay alive than to figure out a way to shoot. If I had to, I could fire my weapon, but I would risk the round in the chamber exploding in my face.

Clipper and I lay fifteen feet from Charlie's entrenched positions. Between the exchanges of small arms fire, I could hear Charlie whispering in Vietnamese from his foxholes. I knew Clipper heard them, too, but he didn't make a move or a sound. My dog and I were in deep shit with no way out. My heart pounded and my adrenaline spiked.

The current situation was much different than with Timber in the armored personnel carrier ambush. This time I was even closer to the enemy, had no helmet, no functional weapon, no grenades, and could be killed by either side. I didn't dare make the slightest movement or noise to draw attention to myself. Unlike the frightened and skittish Timber, I was grateful that Clipper wasn't jumping around or trying to get away.

I prayed, *God, please get us out of this death trap.*

Minutes seemed like hours. I thought that my time on earth must be running out. I wanted to melt into the dirt to get away from it all. I was scared and could feel Clipper shivering underneath my arm.

I found it peculiar that I could simultaneously hear Charlie whispering in Vietnamese and the Americans shouting in English. Not long into the firefight, I heard the deafening sound of artillery rounds exploding behind Charlie's positions. The shrapnel violently splintered the trees and shredded vegetation all around us. The Americans were walking the artillery closer and closer to our positions. Between volleys, Charlie and the Americans exchanged small arms and machine gun fire.

I lay silently holding Clipper and trying not to move a muscle. To my surprise, I felt something touch my foot. I spun my head around and saw a soldier who was one of my designated security guards. We exchanged no words as we made eye contact. He gave me a thumbs-up and motioned me to move back to the rear.

As quietly as I could, I slowly turned around on my belly. Clipper followed me. When I tried to crawl away from the tree, my backpack got caught in some vines and moved the vegetation. Charlie must have spotted the movement. All hell broke loose again. Somehow I broke free and crawled away on my stomach with Clipper at my side. I anticipated feeling the pain of a bullet entering my body or hearing Clipper groan from being shot. Charlie was either shooting too high or we were as flat as the rotting leaves on the jungle floor.

The distinct sound of an M16 echoed through the jungle behind me. The soldier who relieved me was providing cover for my escape. I flinched at the sound of a grenade exploding behind me. I briefly hesitated but didn't turn to look.

As I crawled, an American soldier appeared before me and motioned me to stay down. He fired over my head. As Clipper and I passed, I saw a dead Vietnamese in khaki clothes suspended from a tree by his bare foot. His arms dangled down over his head and almost touched the pool of blood dripping from his body and soaking into the jungle floor. I quickly moved Clipper around the hanging body to take cover behind a nearby tree.

Behind the safety of the American lines, there were dead and wounded on the ground everywhere. I broke down my CAR15 and ran a cleaning rod through the bore to release the clump of mud and took up a defensive firing position. I quickly checked over Clipper's entire body, feeling for holes and looking for blood. Clipper didn't wince in pain as I touched him. He was okay. Artillery had pounded the jungle around us with explosive devastation. It wasn't long before the barrages halted and shooting drizzled to a stop.

That was the usual way that those firefights started and stopped. Charlie had either been eradicated or decided to break contact. It was hard to tell. Reinforcements from another platoon reached the perimeter from the clearing and took up firing positions. A medic frantically worked on a wounded soldier nearby who screamed that he was going to die. The medic tried to stop the bleeding, patch him up, and calm the wounded man. It did no good; the soldier died and the medic quickly moved on to assist another wounded man.

I saw the lieutenant's silent body being carried in a poncho. The platoon sergeant was now in charge. He told me that the company commander had killed a VC who was in a tree after the captain was shot in the foot. I then remembered that before the firing had started Clipper had alerted up in the trees and I had disregarded it. Now I realized that Clipper may have sensed the danger in that tree. Guilt penetrated my heart for the captain who had paid the price for my possible mistake.

The platoon sergeant told me that the soldier who had come to save us while we were trapped in that crossfire had been killed. The Americans had killed several enemy soldiers inside a bunker near that tree.

The platoon sergeant explained that most of the casualties had happened during the first few seconds of fighting as everyone stood around waiting for the lieutenant to check out the bunker. He said there had been a lot of commotion and chaos while getting everyone out of the open clearing and under the cover of the jungle. He believed that his men should have automatically formed a defensive perimeter and assumed firing positions on the ground. Instead, many of them were standing or milling around waiting for something to happen. Charlie had sucked us right into his trap by baiting us with the sniper.

I told the platoon sergeant that Clipper had done his best under the circumstances, and he didn't place any blame on me. The dog had alerted them of danger way before the sniper opened up on us in the clearing, he said. We had done our duty and were lucky to be alive. When the shooting started he had thought that the lieutenant, the dog, and I had been killed instantly.

The last thing I mentioned to the platoon sergeant was that the CO had ignored my request to shell the tree line before sending in his troops. The platoon sergeant replied, "We needlessly lost a lot of good men today." Patting Clipper on the head, the sergeant told him that he was a good dog, shook his head, and walked away.

Helicopters, small arms, and machine gun fire echoed in the distance, signaling that someone else was getting into the shit. The entire area must have been loaded with pockets of hard-core NVA troops. The reconnaissance team who scouted that area before the mission had done a good intelligence job. Now it was up to the infantry to fight smarter and defeat the bastards. Even though there was another fight going on nearby, my platoon wasn't ordered to assist, so I rested under a tree with Clipper and gave him some water. I listened to the squawking of the field radio, the distant noise of a firefight, and watched my fellow soldiers receive medical attention.

A soldier came up to me and asked, "Is your name Burnam?"

"Yes," I answered.

The soldier handed me my helmet with my name written on the headband inside. He said that it was lying near a bunker and next to the bodies of the lieutenant and another soldier. He couldn't understand how the dog and I had survived without a scratch.

Before I put on my helmet, I checked it over. There wasn't a mark on it. Clipper didn't have a scratch either, and he appeared to be dealing with the whole situation better than I was.

Clipper had been a competent and brave soldier that day by alerting us of danger and then showing courage under extreme circumstances. Many of the troops came by to pet Clipper for good luck. One person called Clipper "the invincible scout dog." I chuckled at that comment. I hugged him and said, "Clipper, for all the hell you've been through, you just earned yourself a Bronze Star and a Combat Infantry Badge for all those great alerts."

I knew the army didn't award medals or badges to war dogs for exceptional performance of duty or for bravery and heroism. The army officially recognized scout dogs only as military combat equipment. In four months, I'd be rotating back to the States. Clipper, on the other hand, didn't have a rotation date. His orders were to serve his country in Vietnam for the rest of his natural life. I didn't want to believe the naked truth about what Clipper's fate would be.

What the hell do the army brass and politicians know about Clipper and what he's done to risk his life to save others? I thought Clipper was a soldier, not a piece of equipment. He displayed uncompromising loyalty and obedience. His memory was magnificent and he knew what he had been trained to do. He was a hell of a lot more responsive carrying out his duties than many of the humans I'd met during the war.

How did the army know what my dog could do mentally and physically? How many lives would Clipper have to save to be recognized as something more than equipment? I thought it was cruel and unjust to punish a dog by making him walk point for the entire war. The army had trained Clipper to save lives. Shouldn't they treat him with respect and give him a rotation date, too? These were all questions I could never ask out loud. As a lowly grunt, I had to follow orders and never question the decisions that people in higher levels of authority made. I sat under that tree pondering the mystery of why Clipper and I were still alive, and thinking about my dog's true fate.

Then I heard that the platoon's casualties during that skirmish were considered light, with six men killed and eleven wounded. It was decided that we hadn't suffered enough losses to be relieved of our mission. The platoon sergeant briefed me on our new orders. I was to join the rest of the company to set up a defensive perimeter for the evening in the very field we'd crossed. The next day, the company would continue its mission of hunting NVA along the Cambodian border.

After a short mission briefing that afternoon by the platoon sergeant, it was time to saddle up and move into the clearing and
set up for the night. Clipper and I assumed our usual position out
in the front of the platoon formation. We headed into the
clearing to join the rest of the company. Clipper alerted like
crazy. We didn't have to check out his alerts, because American
soldiers were in the area all around us.

A sister company had reconnoitered the battlefield to clean up
any remaining pockets of enemy troops. They'd discovered a
small but empty enemy base camp. It looked as if Charlie
ambushed us in his backyard. Now, except for leaving a few dead
bodies near our positions, the enemy had disappeared.

The enemy probably ran for the Cambodian border, knowing
that we couldn't pursue them there. If this had been my old unit,
the 1st Battalion, 7th Cavalry, I knew that the CO would have
dropped artillery and napalm before sending one soldier after a
sniper. We all knew that using a sniper to lure Americans into a
trap was a typical Charlie-baiting-the-Americans tactic.

In my mind, I kept reviewing the events of that battle.

Even when the platoon had gotten into the tree line, Clipper
and I had been useless during the commotion. When Clipper
alerted toward the tree where the sniper hid, Charlie had intentionally let us pass through, probably figuring that Clipper and I
were going to be dead meat anyway. I'd missed that alert and felt
responsible for the CO getting shot in the foot.

There was no way Clipper could have alerted on that bunker,
because the lieutenant was walking directly in front of us. But if
Clipper and I had taken the lead, it would have been lights out

for both of us. Clipper and I must have had a guardian angel watching over us that day. I just hoped that angel would stick around.

Moving across the clearing that afternoon, Clipper and I entered a company-size perimeter deep inside with over one hundred American soldiers. They were everywhere, digging chest-deep foxholes, clearing firing lanes, planting claymore mines, and setting up trip flares. The company prepared for a counterattack. Every man was on full alert. There would be little or no sleeping on the perimeter that night. None of us wanted to get caught by surprise.

Clipper and I took up a position where I felt a little more secure, well inside the perimeter behind a bush. We got lucky and didn't have to pull perimeter guard duty that night. In the past, when I pulled guard duty, Clipper was so naturally good at it that I could sleep all night if I wanted to. I wasn't a heavy sleeper, whether I was in the field or at base camp, and tended to wake up at the slightest unusual noise. After all we'd just been through, I knew I would not even catnap easily.

Darkness settled in as a helicopter appeared overhead and landed under the green smoke signal inside the large perimeter. I figured it was a resupply ship and paid little attention to it. Besides, I didn't need any supplies. A few minutes after the chopper took off, I recognized fellow dog handler Sergeant Durbach of the 44th Scout Dog Unit. He slowly walked over to me.

I wondered what Durbach was doing out here without his scout dog. As Durbach approached, I noticed that he looked fresh and clean-shaven and his jungle fatigues weren't dirty. I, on the other hand, was filthy from a long day of humping and crawling along the damp jungle floor.

Sergeant Durbach carried a CAR15 and a light pack strapped to his back. We greeted one another with a smile and shook hands. As we sat on the ground, Durbach stroked Clipper's head and back, but appeared nervous. His facial expressions conveyed that something was bothering him. He forced a smile and asked me how I was doing.

"John," he said, "Ed Hughes and his dog, Sergeant, were killed today."

"What?" I replied.

Durbach filled me in on what had happened. After Ed's chopper had landed, he and Sergeant ran for cover along with the rest of the troops. When Ed reached the jungle wall, he moved inside to seek cover and was shot down at point-blank range. The enemy had hacked Ed's dog to death with a knife or machete. Sergeant Durbach speculated that the dog had died fighting, but that Ed was caught by surprise and probably died instantly without knowing what had hit him. I couldn't believe what I was hearing. My eyes welled up with tears.

Durbach said that the NVA had overwhelmed the rest of Ed's platoon and forced them into a hasty retreat back across the landing zone. The platoon had set up a defensive position and held off an enemy assault. The NVA retreated into the jungle where Ed and his dog lay dead.

I asked Sergeant Durbach how he knew so much if he hadn't

been there. He said that Lieutenant Fenner had received a call from 3rd Brigade headquarters in Dau Tieng. They told him that a dog handler and his dog were killed in action while on patrol near the Cambodian border. All the casualties, they said, except for the dog handler and his dog, had been recovered. It was apparently too risky to try to recover Ed and his dog at that time, so they had left them behind.

I interrupted by saying, "That is a bunch of bullshit! Those fuckers can't leave Ed and Sergeant out there alone all night. So they must have sent you to get me to help recover Ed and Sergeant. Well, I'm ready. Let's fucking go and get some more men and do it!"

Sergeant Durbach put his hand on my shoulder and said, "John, sit down and let me finish."

Then he told me that Lieutenant Fenner had sent him out about three hours earlier to size up the situation and report back. Since the attack, Ed's platoon had been reinforced with two more platoons and set up in defensive position not far from Ed and Sergeant. Durbach had received a status report from the company commander of Ed's unit.

The CO had already decided to assemble two squads and send them across the clearing to locate and recover the bodies. Durbach arrived in time to accompany the patrol. When they'd found Ed and his dog, the NVA were long gone. Ed's body had been stripped of his weapon and gear, including his boots. Sergeant's body was lying near him. The Gooks, Durbach said, had even taken Sergeant's leash and collar. Both bodies were recovered without incident and sent home to Dau Tieng. Durbach's next task had been to locate me.

By using a field radio, Durbach had been able to find my exact position within minutes. I was less than a mile from where Ed and Sergeant had died. Durbach caught a ride on a resupply chopper operating in the area. I told Durbach that I'd heard a firefight in the distance after our battle. I didn't think to realize that it may have been Ed's unit under attack.

Sergeant Durbach asked me for details about our fight. I gave him a blow-by-blow account of our near-fatal encounter with Charlie.

On that Thanksgiving Day of 1967, I was thinking, *What the hell do we have to celebrate or be thankful for?* Even after I listened to every detail about Ed's death, I couldn't believe he was gone. Ed had been killed before he'd even had a chance to fight back.

Durbach and I sat silently for several minutes. I reflected on how much I'd enjoyed Ed's friendship and humor. Even though I'd only known him for six months, I thought that Ed was a wonderful person. Now he was dead, and I'd never see him again. The incident between Ed and Mike Eply at the K-9 Klub, which led to the two of them switching places for that mission, now played over and over in my head. "Eply, if I get killed out there tomorrow," Ed had said, "I'm gonna come back here and kick your fucking ass."

Sergeant Durbach coordinated my return to Dau Tieng so I could provide a field report to my unit. We left in the morning on the first available chopper. Sergeant Durbach briefed Lieutenant

Fenner on Ed Hughes, and I provided the details about what had happened during my mission. After the briefing, all I wanted was to take a shower and put on clean fatigues.

No one in the platoon could believe Ed and Sergeant were dead. Of course, every dog handler wanted to hear about it. I must have repeated that story twenty times that day. I didn't talk to Mike Eply, but could only imagine how he must have felt about that entire incident.

The day after the debriefing, the entire 44th assembled at a chapel to pay their last respects to Ed and Sergeant. The field chapel was a large green tent with several rows of folding chairs and a makeshift altar. We held a funeral service without bodies. By now, Ed was in a morgue somewhere in Saigon.

To my distaste, the chaplain gave a sermon filled with military jargon. He said something like, "Ed hasn't left us. He's gone on to serve a higher commander, the celestial six."

That term "six" was used in common military radio jargon as part of a commanding officer's call sign. I wasn't the only one to cringe at the chaplain's eulogy. Dan Scott and many of the other handlers were livid about the chaplain's choice of military words for that service. We wanted to hear something beautiful and poetic from the Bible, not language that sounded like a military mission in the afterlife. I vowed that that would be the last time I would ever attend a formal religious ceremony for a fallen comrade in Vietnam. I would deal with it in my own way.

A few days after Ed's death, Lieutenant Fenner asked me to join Sergeant Durbach to escort Ed's dog, Sergeant, to a military morgue in Saigon. Apparently, the veterinarians wanted to complete an autopsy on the dog, and Saigon had better veterinary medical facilities. The second part of my mission would be to positively identify Ed's body in a military morgue.

Edward Cowart Hughes III, nineteen years old, now rested in peace. He would be going home to his grieving family in Garden Grove, California.

For me, I'd be returning to Dau Tieng to risk my own life and that of Clipper's in missions yet to come against that same enemy who took Ed and Sergeant's lives.

Booby Traps

Dense forests and jungles surrounded the Ben Cui and Michelin rubber tree plantations that stretched about ten square miles east and north of Dau Tieng. Fifteen hundred yards north of the airstrip stood a small range of steep foothills covered by thick jungle canopy.

On a military grid map, the rubber tree plantations were identified by thousands of tiny green circles divided into square grids crisscrossed with many dirt roads that were used to harvest the thousands of rows of rubber trees. One grid equaled one thousand square meters. Resident Vietnamese workers lived in small hamlets scattered throughout the rubber tree plantation. A combination of numbers and letters were used to mark the location of each hamlet on our military grid maps such as AP 2, AP 12, and AP 13.

Every so often, a blue and white civilian helicopter flew into base camp. It would stick out like a sore thumb, since all the military aircraft and equipment were painted olive drab or camouflage. Civilian choppers belonged to business partners of the Michelin and Ben Cui rubber tree plantations. Scuttlebutt had it that these companies were concerned that the U.S. Army was destroying too many of the precious rubber trees. They apparently wanted payment for each tree we damaged or destroyed. They were also unhappy that we were using the trees to tie our dogs to, because the leashes rubbed the bark raw and the dogs were digging holes around the roots. They complained about all the wooden hooches that the dog handlers had built between rows of their rubber trees.

I never learned if the army ever paid for damaged and destroyed rubber trees. In the K-9 platoon, "Fuck 'em all," was a general response to the businessmen's complaints. I had no idea what kind of diplomatic relations the army had or the deals made with the plantation owners. As a grunt, I didn't care and I didn't want civilian businessmen snooping around our K-9 area.

I had reflected back to what my former first sergeant warned me of in Okinawa. He said, "There are spies out there. They want classified information about what we do. Don't talk or try to figure them out; they are professionals. Report everything immediately to your security officer. Do you understand, soldier?"

We dog handlers figured that we owned the rubber trees while we occupied them and fought the war for the South Vietnamese. Besides, the rubber trees offered no safe haven for Americans. We had to defend every inch of what we maintained. The VC and NVA used the trees and dirt roads between them to booby-trap American troops. We knew that the enemy lived inside the hamlets at night and during the day when we were not patrolling.

I found the scout dog business to be a never-ending learning experience. Since booby traps surrounded us, I needed to know if Clipper could detect trip wires. A bright and a proven combat veteran war dog, I didn't think that Clipper would ever intentionally walk through a trip wire stretched between two trees. I assumed that he would avoid that type of danger, but I had to learn what alert Clipper would give when he came close to one.

One morning, before I cleaned Clipper's run, I walked to the rubber trees behind the hooches. I had a roll of regular olive drab (OD), thin, fairly strong, and easily pliable trip wire taken from a trip flare. I tied a strand about knee-high between two trees and twanged the wire with my finger to assure that it was tight as a guitar string.

After I cleaned the kennel and played with Clipper, I put him on his leash and choke chain and we headed in the direction of the trip wire. Clipper walked ahead without pulling just as we did when working on a mission. We went to an area of short grass clear of obstacles. The trip wire was set up about seventy-five yards away. I didn't want to walk a straight line to the target, so I tugged the leash left or right to direct Clipper through the rubber trees. As we moved farther into the plantation, Clipper didn't alert. We came closer to the trip wire, but I still didn't see any alert signs from him. When he was about fifty yards away from the target, Clipper gave a weak alert with a slight movement of his ears, but he didn't stop walking.

When the wire touched his head, he ducked under it, so I jerked the leash and said, "No, Clipper! No!"

Clipper turned and looked at me as if to say, "What did I do wrong?"

I took Clipper back to the wire and clutched it in my hand. I got down on one knee, looked Clipper in the eye, and showed him the thin green wire. Then I gently tapped the wire on the black tip of Clipper's nose. Each time I tapped Clipper's nose, I raised the inflection in my voice and said, "No, Clipper! No!"

I talked to him as if he were a trainee. I said, "Clipper, that is a fucking trip wire. Do not cross it. Do you understand? Do you have any idea what might happen to us if you crossed it? BOOM! That's right, BOOM!"

Clipper responded to the word *no,* but I doubt that he understood anything else.

I walked Clipper around a bit to calm him, then let him approach the wire again. This time, Clipper gave a weak alert and, as before, he walked under the wire. We continued to practice with the wire, but Clipper did the same thing each time. He surely must have tired of hearing me say, "No, Clipper! No, Clipper!" Finally, Clipper stopped and sat a few feet in front of the trip wire. I was so excited and proud of him that I hugged him and said, "You're the greatest fucking dog in the world! The best scout dog in the platoon! Good boy! Good boy!" I had taught an old veteran a new trick.

Then I made Clipper repeat the exercise. I wanted to be sure his behavior hadn't been a fluke and that we were on the same brain wave. Sure enough, Clipper had really learned not to go through the trip wire. He completely avoided it by going around it. We continued to practice the trip wire exercise for several hours that day, and Clipper routinely went around it. It had been a good learning session for both of us.

We practiced the trip wire routine for a few hours a day over the next several days. To make the training tougher, I put several wires in different locations. I wanted to examine how Clipper would negotiate more than one trip wire. I learned that if

Clipper came directly upon a trip wire, he'd sit in front of it more often than he'd go around it. I also learned that if Clipper sensed the wire from a distance, he'd go around it. I was quite pleased that I'd made so much progress with Clipper in only one week of training.

I still had no idea how effective the trip wire training would be when Clipper worked in thick brush, across wooded terrain, or moving down trails. I always dreaded going down trails and tried to avoid them, especially in very remote jungle. Common sense dictated that staying inside the bush was safer than walking on smooth dirt paths. Jungle trails were perfect places for the enemy to set up ambushes and booby traps.

The Viet Cong were smarter bushmen than Americans, because the bush was their natural turf. Most of us grunts had never traveled outside the United States, let alone seen a jungle. The closest I'd ever come to a jungle was thumbing through the pictures of a *National Geographic* magazine. The NVA had mastered guerilla warfare tactics long before I was born. We Americans were infants, still learning how to walk and talk our way through that kind of war.

By conducting these training sessions, I'd learned one more way to keep my dog and me alive while we walked point. Still, I didn't intend to volunteer our services as an expert booby trap detection team.

The day came when my name came up on the rotation schedule for another mission. This time I'd be working with the 2nd Battalion, 12th Infantry (White Warriors) who had the motto "Led by Love of Country." That unit was organized back in 1861 during the Indian Wars.

The 2/12 consisted primarily of foot soldiers sometimes transported in trucks or choppers to air assault into an LZ. I preferred working with foot soldiers, especially after my ambush experience with a sister battalion of armored personnel carriers. Working with the mechanized infantry had become one of my greatest fears in Vietnam.

I reported to the 2/12 down the road from the K-9 compound. I thought, *There's one good thing about living in a small base camp—everything is within walking distance.* Brigade S2 (military intelligence) had information concerning a VC buildup around Dau Tieng. The enemy was reported to be operating out of hidden base camps in the nearby jungles surrounding the rubber tree plantations. At night, the VC were infiltrating the hamlets and reconnoitering our base camp's perimeter for our strengths and weaknesses. They knew a lot about our capabilities, such as how many helicopters we had, the exact locations of our ammunition dumps, where our main communications bunkers were, and how many troops were inside.

At least twice a week, they were attacking our airstrip with mortars and creating too much havoc for our aircraft operations. The mortars were mainly coming from the foothills north of Dau Tieng and east from somewhere in the rubber trees and surrounding jungle. Retaliatory artillery and air strikes at the suspected locations couldn't silence the problem. Helicopter gunships weren't effective enough without someone on the ground helping them to pinpoint their air strikes.

Now the infantry foot soldiers and scout dog teams had to find the VC's hidden base camps. Someone once told me that the infantry was called the *Queen of Battle*. When no one else could get the desired results, the Queen of Battle finished the job. I thought that the Queen of Battle sounded a little to effeminate to be the name of a military fighting force. The army should have called the infantry by the manlier name *King of Battle,* but that title was already taken by the artillerymen.

Clipper and I were going on a two-day mission with the 2/12. My assigned platoon was to fly by helicopter several miles east of Dau Tieng. We were to be dropped off in a clearing and then search the surrounding jungle. On day one, our job was to patrol the jungles east of the Michelin rubber tree plantation to search for VC base camps. On day two, we were to sweep west through the rubber tree plantation and then go back to our base camp.

Another company of the 2/12 had the job of conducting search-and-destroy operations in the northern mountain sector of the rugged foothills. Most of the VC mortar attacks had been coming from that area.

Charlie's shelling equipment consisted of an 81mm mortar tube, base plate, sighting mechanism, and a bunch of mortar rounds. Charlie easily and quickly assembled, fired, disassembled, and moved before any retaliatory strike was effective. These highly mobile mortar squads were deadly accurate and difficult to detect without flushing them out with ground troops.

The Americans had similar capability within their infantry arsenal of weapons, but American artillery required vehicular or aircraft transportation. Even the smallest artillery pieces, the 105mm Howitzers, were bigger and more deadly than a mortar round. Charlie wasn't equipped with such large artillery pieces. All the weapons Charlie used against us were carried on his back.

The 2/12 was given the order to hunt down and eliminate Charlie's mortar teams. To get to the mission site, we flew east by chopper with gunship escorts. Clipper and I were in the lead formation's second ship. The door gunners had post-mounted their M60 machine guns, loaded and ready for firing. After the short ride over the rubber trees to the nearby jungle, the choppers descended into a small clearing and landed under the all-clear green smoke signal.

Clipper and I jumped out and darted to the jungle wall to our front. Its outer skirt was too thick to get through without a machete. The platoon leader ordered one of his men to take point and cut a path for the rest of us. Clipper and I followed the man with the machete as he hacked his way forward. We were useless at that point in the mission. The machete's loud hacking noise distracted Clipper's capability to sense if there was danger ahead.

With such thick vegetation, the platoon leader had to pull in the flank guards. He tightened up the column so he could maintain tighter control of the platoon. The point man continued to slowly cut his way through the vegetation. It was the thickest jungle that Clipper and I had been through, and it reminded me of some of the vegetation in the central highlands where I'd been a year earlier with the 7th Cavalry. Back then I had no dog, but we sure could have used a great dog like Clipper.

The platoon continued to slowly make its way deeper and

deeper into the dark, green jungle. When I looked up, I couldn't see the sky or sun through the canopy. My right knee had begun to ache a bit more during each mission. I had hoped it would hold up for a few more months until I left Vietnam.

If we were to get hit by Charlie, our position would pose a major problem. We would be difficult to locate on a map for air and artillery support. Our AO was colored dark green for thousands of yards around us. If we needed artillery support, it would have to be walked in from a map's point of reference. If we relayed the wrong map coordinates, we risked having artillery dropped on our heads. Regardless of the what–if factors, we had no choice but to keep moving under that thick canopy of vegetation. Since another entire company of infantrymen was operating in our same area, we had the assurance of support, if only we could get to one another in time.

Not long into the journey, the sound of thunder roared overhead. It began to rain, and drops of water made their way through the thick canopy and down on top of the platoon. Millions of raindrops, splashing on the leaves and branches, helped to muffle the sounds of our movement. The man with the machete kept switching it from hand to hand, so we could walk at a steady pace through the rain-soaked jungle. The pace man walked behind Clipper and me. His job was to count the number of steps we'd traveled. Periodically, the lieutenant halted our progress to get the pace man's count, and use his map and compass to check our distance and direction of travel.

Our jungle fatigues and boots were sopping wet from the constant rain and tromping through the soaked and rotting debris. That trail we had forged with machete and boots would disappear in a few days. That seemed to be how fast vegetation grew back after it was cut or mashed into the soil.

Then there was the unavoidable thorny vegetation we called *wait-a-minute vines*. They scratched deep into the exposed wet arms and hands and ripped holes in fatigues. The rain and sweat washed away the trickles of blood. When a grunt rolled up his sleeves, the cuts, scratches, and thin scars ran up and down both arms. These flesh wounds were immediate identity tags of an infantryman in a crowd of new men or REMFs (Rear Echelon Mother Fuckers). One could almost guess the amount of time a grunt had spent in the bush by the number and age of the scars on his body. A veteran took his licks from Mother Nature without crying about it. A new guy had to learn how to just take it and forget about it.

The jungle was alive with insects, spiders, snakes, and other weird-looking critters crawling on the ground and sitting on the leaves and branches around us. The rain made it easy to spot the huge spider webs. When someone located a snake, each man quickly passed on the word "snake!" I don't think any of us youngsters knew a poisonous snake from a nonpoisonous one, but we feared them all.

As we moved forward, Clipper startled me by jumping up and down as if he had stepped on hot coals. I looked down at Clipper dancing around, groaning and furiously biting at his paws. The point man had apparently stepped on a decaying log and crushed it open. Hundreds of large wingless insects had swarmed out. Clipper had stepped right on top of them and they attacked. I leaped over the decaying log, pulling Clipper away, and tried my best to slap and brush off as many bugs as I could. I stomped on the ground to keep the disturbed nest of insects from climbing up my boots and pant legs.

A man behind us commented, "Your dog is going to get eaten up out here."

"No shit, Sherlock!" I replied.

I moved to the side and let the others pass. A soldier stopped to help me get the pests off Clipper. Clipper eventually calmed down, so we moved on to catch up to the man with the machete. I'm sure that if Clipper could talk, he would have asked me for some boots to wear and a chopper ride back home.

The rain finally stopped and there were still no signs of Charlie. All I heard was the sounds of birds and flying insects and grunts slapping their exposed skin to kill their tiny attackers. The sound of the machete cutting through vegetation was becoming less frequent as the jungle thinned out. The platoon leader decided to halt and give the platoon a short lunch break, posting flank guards and machine guns to the front and rear of the column.

I sat on the wet jungle floor against a big tree. Clipper didn't seem to mind when I examined him for bugs and bites, finding a lot of bite marks on the tender areas of his paws. I brushed my fingers like a comb through his furry back and neck checking for ticks. Clipper enjoyed the grooming. I felt some bloated purple peanut-size wood ticks attached to Clipper's skin. I lit a cigarette, got it red hot, and burned them off, one by one. Clipper was happy to have me get rid of his little pests. Besides, it was what best friends are supposed to do. Clipper would get a dipping in a vat of insect medicine when we got home.

I expressed my love for Clipper by hugging him and telling

him that he was doing a good job, and that he was brave. I gave him some fresh water and a package of dog food. Clipper showed his appreciation by licking all over my filthy sweaty face. After he ate, he lay down on his side leaning against me and licked his sore paws. I ate a jungle-temperature can of ham and lima beans and washed it down with some cool water from my canteen. While we relaxed, the smell of cigarette smoke filled the air. I wondered if letting Clipper breathe in that smoke might dull his sense of smell.

As I glanced around my surroundings, I saw steam rising from damp jungle fatigues. Squad leaders quietly moved around to make sure that we were all okay and that we buried our trash. All too soon, the order was given to saddle up. I spotted the lieutenant talking into the handset carried by the radio telephone operator. After he finished, I asked him if Clipper and I could take point since the jungle was no longer very dense. He nodded in agreement.

A West Point graduate, the lieutenant possessed impressive leadership skills. He walked and talked with the confidence of an organized and well-trained officer. I noticed that when he spoke, his squad leaders listened and obeyed his instructions. I preferred being with a unit that had discipline like that.

Working with different units was the nature of my job as a scout dog team for hire. I found that the organizational structure was pretty much the same from unit to unit, but the leadership and discipline ranged from poor to outstanding.

It was more difficult for me to get to know anyone for very long in the field as a scout dog handler, and working with that platoon was no different. Names didn't seem to stick in my head very long. But one thing that made me welcome was that the grunts loved to see and pet a dog. Clipper gave them some comfort when they'd say "Shake!" and he would offer up his paw.

Kenny Mook had been my last best human buddy. He would have loved Clipper. But Clipper was my new best friend and we'd been together longer than Kenny and I had. Sure, I had a lot of scout dog handler friends back in base camp, but we never traveled together on the same missions. I had no idea how they worked in the field or reacted under fire. I assumed that when they were in the bush they managed things the same way I did. Most dog handlers rarely worked with one unit long enough to develop friendships, and besides, we were walking point most of the time. My relationships with the infantrymen I worked with amounted to casual conversations at best. We were never together long enough to form very strong bonds.

After the lieutenant approved my request, I took the point and told the flank guards not to get ahead of Clipper. I explained that they would diminish his scouting effectiveness. Clipper started forward and slowly picked his way through the jungle. I watched his head and ears for any signs of an alert.

Soon, Clipper alerted with his ears up high. The platoon leader sent a fire team to investigate as the rest of the platoon got down and security was implemented. The fire team returned with a negative report. Clipper and I continued forward and he alerted a second time. The platoon leader again took no chances and dispatched a fire team. They again returned with a negative report. The platoon leader asked why I thought Clipper was alerting. I told him that I wasn't sure what was out there, but maybe Charlie had left a fresh scent or was hiding up ahead. Or a base camp could be nearby. I admitted that I didn't know exactly why Clipper was alerting.

Suddenly, something came dashing and crashing through the brush a few feet in front of Clipper. Clipper alerted in amazement as I flinched with surprise. Before I knew it, whatever had crossed our path quickly disappeared.

The lieutenant came up and asked what we'd seen. I told him that I thought it had been a small animal that was spooked and that all I could see was the vegetation moving as it blew by us in high gear.

The platoon leader decided to send out a patrol to sweep the area another fifty yards to the front. Upon returning, the fire team reported finding the edge of a base camp with worn trails directly ahead. The platoon leader assembled his squad leaders to check out the report. He had assumed that since Charlie hadn't engaged the fire team, he was either gone or hiding in wait.

The platoon leader came up to my position and said I was doing a good job and gave Clipper a pat on the head and thanked him for the alert. He told me to enter the base camp with the first squad and an M60 machine gun team. I followed the first squad as it spread out and cautiously began to step through the jungle at the edge of the base camp with the second squad right behind us. The rest of the platoon remained in reserve.

I had a flashback to the time I'd followed the platoon leader to check out a bunker. He had been killed in front of me. I tried to quickly erase the memory from my mind. Not long into our forward progress, everyone in front of me promptly got down on one knee. I knelt right behind them ready to fire my CAR15. I had made sure to pack several grenades. I wasn't going to ever get caught again without grenades.

A soldier signaled me to move up. Clipper led the way. We were now a few short steps inside the edge of a Viet Cong base camp. The first squad spread out and carefully penetrated its interior with their weapons on the ready.

VC base camps varied in size, depending on their purpose and how much of a force they housed. Some base camps were used as training sites for local guerrillas, while others were fortresses. For the most part, VC camps were underground, leaving only a few exposed signs of their existence. The vegetation was carefully cleared away, leaving a few paths. The base camp we now explored had recently disturbed vegetation on the jungle floor but no occupants.

Clipper alerted wildly, but there were too many Americans moving all around for me to get too excited. The VC base camp appeared to be about one acre in size and probably accommodating a company-size VC unit of maybe fifty to one hundred soldiers. It had tiny bunkers (*spider holes*) all around and well-worn paths throughout. Even though it appeared empty, it had been well used. Charlie could spring up at any time. Clipper and I continued to search the base camp with two other soldiers following us for security.

Inside one of the bunkers, someone found a pile of Chinese grenades. I knew from past experience never to touch a pile of enemy grenades that were lying around, because they might be booby-trapped. Someone used C ration toilet paper to mark the bunker with the grenades to warn others to leave them alone. Those primitive grenades, filled with black powder, had a cast-iron head, shaped like a tiny pineapple, attached to a hollow wooden handle with a string that hung out of it. Pull the string, throw the grenade by the handle, and *boom*! These grenades worked well, but the American grenades had a more complex design and were a lot deadlier.

Clipper alerted to something on the ground and started sniffing at a clump of cut branches. I recognized it as a cover for something hidden below. I pulled Clipper away in case it was booby-trapped. I motioned everyone nearby to find something for cover. From behind a tree, I used a bamboo stick to move the brush away, thankfully not triggering an explosion. As I peered from behind the tree into what Clipper had found, I saw a buried fifty-gallon drum full of what looked like crushed green weeds. As I got closer, I smelled marijuana. I couldn't believe it. Clipper had found Charlie's stash of Mary Jane!

Word quickly spread throughout the platoon about the great marijuana find. No one said anything when some grunts grabbed and stuffed handfuls of weed into their pockets. Everybody who came by wanted to know who had found the stash. Well, Clipper was once again a hero. It didn't take much to excite a bunch of grunts.

The platoon leader got on the radio and reported the findings and ordered the marijuana destroyed. One of the squad leaders stuck a flare down inside the drum of marijuana and ignited it. The scent of marijuana smoke carried throughout the base camp. I got out of there before I got high and because I wasn't sure how it would affect Clipper's senses if he got loaded.

After we completed our search, we moved a safe distance from the base camp. The bunkers containing war supplies were blown up with composition C-4 (plastic explosive). The force of the explosions scattered dirt and debris all around us, but no one got hurt.

The lieutenant called for a spotter round of artillery so he could pinpoint our location. A little later, an artillery round whistled through the air and exploded a few hundred yards away. The spotter round satisfied the platoon leader and he marked his map. The map coordinates could be used later to destroy the VC base camp by an artillery or a bombing run.

The vegetation was thin as Clipper and I moved out on point. Flank guards were posted about ten yards on either side of the column formation. We departed without incident and reached a small clearing.

It was getting too late to travel any farther, so the lieutenant decided that we should set up camp for the evening inside the small clearing. Clipper and I took a position inside the platoon perimeter near the platoon leader's control point (CP).

Half of the platoon had to be awake at any point throughout the night. The lieutenant was hoping the VC would pass our way when they returned to their base camp. Clipper remained alert, but nothing out of the ordinary happened that night.

The next morning, Clipper and I assumed the point position and slowly moved through a heavily wooded area with knee-high vegetation. Clipper stopped at the edge of a tiny clearing with ankle-high grass. It was about half the size of a basketball court with a small tree near the center. I followed Clipper as he crossed the clearing, and when he reached the tree, he sprang up and over me as if he had been launched by a catapult. He let out a loud yelp. I hit the ground thinking that Clipper must have been hit.

As I lay on the ground, Clipper stood on his hind legs with his right front paw stretched high above him. He twisted and turned, trying to get loose from something that was suspending him. No shots had been fired. I was completely confused, but soon realized that Clipper had been caught in an animal snare. I released his paw and checked him for injury. He was shaken but okay. I turned around and saw two soldiers lying on the ground, shaking their heads in disgust but not saying anything. I felt embarrassed that Clipper hadn't sensed and avoided the animal trap. I hurried to the other side of the clearing to continue the mission.

As we walked, I kept wondering what had happened back there. Thoughts hurried through my mind like *How could Clipper step into an animal snare? We had so much trip wire training. Maybe I should have trained him to detect animal snares, too. Has my dog lost his instinctive edge? Did the pot smoke impair his senses? Maybe Clipper is tired of the bush and getting lackadaisical. Has he had enough rest, food, and water? How could he need anything when we've only been on the move for a short time this morning?*

Finally, I concluded that Clipper had made a mistake and thought, *So what? It happens to everyone. What about me and that aftershave lotion incident in the Ia Drang valley, or the time I almost killed the squad leaders by accidentally discharging my M16 on full automatic? Besides, Clipper is just a dog, not a machine.*

More importantly, no one had been hurt. I realized that I couldn't blame Clipper. I needed to clear my mind of all these thoughts and doubts and stay focused. A lot of people were depending on us. I was grateful when Clipper and I made it to the edge of the rubber tree plantation without further incident.

Then the platoon leader stopped us and reset the tactical formation for movement through a large open area. I felt relieved when no one said anything to me about what had happened with Clipper and the animal trap. The squad leaders spread their men out. They moved flank guards out to the far right and left wings of the main element.

After the leader changed our platoon's formation, Clipper and I continued to walk point. We passed row after row of rubber trees. It was quiet and we didn't spot any Vietnamese working that sector of trees. The age and thickness of vegetation between and around the rubber trees made it easy to tell the difference between sectors that the Vietnamese had or hadn't worked. We knew the hamlets had to be approached with caution. However, we were under orders not to fire inside a hamlet for fear of wounding or killing noncombatants.

After we were about one hundred yards into the advancement, several explosions echoed in the near distance followed by small arms fire. The platoon leader halted us in place. I looked back and saw him talking on the radio, and then he started running and passed me. He pumped his fist up and down over his head and yelled, "Double time! Double time!"

The entire platoon started running to keep up. The fast pace didn't last long, because we quickly tired under the weight of our heavy packs. The platoon leader stayed in the lead with his radio/telephone operator (RTO) and finally slowed to a quick step. Clipper and I were right behind him trying to keep up. The rest of the platoon spread out behind us to maintain the formation's quick pace and discipline through that open area.

The sound of small arms fire stopped. I waited for shooting to start again, but it didn't. Minutes continued to pass and still I heard no rifle fire, so I assumed the attack to be over. Then, I heard choppers in the distance, but couldn't see them through the rubber trees. It sounded as if we were still several hundred yards away from the action. The squad leaders shouted to their troops to stay alert. We began to move at a brisk pace through the tall grass and weeds between the rubber trees.

We abruptly halted our forward progress when Clipper came upon a steep ravine with a creek below. A narrow footpath led to a log that bridged to the other side of the creek. The platoon leader directed two riflemen to cross the creek first, a distance of about thirty feet, while the rest of us provided cover. After the advance team reached and secured the other side, one by one, we carefully crossed over the thick log.

Clipper cautiously stepped onto the log. He crouched low and looked as if he was hugging it. Step by step, he cautiously and steadily picked his way across in a crouching movement. I was careful to give him enough slack in the leash as I followed behind him. It took us a little longer than the others to get across, but we made it. I was glad that I had him in a harness. With a collar or choke chain on, the leash would have snapped his neck if he fell from the log. I had no doubt that our crossing-the-log training course had helped to prepare Clipper for that real-life obstacle. When we got to the other side, I gave Clipper a big hug and praised him for a job well-done.

Fortunately, we reached the other side without anyone losing balance and falling into the creek. The platoon leader motioned the lead squad to move out quickly. Clipper and I assumed the point man position. The platoon leader, his RTO, and two riflemen were directly behind us. The rest of the platoon spread out in a tactical formation to the left, right, and behind. The platoon leader kept instructing me to move faster, so Clipper and I quickened our pace.

Clipper gave a strong alert to the right front. He stopped and stood rigidly with his head and ears pointing to the right. I got down on one knee and quickly looked in that direction and spotted troop movement about one hundred yards away through the rubber trees. I immediately praised Clipper, "Good boy, Clipper! Good boy!"

The platoon leader got flat on the ground directly beside me with his RTO. He got on the radio and learned that we were on the back side of a sister platoon ahead of us. He then directed me to move in the direction where Clipper had spotted the troop movement. I got up, tapped the bottom of the twenty-round magazine to ensure it was properly seated in my CAR15, and made sure that the safety lever was on safe. I yanked on Clipper's leash to motion him to move out.

It was quiet as we penetrated farther into the rubber trees toward the American lines. Even though Clipper kept alerting directly ahead, I didn't stop until we spotted an American soldier waving for us to come forward. When I reached him, the platoon leader stopped me from going any farther. I knelt on one knee and Clipper got down on all fours.

We had arrived twenty minutes after we'd first heard the sound of shooting, with crossing the creek occupying most of the time. The platoon leader headed for our sister platoon's control point while we stayed put. I sat quietly next to a soldier from the other platoon and asked him what had happened. He told me that the platoon had spread out and moved through the rubber trees. Then command-detonated mines planted by the VC struck down the front of his platoon. When the platoon got into the killing zone, the VC had detonated the mines. A few men had been killed instantly and several others were wounded. He said the rest of the platoon had fired in the direction of the explosions, but Charlie never returned their fire. The platoon's advancement halted while they waited for medevacs and reinforcements.

I saw gunships and slicks in the air. Several slicks landed on a road not far from us to pick up the dead and wounded. When the platoon leader returned, he changed our mission, ordering us to merge with the platoon ahead and sweep through the hamlet area. There was a possibility that the VC who had detonated those mines might still be hiding in the hamlet along with women and children who lived there. We were not to shoot while inside the hamlet unless we had a clear target of aggression. As he talked, I noticed that the nearby area of rubber trees had been well-worked by the Vietnamese. There was little to no grass or weeds between the rows.

We cautiously moved out with weapons at the ready with Clipper leading the rear squad of our sister platoon. Farther on, I stepped on something that felt weird and rubbery under my boot. I looked down and saw a human hand, but I didn't stop to think about it. I had to keep moving until I reached the outer perimeter of the lead platoon.

American soldiers were spread throughout the rubber trees and moving forward along with us. We weren't far from the hamlet when Clipper's ears perked up. I didn't stop, because I assumed that Clipper was alerting on the hamlet's inhabitants.

A soldier to my right said, "Hey, dog man, check out the bomb lying against the trunk of that rubber tree."

I glanced at the tree trunk and saw a huge warhead at its base. The soldier told me that his platoon had discovered it after they were hit by the mines. He explained that the VC probably hadn't had time to rig it as a booby trap or they would have already detonated it. Instead, an American soldier had booby-trapped it for the VC. If anyone tried to move or tamper with it, that bomb would explode. Clipper couldn't stop alerting on that booby trap until he had completely lost sight of it.

When we arrived at the hamlet, Vietnamese women and children quickly came out of their huts to greet us. Clipper became agitated and growled as they approached. I held him back as the other soldiers entered the hamlet. I also held my finger on the safety of my weapon, just in case I had to flick it to automatic and shoot. More soldiers entered the village and started searching the huts, one by one. They looked for the VC who had detonated the mines that had killed and wounded our comrades.

As they searched, I heard someone shout inside one of the huts, "You VC? You kill Americans? Where VC? Bullshit! You lie!"

A thorough search of the hamlet, inside and out, revealed only the hiding places of women, children, and old men. We couldn't figure out where the VC were hidden, but we knew that they couldn't have vanished. I had begun to think that probably one of these women, an old man, or even a child had detonated the mines. I trusted no one.

I watched the hamlet fill with commotion and confusion as the soldiers completely surrounded its twenty or thirty huts. Several squads searched inside each hut. The Americans were having major communication problems with the Vietnamese. After several hours, a few Vietnamese interpreters flew in to help translate and interrogate every adult in the hamlet.

The Vietnamese were afraid of Clipper, so I stayed outside and didn't participate in the search for fear that Clipper might bite someone. If I let Clipper loose, he'd attack the first Vietnamese he found. I decided to take advantage of Clipper's aggressive behavior and use him as my guard against any personal attack.

When the village situation calmed down, several Vietnamese women moved quickly past Clipper and me with baskets of bananas, offering them to the American troops.

Several Vietnamese were taken into custody and later loaded into choppers for further interrogation in Dau Tieng. I was part of the first group of soldiers ordered to move out of the village and across a dirt road back into the rubber trees heading toward Dau Tieng.

Now we were on the last leg of our mission heading home to Dau Tieng. Our final objective was to form a long, linear sweeping formation to cover as much ground as possible and hunt for VC hideouts. After Clipper and I moved past a few rows of rubber trees, we were ordered to stop.

We waited for several minutes for the rest of the platoon to leave the hamlet and join the main element inside the rubber trees. Finally, the signal was given to move out again. Clipper and I carefully moved out on line among the trees. Two men walked by my side between the dirt road on my left and me. The rest of the platoon was strung out to the right and rear.

As Clipper and I passed between two trees, I heard a shattering explosion to our immediate right. I hit the ground and dragged Clipper down beside me. We didn't hear any shots being fired, but then I heard the sounds of a hurt soldier a few feet away from me. I quickly crawled over to him. He was lying on his back rocking in pain with his legs and boots covered in blood.

I yelled, "Medic! Medic!"

When the medic arrived, he cut the young soldier's boots off and treated the wounds on his legs and feet. Looking around on the ground, I discovered a broken trip wire attached to a short stick that was stuck in the ground. The other end of the wire was tied to a rubber tree. I immediately thought, *That could have been me if I'd moved one more tree over before I stopped,* I thought. *Would Clipper have alerted on that booby trap?* I would never know the answer to that question.

I decided that it was time to put to the test all the training that Clipper and I had gone through. Clipper had shown in our recent training sessions that he knew how to detect booby trap trip wires. He'd have to do it for real now, or more of these men would be injured or killed.

After the soldier was medevacked, I told the platoon leader that I would take the lead. I asked him to move the rest of the platoon into a column and follow behind me. I didn't give the platoon leader a chance to respond as I turned away. Out front, I slowly moved forward and began to follow Clipper's lead. As I glanced behind, I noticed that the platoon leader had ordered the troops to form a single column.

I thought, *Clipper is in charge now, even if he doesn't realize it. If anyone can do it, Clipper can get us through this area and safely home to Dau Tieng.*

With the outer perimeter of our Dau Tieng base camp less than a half mile away, I kept my attention glued to Clipper's head and ears while he guided me forward. Clipper gave a faint alert to the left, briefly hesitated, and then moved right. I glanced in that direction and saw nothing, so I didn't stop. I had to trust Clipper because my field of vision was only clear at eye level. The ground below was overgrown with knee-high weeds and grass. It was easy to walk through, and Clipper didn't have a problem negotiating a path.

Clipper gave another weak alert to his right and then moved left. He performed that maneuver again and again without much hesitation or stopping. A short time later a voice from behind ordered me to stop. As I looked back, I saw a long column of American troops snaking through the rubber trees behind me. We stopped only briefly and then moved out again. That stop-and-go situation occurred several times during the journey. I wasn't completely sure why we were stopping. No one behind me said anything about it, and I didn't ask, because I was too far forward. They could have been checking something out or reviewing the map for direction of travel. Someone may have spotted trip wires or booby traps. I had no way of knowing.

I didn't think Clipper's alerts were strong enough for me to worry about danger. The way he was moving, it looked as if he was deliberately going around things that could be trip wires or booby traps. Clipper had performed that kind of maneuver during our training sessions in base camp, but now when he moved from one direction to another, I couldn't see anything out of the ordinary. I decided to focus on watching Clipper instead of trying to figure out why he was walking from left to right so much. I was grateful that there had been no more explosions; Clipper was leading us on a safe path.

We finally reached the outskirts of Dau Tieng's base camp. I stopped short of the concertina wire and spotted soldiers standing on the other side next to their sand-bagged bunkers and staring at us. I dropped to one knee and waited for the rest of the platoon to catch up. My right knee was aching again, but I knew that I'd soon be safe inside the K-9 compound.

While I knelt and rubbed my right knee, several soldiers caught up with us. One of them stopped and told me to wait for the platoon leader. Another soldier smiled as he passed by. The soldiers moved along the fence of concertina wire in a column toward the base camp's entrance gate.

The lieutenant I had worked with throughout the mission finally showed up. I stood up to greet him, and he smiled and thanked me for getting his men through all the other booby traps. Then he knelt and gave Clipper a hug and told him what a great dog he was.

I was puzzled, so I asked, "What other booby traps?"

The platoon leader looked at me as though I should have known the answer to that question. He told me that when Clipper had changed directions for the first time, one of his men had spotted a grenade tied to the base of a rubber tree, right where the dog had changed directions.

He stated, "After you and your dog changed directions several times, my men got wise to what was going on, so they started searching for booby traps. The times we had stopped were used to mark the booby traps Clipper had avoided." He explained that the marked booby traps would be detonated after the entire company was safely through the area.

I was happy to hear that I'd been right. Clipper had been deliberately going around booby traps and trip wires. I hadn't seen any of them, because I didn't stop to search.

The platoon leader told me that it had been brave of me to take the lead when I didn't have to. He said that if it hadn't been for Clipper some of his men could have been wounded or killed by those booby traps. He said that he was going to recommend us for a Bronze Star medal. Then he shook my hand. As he walked away, he turned to me and said, "I'm going to ask for you the next time I need a scout."

That was the finest compliment I'd ever received for doing my job.

I smiled, waved, and gave the lieutenant a thumbs-up signal. I looked down at Clipper and tapped my chest. Clipper jumped up and rested his front paws on my shoulders. I looked into his big brown eyes and gave him a bear hug. I told him what a great warrior he was and how proud I felt to have him as my friend and scout.

I thought about the lieutenant's words. That was the first time anyone had ever wanted to recommend me for a medal. I felt honored but knew that all the credit belonged to my dog. He'd been the hero of the day. I was the lucky guy behind the leash and grateful to have such a wonderful companion to lead us to safety. I felt that there was nothing more valuable or rewarding than knowing that others had lived because of my dog. My trust and confidence in Clipper dramatically increased that day.

Clipper and I moved out behind the rest of the troops through the gate entrance. I walked with my head and shoulders high and smiled all the way home to the 44th Scout Dog Platoon. On the way, I thought about the trip wire training I'd put Clipper through. I remembered how Clipper had given faint alerts and avoided the trip wires by going around them. The training had paid off. Lives had been saved. I was relieved that another mission was over. As I watched my dog walk ahead of me I thought to myself, *Thanks again for another safe mission, Clipper!*

The Capture

Later on, Clipper and I were assigned to support Company A, 2nd Battalion, 12th Infantry. Brigade S-2 intelligence had reported that an NVA courier routinely traveled alone between the provinces of Tay Ninh and Dau Tieng. They wanted him captured and interrogated.

The platoon leader's field map marked the most probable places to trap and bag the courier. This type of mission was normally reserved for the long-range reconnaissance patrol (LRRP) teams, but the teams must have been busy with other missions at the time, so the 2/12 infantry had been signed up for the two-day assignment.

Choppers lifted us off at the crack of dawn. We headed toward the majestic Black Virgin Mountain, an inactive volcano. Nui Ba Den, as the Vietnamese called it, jutted up from the ground about three thousand feet and towered over the Tay Ninh province about eighty miles west of Saigon. Its summit was usually shrouded by clouds and mist and covered in a thick, green blanket of steep and dense rugged jungle. As the tallest landmass in the area, Nui Ba Den could easily be seen from miles around. From the air, the mountain was a beautiful sight to behold.

The U.S. Army 5th Special Forces Group had captured the summit in 1964. When we flew close to Nui Ba Den, we could see the 25th Infantry Division's signal corps VHF and FM relay station radio towers and some other tall antennas on top of the mountain. The signal corps relayed communication between units of the 25th Infantry Division located in Cu Chi, Tay Ninh, and Dau Tieng. The peak of Nui Ba Den was heavily fortified and appeared nearly impossible to reach by foot from below. The VC used the lower slopes of Nui Ba Den as observation posts and radio relay positions. The VC constantly harassed the American troops stationed on top with sniper fire and mortar attacks.

Four combat infantry platoons were assigned to this mission to capture the enemy courier. Each had separate areas to reconnoiter suitable ambush sites with which to catch him. I didn't know why I'd been the only dog handler assigned to the mission; we could have used four scout dog teams, one attached to each combat platoon.

Green smoke signaled our landing zone in a small clearing less than a mile from the base of Nui Ba Den. We quickly moved away from the aircraft and under the cover of the surrounding jungle. The patrol leader motioned me to take the lead. Clipper and I moved into the jungle, which wasn't too thick to navigate, and soon we had distanced ourselves about one hundred feet ahead of everyone else.

The patrol leader frequently signaled me to stop while he checked the map for the location and distance to a trail we were trying to reach. We cautiously moved parallel to Nui Ba Den for several hours. Clipper eventually gave a strong alert with his ears and head held high. I stopped, dropped to one knee, and motioned the nearest man forward. A fire team of three men was dispatched to check out the alert. When they returned, they reported a well-used trail less than two hundred feet ahead. The patrol leader moved up to my position and evaluated the map coordinates. We were on target according to the map.

Clipper and I quietly approached the trail under the cover of the surrounding vegetation. The platoon didn't want to get on the trail and risk exposure, yet, and I didn't want them to get ahead of me for fear of contaminating the area with their scent and throwing off Clipper's sense of smell. We moved quietly and undetected by using all the ingredients of a successful patrol—radio silence, camouflage, and concealment. We eventually set up an ambush alongside a fork where two trails intersected. It was a spot that provided excellent concealment and lines of sight in either direction. The platoon leader strategically positioned each man about five feet inside the jungle overlooking the narrow pathways. Clipper and I were positioned at one end of the ambush, which gave Clipper the best chance to alert if someone came bopping down the trail. The other platoons supporting that operation were within a mile radius of our position.

The plan was to surprise and capture the courier, not kill him. The ambush platoon waited for several hours, quietly swatting mosquitoes and killing bugs, ants, and spiders. Some men catnapped during the long wait, but most stayed vigilant. It reminded me of a spider in a web waiting for its prey. As the hours went by, the sky grew darker until nothing even within a few feet remained visible. We stayed alert in stationary positions all night, but nothing happened.

As early morning light chased the long shadows away, the men stirred. No one was allowed to smoke cigarettes because the smoke might alert the enemy to our presence. Of course, we never really knew if Charlie had already located us, or if we were going to succeed in ambushing him.

As the morning progressed, Clipper suddenly alerted toward the trail. I immediately informed the man next to me, who passed the warning signal down the line. In the dim morning light, I spotted the target of Clipper's alert—an NVA soldier in khaki uniform riding a bicycle, wearing a straw hat, and with a rifle slung over his back. I got a major rush of adrenaline as I watched the enemy come closer. I realized that I'd be the first man he would reach. Clipper remained silent and ready to pounce. The enemy soldier appeared to be alone and relaxed. He had two canvas bags draped over his bicycle's back fender.

That must be our man, I thought.

When the courier was right in front of me, I turned Clipper loose and he darted into the road, lunged, and knocked the NVA soldier off his bicycle. The man hit the ground landing on his back. I gave Clipper the command, "Watch him!" Clipper growled and showed his teeth but didn't attack. The enemy soldier looked so completely surprised that I thought his eyeballs were going to pop out of his head. Immediately, the rest of the patrol surrounded the soldier at gunpoint. Clipper's growling and barking kept the frightened man squirming on his back in the dirt. Someone quickly stripped him of his rifle.

I handed my CAR15 and Clipper's leash to the nearest soldier and told him to hold back the dog. I harkened back to my high school wrestling days, convinced that I could contain the prisoner without using a weapon. I reached down and rolled the prisoner over to his stomach, straddled his body, and spread his arms and legs. The prisoner was so scared that he pissed in his pants while I searched him.

In his pocket, I found a worn American Zippo lighter that was engraved with a 1st Infantry Division shoulder patch and the slogan "Big Red One." The Big Red One didn't operate near the Tay Ninh province as far as I knew. I thought they were up north a way. The canvas bags attached to the bicycle were filled with Vietnamese currency and documents. I was sure that we had the NVA courier that army intelligence was so eager to capture.

I didn't want to know how that North Vietnamese soldier had gotten that lighter. I thought, *The bastard must have taken it from a dead American.*

It was honorable for a soldier to die on the battlefield. Normal procedure is to take weapons, ammunition, and military documents from a wounded or dead man. But it is disgraceful to rob the wounded or dead of anything else. The soldier's personal effects should be returned to his surviving family no matter which side he's on. But the war in Vietnam wasn't a gentleman's war. It was as brutal and ugly as the death and destruction it left in its wake.

I was in complete control of the prisoner now. If he tried to escape, I would tackle and put him in a wrestling hold that he couldn't wiggle away from. I could also command Clipper to attack him. *There's no damn way that prisoner is going to get away,* I thought, as my blood boiled. I was hoping that he would try to resist or escape. If he did, I'd have an excuse to vent my anger. But the prisoner was too scared to move a muscle.

After I completed the body search, two soldiers took over for me. They tied the prisoner's hands behind his back, taped his mouth shut, and blindfolded him. The patrol leader radioed for a chopper to get us out of the area immediately. We quickly moved under jungle cover to the pickup point.

Later that morning, several choppers arrived. They flew the prisoner and my platoon back to Dau Tieng. I was grateful that Clipper and I had accomplished another mission and had no American casualties. I hoped that the rest of my future missions in Vietnam would be that successful, but safety was never a guarantee in that *undeclared war*.

Life between Missions

It was always a welcome comfort to return to base camp after a mission, like coming home from work and spending time relaxing with friends. Our K-9 Klub was the best place for us to unwind and try to forget our troubles on the job.

Huddled within the wooden buildings of our sleeping area, the K-9 Klub served as the mailroom lounge. It was modestly furnished with tables, chairs, a refrigerator, a bar, and portable air conditioners. Screened-in windows, covered with scrapped sheets of clear plastic, kept cool air inside. The club was even wired for electricity to accommodate those modest but important morale-lifting conveniences.

The good and bad times with family and friends back home was always a hot topic of conversation. Some bragged about all the girls waiting for them back home. Others talked about going to college, getting a job, and starting a business. Nobody had aspirations of making army life a career.

The local *Stars and Stripes* newspaper reported the war's current events throughout Vietnam. Many of the dog handlers passed time reading books, magazines, and hometown newspapers. They played cards and drank soda pop and Ballantine and Pabst Blue

Ribbon beer. They especially enjoyed drinking Kool-Aid, because it sweetly masked the nasty taste of the local water supply.

News of our fellow dog handlers who were in hospitals recovering from wounds was always a major topic. Kentucky, wounded during the kennel attack, was wounded a second time when he was shot in the buttocks by a VC sniper during a search-and-destroy mission. Another dog handler, Randy Cox, was severely burned with his dog while inside an armored personnel carrier that got hit by an enemy rocket. Randy was evacuated to a hospital burn unit in the States and did not return to active military service. His dog died of severe burns.

In May 1967, I read a story in the 3rd Brigade's newspaper about Mike Phillips and his scout dog, Beau. Mike was a twenty-year-old, curly-haired redhead from Cleveland. Beau was his German shepherd and had an aggressive attitude. They had trained together at the Scout Dog Training Center in Fort Benning and arrived in Vietnam with the original members of the 44th Scout Dog Platoon in January. Both had tasted the bitterness of war for five months.

According to the story, Beau had been wounded two different times, first during a three-day mission. Phillips and Beau had been scouting for an infantry unit near a large clearing when Beau alerted. Phillips had immediately recognized the danger, signaled the men behind him, and dove for cover. The Viet Cong opened fire, but Beau's alert had halted the American patrol short of the deadliest area within the ambush zone.

During the ensuing firefight, a bullet from an enemy AK-47 rifle had struck Beau in the front leg. Phillips protected his dog by covering him with his body while he returned fire. The Americans suffered only light casualties in that battle and defeated the enemy. If it hadn't been for Beau's alert, American casualties would have been greater. Beau's wound turned out to be mild and Doc Glydon patched him up.

That put Mike and Beau back in action for Operation Junction City in the rugged area of War Zone C. Mike and Beau were sitting in a clearing preparing to move out when enemy mortar rounds began piercing the air and exploding all around them. During the mortar attack, Beau and Phillips were wounded. A piece of shrapnel passed completely through Beau's middle, breaking part of his backbone. Phillips's right arm was pierced with another piece of shrapnel. Beau was so seriously wounded that he was evacuated to a hospital in Saigon. A death certificate was filed in Dau Tieng because no one expected Beau to survive, let alone to rejoin his war dog platoon. Beau was a tough dog, however, and refused to give up. He made it through the surgery and was rehabilitated back to health.

A month later, Beau returned to duty with the 44th, and his death certificate was torn up and thrown away.

I preferred to work Timber and Clipper on-leash, while Ollie, Mac, and other dog handlers worked their dogs off-leash without problems. Roger Jones was no exception. Roger had won the Trainee of the Cycle award at the Scout Dog Training Center in Fort Benning, Georgia.

In June 1967, Roger and his dog, Ringo, were supporting a

platoon on a mission when they got into a firefight with the enemy. Ringo, unleashed, bolted from the chaotic scene. Lieutenant Fenner and Doc Bob Glydon felt accountable for every scout dog and handler and were furious that Roger returned without Ringo. They filed a Report of Survey form charging Roger with suspicion of negligence. The incident could have resulted in court-martial proceedings, but Roger was never punished.

A few weeks after Roger had lost Ringo, the local *Stars and Stripes* carried the story of a wounded German shepherd who had followed an American combat patrol into the Cu Chi base camp. According to the story, the dog had been badly wounded in the jaw, dehydrated, and hungry. The wounded dog had survived several days hiding in the jungle on his own.

The dog had been taken to the 38th Scout Dog Platoon for medical attention. The 38th was a sister scout dog platoon based at Cu Chi. Because each dog had a serial number tattooed into his left ear, Doc Glydon was able to verify that the wounded dog's serial number matched that of Roger's missing scout dog, Ringo.

Ringo had suffered from a close-range gunshot wound in the face. The bullet had entered one side of his jaw and exited the other side. Ringo was evacuated to Saigon, where he underwent a special surgical operation performed by a well-known military dental surgeon. Roger flew to Saigon to accompany his dog through his successful surgery, and a month later, Roger and Ringo returned home to the 44th. Ringo eventually recovered from his wounds, except for his tongue. When it hung from his mouth, it was evident that part of it was missing.

For surviving his wound, hiding in the bush, and finding an American patrol to follow home, Ringo was our hero. We admired his courage and strength to evade being killed by the enemy.

Dog handlers all had their own personalities and ways of expressing their individuality. For example, my hooch-mate, Dan Scott, always seemed to have a book sticking out of his back pocket, because he liked to read every chance he got. After dropping out of Officer Candidate School, Scott was reassigned to scout dog training. Upon graduation, Scott had been shipped to Vietnam and assigned to the 44th in March 1967, the same month that I returned for my second tour of duty.

Somehow Scott had acquired a World War II, twenty-five-inch-long .45-caliber machine gun commonly called a *grease gun*. Although .45-caliber ammunition was a standard item within the Dau Tieng supply channels, Dan had also acquired several thirty-round ammunition clips to go along with his new weapon. The gun was designed to be slung from a shoulder strap and fired from the hip with one hand.

Lieutenant Fenner didn't seem to care that some of his men preferred weapons other than the standard-issue CAR15 or M16. For example, Mac McClellan insisted on carrying his M1 rifle to the field and wouldn't trade for anything else. Scott toted his grease gun on every mission and swore that it never jammed when fired. It didn't have a semiautomatic selector switch like the CAR15, because it was designed to fire on full automatic. I didn't think that grease gun could hit the broad side of a barn beyond twenty feet, but everyone agreed that if the bullets didn't kill the enemy, the noise would scare him to death.

One day Scott stood outside my hooch and called, "Hey, Burnam! Get out here! I have something to show you!"

I went out to see what the fuss was and found Scott holding two jars in his hands. Inside of one jar was the largest centipede I'd ever seen. In the other jar was a monster scorpion. Before long, several other dog handlers gathered around while Scott placed the two jars on the ground. We started placing bets on which of the critters would survive in a fight. I put my money on the scorpion, because it looked meaner. When all the bets were in—about fifty-fifty on the scorpion and the centipede— Scott emptied the jars and forced the critters into a fight that didn't last long. Less than a minute into the first round, the centipede killed the scorpion, and I lost my bet.

Everyone's sense of humor was not only a way of expressing one's identity but also of staying mentally healthy in Vietnam, so we often looked for ways to have some fun.

One day, Dan Scott, Mike Phillips, and I acquired a torn camouflage parachute from a logistics sergeant and decided to liven up our hooch with it. We centered the parachute's apex onto the ceiling and painted it black. We glued strands of steel wool around the dark center and spread out and nailed the rest of the parachute material to the rafters and walls. We called our creative decoration "The Pussy That Swallowed Vietnam."

While Dan, Mike, and I fantasized about women, Bill Zantos, a fellow scout handler managed to find himself a girlfriend. Two local women, whom we called Mama Sans, operated a laundry and boot-shine service inside a large military canvas tent across the road from the K-9 compound. A black chalkboard listed the prices they charged for each laundry item as well as the cost of boot-polishing services. We used military pay currency, or paper money, to pay for their services.

One of the older Vietnamese women who worked in the laundry tent took a shining to Bill Zantos. Compared to the rest of us, Bill had a robust body, which quickly earned him the nickname "Heavy." When the dog handlers found out that Heavy was doing the boom-boom thing with a Mama San in the back of the laundry tent, they had a great time poking fun at him. Fortunately, Bill had a good sense of humor and he laughed right along with us.

———————

The 44th set up a volleyball net between two rubber trees inside the K-9 compound. Playing volleyball gave us some exercise and helped take our minds off our troubles. There always seemed to be plenty of dog handlers who wanted to play, and we played for hours without shirts under cover of the fully leafed rubber trees.

About once a week, from a small range of mountains north of our K-9 compound, Charlie launched mortar rounds at the Dau Tieng airstrip. We quickly learned that the maximum range of Charlie's mortar rounds was about two hundred yards short of the volleyball court. So whenever we heard mortars exploding on the airstrip, we'd stop the volleyball game and watch.

Since the shrapnel from the mortar rounds never reached us during those random daytime mortar attacks, we didn't need to run and seek shelter in the bunkers. We stood on the volleyball court and watched the fireworks. Most of the shells exploded in and around the airfield's runway and the helicopters would scramble to get airborne. During each mortar attack, Dau Tieng sounded a siren like the one used for an air raid. The mortar attacks never lasted long. It was just Charlie's way of saying hello.

Occasionally, Charlie would get lucky and blow up a helicopter or ground vehicle, or hit a building near the runway. American retaliatory artillery strikes were immediate and our gunships were airborne. With a vengeance, the Americans would fire volley after volley of artillery rounds. The infantry would patrol on foot and search through the rugged and difficult mountainous terrain. Scout dog teams would also be sent out to locate Charlie's mortar squads. Once in a while we got lucky and surprised Charlie, killing him and capturing some of his mortar tubes. For the most part, however, it was a cat-and-mouse game. Charlie was too smart and usually got away in time only to return another day and launch more shells. We learned to respect those tenacious little bastards, because they were so good at guerilla warfare.

On September 2, 1967, a beautiful, hot and humid morning with not a cloud in the sky, Lieutenant Fenner decided that we should go on a road march, because he thought we weren't getting enough exercise in base camp. He directed the entire platoon of fifteen or so scout dog teams to assemble. We were to march around the entire perimeter of Dau Tieng. We decided to travel light with only our helmets, weapons, one canteen of water each, and dog on-leash. With the hot sun and balmy air, none of us were too happy with the idea of a road march. But shortly after lunch, we formed up in single file for the trip.

As we headed out of the K-9 compound, we must have made a magnificent sight with German shepherds and scout dog handlers stretched out for a quarter mile. When the platoon moved along the shoulder of the road, I realized that that was the first time I'd seen an organized march since my assignment with the sentry dog platoon in Okinawa. Back then, it was routine to march around in formations. In Vietnam, emphasis wasn't placed on organized training activities. Usually, we rested while in base camp, and trained at our individual discretion.

Because our base camp wasn't very large, the dogs drew immediate attention as we passed infantry company areas, battalion and brigade headquarters, the field hospital, motor pools, the airstrip, maintenance hangers, and trucks and jeeps that were driving down the road. We figured that we'd be gone for only a short time. It must have been 110 degrees that afternoon, and the dusty road offered no cover or protection from the sun and heat. We marched at a slow pace, and after about two hours, the column of scout dog teams had made a complete nonstop loop around the entire base camp of Dau Tieng. The dogs' tongues were dragging the dirt.

We were within a few hundred yards of walking through the

entrance of our K-9 compound when the worst possible thing happened. Tony Pettingill's dog, Prince, gasped for air and collapsed near the entrance to the K-9 compound. Doc Glydon wasn't able to revive Prince, and he died of dehydration. I watched as Tony cradled Prince in his arms and sobbed. There was nothing anyone could do for him. Prince was the only casualty of that road march, just another tragic accident that took the life of a war dog.

We buried Prince in the cemetery inside the K-9 compound next to the dogs that had died before him—Erik, Shadow, Sergeant, 44, Hardcore, and others. The grave markers were starting to add up.

The army never let a grunt rest for very long. Even when we were back at base camp between jungle missions and assignments, we had to pull duty with the 3rd Brigade, 25th Infantry Division military police detachment. That served to keep us occupied and useful.

The military police detachment was responsible for law and order inside the Dau Tieng base camp and they controlled the traffic in and out of the gates. The village of Dau Tieng was off-limits to American grunts at all times; liberty passes were never issued for us to enter the town. Besides, there was really nothing to see or anything worth buying there. The MPs also patrolled inside the village at night.

The primary reason American troops occupied Dau Tieng was that the rubber tree plantations happened to be strategically located for military use as a forward fire base and as a buffer between Cambodia and Saigon. The Vietnamese used the Saigon River, which ran right through the village, for fishing, bathing, and transport.

So the 44th IPSD got involved supporting MP night patrols in the Dau Tieng village. Lieutenant Fenner maintained the duty roster and made sure that every scout dog handler was on his list. When we weren't in the field, dog handlers were expected to go on what was dubbed "Rat Patrol."

Rat Patrol was never conducted during daylight hours. It started after midnight and lasted for several hours. Mainly a show of force, a scout dog team would accompany a small detachment of MPs into the village several nights during the week. A dog handler traveled light, carrying a CAR15, bandolier of ammunition, flashlight, and a few canteens of water for the dog. He wore a soft flop hat instead of a steel pot. The MPs carried M16s and .45-caliber pistols as side arms. One member of the MP team carried the PRC/25 radio to use in getting help and relaying situation reports.

The local whorehouse, off-limits to Americans, was one of the village's checkpoints. An ARVN and an American Military Assistance Command Vietnam (MACV) command post near the center of town was heavily guarded and surrounded by barbed wire and sandbags. The Rat Patrol used it as a pit stop for a cup of coffee and as a place to hang out and talk with the American advisors who were on duty there.

Rat Patrol was conducted with clockwork precision and didn't surprise any of the locals. Every villager knew where we went and how many of us were on a team. The patrol walked the main dirt road and beaten paths of the village. Every now and then the patrol had to chase some Vietnamese through the darkness, but they always seemed to get away. The Rat Patrol wouldn't be surprising a lone Viet Cong and never snuck up on a squad of North Vietnamese Regulars sitting around smoking pot or setting up a mortar tube. Charlie was too slick for that.

Dau Tieng didn't have streetlamps, traffic signals, or a town square with a huge lit-up clock. It was a poor town where people lived in small huts and mostly traveled on foot or by bicycle. Their dirt yards had chickens, oxen, pigs, and tiny dogs hanging around. There were no paved roads. In fact, everything seemed to be dirt, including most of the floors inside the homes. While some of the businesses in town had a more permanent look, heavily influenced by the French style of architecture, permanent-looking structures were few and far between in the village of Dau Tieng.

We enjoyed going on Rat Patrol for one reason—we could visit the local bakery. Dau Tieng's Vietnamese baker used a primitive brick oven with a cast-iron door to bake small loaves of bread. What a treat it was to smell and taste hot baked rolls at two o'clock in the morning! The baker never charged us for his goods, saying that the Rat Patrol kept away the VC. Part of every scout dog handler's mission on Rat Patrol was to bring back some bread or rolls for his friends.

I figured that the military police were like the local police back home. Instead of free donuts and coffee at the local late-night convenience store, they enjoyed free bread at the local

Vietnamese bakery. The only redeeming value of going on Rat Patrol was bringing home this welcome treat, which was just another way of relieving some of the tension of serving as a scout dog handler. But despite the great food, Rat Patrol—along with combat missions—was wearing on my bad knee.

Soon, my old injury would force me to leave Dau Tieng and my best friend, Clipper.

Short-Timer

On Christmas Day, 1967, the battalion mess hall served a big lunch of turkey with all the trimmings. The past week had seen a major increase in incoming mail and packages from the States.

I woke up early that Christmas morning and felt great, even though it was hot and muggy outside. Everyone I ran into seemed to be in a good mood and the dogs were barking and hungry. It was a day like any other in Vietnam for Clipper and his pals in the kennel. Same old dog food, same old rubber tree, same old water pail, same old kennel run, and the same old mutts as neighbors. He didn't even know that he had no chance in hell of ever going back to the States as my pet in my backyard. That was too depressing a thought, so we dog handlers didn't talk about it much.

That Christmas, I thought about two Christmases past.

On Christmas in 1965, I'd been in Littleton, Colorado, living it up on a week's furlough from infantry recruit training. I had no idea that the army would be shipping my butt off to Vietnam in March 1966.

On Christmas Day in 1966, I was in a sentry dog platoon with the 267th Chemical Company in Okinawa. My fear of guarding chemical weapons of mass destruction was one of many reasons I chose to return to Vietnam.

Now, on this, my first Christmas in South Vietnam, the radio played Christmas music, courtesy of the armed services radio station. Since the Vietnamese culture was largely Buddhist, there were no colored lights or Christmas trees in town. Separated from families and friends on the other side of the planet, no children surrounded us and shared their excitement about Santa Claus or a special Christmas toy. We couldn't shop for Christmas gifts, because there were no real stores nearby. Civilian life was only a nice memory, even though many of us had been civilian teenagers less than a year earlier. Although we felt light-years away from the comforts and traditions of an American Christmas season, we enjoyed each other's company and shared packages of food from home.

The nearby chapel offered a variety of religious services throughout the day. I still felt bitter over the sermon the chaplain had given for Ed Hughes, so I had stopped attending church services. However, I was truly thankful that I was well and had been spared from falling sick with malaria, dysentery, or Asian flu, and that I wasn't lying in some hospital bed suffering from another combat wound.

We shared care packages of food from home that all seemed to contain various types of fruitcakes. People back home figured that fruitcake wouldn't spoil on the long journey to South Vietnam. I hated fruitcake! In this, I wasn't alone. We all disliked the taste of fruitcake. We wouldn't even feed it to the dogs, because we thought they'd puke from the taste. Nonetheless, we were grateful to receive it, and there was always someone who'd eat the fruitcakes. Our fellow dog handler Coonrod would eat about anything. Coonrod was known to swallow large chunks of cooked hog fat just to gross people out.

A fellow wouldn't think of writing home to complain about the contents of a care package, not even if it contained fruitcake. Homemade chocolate chip, oatmeal-and-raisin cookies, and chocolate cakes were our favorites. They arrived in cardboard boxes, wrapped and taped in plastic and tin foil, and packed in popcorn. Those goodies never lasted long, because you couldn't eat one cookie without eating another and another. Sometimes the packages took a beating during the long trip. The cookies arrived broken and crumbled, and the cakes were mashed, but they still tasted great. We ate all the crumbs.

Rumor had it that if the United States declared war on North Vietnam, we would all be in Vietnam for the duration. The war could go on for several years, which would've been the biggest of all bummers. I didn't figure I'd last the duration of a full-blown war with North Vietnam. In my line of work, walking point and being the first exposed to the enemy, people got killed sooner or later. But it was taboo to allow yourself to think about death, so I convinced myself that I would survive in Vietnam.

I believed the Americans could kick ass and take names all the way to Hanoi if the Army would only unchain us from all the war restrictions and let us keep the ground we fought so hard to capture. As it stood, we operated out of base camps, fought the enemy, and returned to base camps only to go out another day to the same places and do the same things over again. It was like continuously mopping up the water from a leaking pipe but never fixing the plumbing problem.

A Christmas cease-fire to last a few days into the New Year of 1968 was announced throughout Vietnam. There would be no major offensive, and no search-and-destroy operations. They called this *standing down*. However, the defensive perimeter circling the Dau Tieng base camp still had to be manned around the clock. Patrols were scheduled, as a minimum security, to probe right outside the perimeter during the cease-fire period. This was our only insurance against one of Charlie's surprises. No one wanted to get caught with his pants down, and even though the 3rd Brigade's infantry units were standing down, they remained on a one-hour-alert status.

All the scout dog teams were in base camp for the week but ready for deployment if needed. Charlie was supposed to honor the holiday cease-fire, and we didn't expect him to attack our base camp with mortars, rockets, or snipers, but there was no telling if all of Charlie's units, hiding in the jungle, had gotten the message or would obey the cease-fire.

The Vietnamese, in general, didn't recognize or honor Christian holidays. For me, the Christmas holiday was another day off from the war, which was a good thing. Any day I didn't have to expose Clipper and me to the enemy was a good day, and I was only two and a half months away from ending my tour of duty in Vietnam. My rotation month was the middle of March 1968 and my twelve-month stint would soon be over. Soon, I would have accomplished my mission in Southeast Asia, even though the army had reneged on my promised assignment when I volunteered to return to that hellhole. I didn't want to think about that broken agreement, because it still upset me.

My hope was that the army would get me home in time to celebrate my twenty-first birthday on March 16, 1968.

In Vietnam, there was no such thing as a travel agent at headquarters who took requests for plane reservations and a window seat. I knew exactly how the army operated. I was just a number, a man without a face, who would be processed out when my time was up. I had grown used to expecting the routine of hurry-up-and-wait for the unknown. I couldn't understand how career soldiers, dubbed *lifers,* dealt with the army for five, ten, or even fifteen years. I could barely figure out how I would deal with the next two-and-a-half months.

The combat missions, combined with walking, running, jumping, and carrying a loaded backpack, had taken a heavy toll on my right knee. Over the last few months, I'd been feeling more and more discomfort, as if my knee was wearing out on me. After a mission, it stayed inflamed, puffy, and red for days. Every now and then it would lock up, and I would walk stiff-legged until it unlocked. After the swelling went down, I'd feel okay, but then I'd have to get ready for another mission. I began walking with a noticeable limp, but I wasn't a complainer, slacker, ghost, or skater when it came to pulling my load.

When I talked to Lieutenant Fenner about my knee injury, he agreed that I should see a doctor. After an initial medical evaluation at the local field hospital, the news the doctor gave me wasn't good. I had damaged ligaments around the fleshy area of my old bamboo *punji* stick wound. I also had the beginnings of degenerative arthritis developing in the joint. The doctor told me that this condition could worsen with age.

Age? I thought. *I'm only twenty years old!* I wondered what my knee would be like when I became an old man of thirty.

The doctor said that further aggravation of my knee would cause more discomfort or even permanent damage, and then I'd need another operation to repair the ligaments. For at least a year since my operation, I had been pounding hard on that knee, but I didn't want to go under the knife again. The recuperation period was too long and I was almost through with my tour. I knew that I had to hang in there for a few more months before I went home.

The doctor at the Dau Tieng field hospital scheduled an appointment for me to see an orthopedic specialist in Cu Chi, the home of the 25th Infantry Division. The 3rd Brigade, in Dau Tieng, was a subordinate command of the 25th Infantry Division. The medical facilities at Cu Chi were more permanent and better staffed than the small field hospital in dusty old Dau Tieng.

In the middle of January 1968, I flew in a supply chopper to visit the orthopedic specialist in Cu Chi. I expected to be gone from Clipper for only a few days.

Boy, was I wrong!

When I met with the doctor, I underwent another complete medical examination, including a blood workup. The doctor told me that he was going to put a cast on my leg to immobilize it for one month. He asked me how much time I had left in Vietnam and I explained that I was scheduled to rotate back to the States in two months. Based on the condition of my knee, he said that I wouldn't be leaving Cu Chi. He placed me under medical observation and care in the Cu Chi hospital for my remaining time in Vietnam.

I thought that this news was fine and dandy, but I really needed to get back to Dau Tieng to collect my personal effects and see Clipper. I'd always been bothered by this kind of quick decision making so typical of the army.

The hospital issued me a temporary physical profile signed by the doctor who had performed the examination. It stipulated that I was to do no more strenuous activity. I was restricted from running, jumping, crawling, prolonged standing, or marching. The term of the temporary physical profile was three months, which would carry past my rotation date in March. I had to carry the document in my pocket at all times. It was my special-duty pass.

Not having to hump the boonies anymore was great, but I really missed Clipper. My only comfort was that I knew my hooch buddies, Dan Scott and Mike Phillips, would take good care of him while I was gone.

The doctor told me that he was obligated to properly look after and ensure my health and welfare. My knee would get better only if I quit abusing it. In his eyes, I was "just a kid," and he told me so. I decided to educate the doctor on my definition of a man.

I said, "I resent being called a kid or a boy. If I'm old enough to fight a war and spill blood for my country, I'm old enough to be called a man."

The graying old guy smiled and told me that he had boys my age, but they were in school. My initial thought was that his sons would probably be drafted for Vietnam duty if the war continued.

I also had the impression that the doctor was trying to give me the gift of having a valid medical reason for staying out of a combat unit. I decided not to push the "man" argument with him. My health was important to me, and although I may have been a little crazy in the head to return to Vietnam for a second tour of duty, I sure as hell wasn't so stupid as to pass up this opportunity not to get shot at anymore.

I had never discussed with any military doctor how they felt about war, but I'd been forming my opinions about doctors' attitudes by observing them. I remembered the kindness of Dr. George Bogumill, the physician in Japan who had performed surgery on my knee. He wasn't motivated by the war, like a field commander in constant need of warm, fresh, and healthy bodies to fight the enemy. Field commanders expected a certain amount of casualties and considered infantrymen to be replaceable. I'd experienced that attitude many times during my short time in the service. Doctors, on the other hand, had more caring and sensitive natures. They didn't see or experience battle, they dealt with the aftermath. They helped mend the bloody young bodies toted on stretchers fresh from the battlefield. Sadly, many times a doctor and his medical staff were unable to save those young lives. I concluded that doctors were truly a breed apart from the military infantry world where I lived and breathed.

Because it meant having to watch my fellow soldiers suffering, I didn't like being in a field hospital. When I milled around the tents of Cu Chi hospital, I saw naked men sitting inside ice-filled metal bathtubs on dirt floors. Those men were burning up with fever caused by malaria, and the sight of them made me glad I'd taken my malaria pills regularly. I'd heard that some of those men would die if the doctors couldn't break the fever in time. What a way to go out of that lousy war—shaking all over, high temperature, sitting in cold water, and then dying. I could sense the pain those young guys must have been going through, but I could only watch, wait, and hope for the best.

For me, though, the most depressing aspect of being a patient in the hospital at Cu Chi was that I wouldn't get a chance to say good-bye to Clipper or my dog handler friends. Because of the distance between base camps, communication had to be made by some kind of radio operator patching system. I felt a little uncomfortable going into some unit's headquarters and asking if I could make a long-distance call to check on my dog. I felt helpless to do anything out of the ordinary, since I was a stranger in these new surroundings. The hospital personnel clerk advised me that he'd contact the 44th Scout Dog platoon and forward the paperwork authorizing my reassignment to the Cu Chi field hospital.

The doctor eventually decided not to cover my leg in a cast. Instead, he wrapped it in a large flexible bandage. He told me not to overdo physical activity, and that I was to see him for checkups every few days until the swelling went down. If my knee continued to swell with fluid, it would have to be drained with a syringe. I hated needles ever since a doctor back in Littleton, Colorado, had stuck a needle in my left ear to drain the fluid that had accumulated from the punishment of high school wrestling.

I was assigned to living quarters at Headquarters Company, 25th Supply and Transportation Battalion (S & T). I reported to First Sergeant Milanowski, who noticed the CIB and Jump Wings sewn above my left breast pocket. He smiled and said,

"Welcome, Sergeant Burnam!" I had finally been promoted to Sergeant E5 in December 1967. My scout dog platoon sergeant, Sergeant D, had pinned my stripes on me in the K-9 Klub. Rear echelon troops couldn't earn a CIB unless they were assigned as infantryman in an infantry unit, but they respected anyone who wore it.

I'd been promoted a few weeks after Private First Class Ed Hughes had been killed in action. The timing of the promotion and celebration was poor, but to ease the memories of Ed's death, I had a few beers and a couple hits off a marijuana cigarette with my fellow dog handlers. My stripes had been merit-based, unlike *blood stripes*—given when a sergeant gets killed in battle and his stripes are handed down to the next person in line for a promotion. So I wore my new three-stripe chevrons on my sleeve with pride. I felt pretty cool and cocky to be a sergeant—equivalent to a squad leader in rank and authority—especially when I was addressed as "Sarge."

The first sergeant at my new base camp, "Top," was trim, short, with about the same build and height as me. He sported a typical military haircut with his head covered in a clean military OD baseball hat. He wore properly fitting and pressed jungle fatigues and brush-shined jungle boots. He was the perfect example of a professional career soldier. My first impression was that I liked him, and he seemed to like me, too.

Since I was a sergeant, Top assigned me to the noncommission officers' (NCO) quarters, nothing more than an army green canvas tent with no special accouterments. I had better quarters in Dau Tieng. No one below the rank of sergeant was allowed to live there. NCOs were separated from the lower enlisted men and not allowed to fraternize with them. I violated the hell out of that military protocol rule.

After I settled into my new digs, a runner came by to tell me to report to First Sergeant Milanowski. I hustled my butt over to Top's office in the *head shed*—the headquarters building. Top informed me that I had been assigned to work at the post exchange. I was to report to Sergeant Major Kelly, who ran the place. With a smile, Top told me that it was the best job he could find for me, and I believed him. I thanked him and cautiously headed out in search of SGM Kelly. SGM (E-9) was the highest enlisted rank in the army. High-ranking soldiers always made me nervous.

The PX was about a mile away from the 25th S&T. I walked along a dirt road that wound its way around the entire inside perimeter of Cu Chi. My knee was wrapped tightly and I limped a little, but at least I no longer had to carry a sixty-pound pack and rifle.

I found SGM Kelly's office in a small detached building behind the huge PX. I spotted him through the screen door, sitting at his desk with his back to the door. I knocked lightly on the wooden screen door, and without looking, a deep voice told me to enter. I walked in, removed my headgear, stood at attention, and announced myself by saying, "Sergeant Burnam reporting as directed, Sergeant Major!"

The SGM swiveled his chair around and faced me. "Do you have any experience working in a store, Buck Sergeant?" he asked. (*Buck Sergeant* was a common nickname for a three-striper.)

"No, Sergeant Major!"

"Well, you'll learn."

He told me to stand at ease and tell him about myself.

I noticed that the SGM had a Combat Infantry Badge with two stars connecting the top of the wreath, which meant that he'd been awarded the CIB three times—in WWII, Korea, and Vietnam. He looked old and wrinkled around his eyes and cheeks and was obviously well-traveled in the army. *One war is enough for me,* I thought. I couldn't imagine serving in three wars as an infantryman. That old soldier must have been born with Army blood in his veins or just plain crazy but he deserved my ultimate respect. I wasn't about to ask him how he'd ended up as the SGM for the PX.

SGM Kelly assigned me to new quarters near the PX. He told me that when he needed someone he didn't like waiting.

My new accommodations were in a wooden building with a wooden floor. I had a metal bunk bed with a mosquito net rigged above it. The hooch was equipped with a refrigerator stocked with food, soft drinks, and beer. It had tables, floor lamps, chairs, and a small bookshelf stocked with paperbacks. That was the nicest place I'd lived in since entering the army.

By that time, I'd been in Cu Chi a few weeks. When I asked the SGM for a chance to visit Clipper in Dau Tieng, he denied my request. Officially, I was no longer a scout dog handler assigned to the 44th. The SGM told me that I hadn't worked long enough to earn time off, but he promised me a convoy trip or chopper ride to Dau Tieng before I left Vietnam in March.

I'd heard army promises before, though, so I wasn't sure if that one would be kept. I hoped it would be. I sure did miss Clipper and my buddies.

My new job was to drive a tractor-trailer rig to the infantry units throughout the base camp. My fully enclosed trailer was stocked with assorted sundries such as candy, peanuts, canned finger food, canned soda and beer, cigarettes, and Zippo cigarette lighters. The truck was really a mobile store and a morale booster for the troops. *What a job!* I thought. *To have all the food and drink I could handle.*

When I pulled up to an infantry company area and opened the doors for business, I had no problem selling the stocked items and collecting money. I had to turn in all the money to SGM Kelly at the end of the day, and he didn't require an inventory of stock. He left that up to me. My job was to keep the truck resupplied. Needless to say, it was tempting to take anything and as much of it as I wanted. If I ever got caught stealing, I'd have probably ended up in LBJ (Long Bin Jail). I wasn't about to mess up that job for some petty theft rap, especially with only one-and-a-half months to serve in Vietnam.

When I parked the rig within the compound of an infantry company, it was like the Good Humor man had arrived. After opening the large metal door and lowering the stairs for business, a line would quickly form to come aboard. I'd position myself at the small cash register near the entrance, which also served as the exit. Due to the cramped space inside, I could only let in a handful of soldiers at a time. As the troops entered, their eyes would light up when they saw the rows of metal baskets filled with packaged candy, canned food, and drinks.

Infantrymen were very special to me, and I knew how hard they worked in South Vietnam. I'd always smile and welcome each of them as they entered my store. I liked to make up my own rules for them. When I serviced an infantry unit smelling of fresh muck from the field, I'd yell, "It's a two-for-one sale today, men!" They'd smile and go crazy, buying all they could carry. I knew that some of those young guys would never make it home to the States. Many of them looked as green as I had when I first got to Vietnam almost two years earlier.

I would visit a bunch of different units each day, seven days a week. When I'd get a day off, I liked staying busy hanging out with the other short-timers that worked in the PX. It helped me keep my mind off of missing Clipper and my other friends in the 44th.

While I couldn't believe my time in Vietnam would be coming to an end, one-and-a-half months seemed like an eternity, and anything could happen before I went home. I certainly didn't want to become a casualty during my last month. But I knew that if I dwelled on these thoughts, each day would take forever to go by. I tried not to worry about things I had no control over. I had to remain positive and do my job. I knew that there'd be plenty of time to reflect on my experiences after I left and was safely back in the United States.

A soldier with thirty days or less to serve was called a *short-timer*. Some field commanders did their best to keep short-timers out of harm's way. But a good number of short-timers still humped the boonies, getting killed or wounded weeks or even days before they were scheduled to leave Vietnam. The goal of an infantry short-timer was to become an REMF (Rear Echelon Mother Fucker). Some examples of REMFs were truck drivers, supply clerks, vehicle mechanics, hospital technicians, personnel and finance clerks, cooks, and engineers. They manned the base camp perimeter when the infantry was out looking for a fight. After an infantryman became a short-timer, he started hunting for a job as a REMF to justify staying away from combat until he left Vietnam.

Once a guy reached short-timer status, it was also tradition to carry around a short-timer stick. Some short-timers carved fancy sticks from tree branches and notched them to show how many days they had left in Vietnam. As each day passed, they'd cut the stick off a notch until only a stub was left. A short-timer also marked a big *X* on his calendar as each day ended. Many of them spent much of their free time writing letters and sending stuff home.

You'd be surprised at some of the things short-timers tried to mail home, though their attempts at having keepsakes of their time in Vietnam were more funny than shocking. For example, there was the story of a soldier who sent home an M60 machine gun. He broke it down into little pieces and mailed each piece in a separate package. The recipient wrote back to report what had arrived and what didn't. The operation took several months, but the man was finally successful. The military postal system had so many packages coming in and out of Vietnam that it must have become impossible for them to check each one for illegal contents.

Some short-timers got superstitious. They acted very weird and would only do things they believed wouldn't put them in any danger. They would avoid walking too close to the perimeter for fear of getting shot by a sniper. If they walked around base camp with several other men, they'd refuse to take the lead or bring up the rear. They ate with their backs to the wall so they could keep an eye on everything, and some wore a flack vest everyday while they were in base camp. Others had been known to live and sleep inside a bunker during the last thirty days. The list went on and on.

One short-timer jokingly told me, "I'm so short and bold that I can look a fire ant in the eye and still kick his ass!"

No one wanted to hang around short-timers, especially an FNG, who had twelve months ahead of him to serve. It was tough enough for the veterans to have to listen to short-timer bullshit.

I hoped that I wouldn't develop any superstitions when I had only thirty days left to serve in Vietnam. If it was my time to meet my Maker, nothing on earth was going to save me. Period.

I also knew this fact to be true: I was going to find a way to see Clipper and my fellow scout dog handlers before I left Vietnam.

TET and Convoy

On January 31, 1968, the Chinese Lunar New Year, the North Vietnamese Army launched an all-out attack on Saigon's military district, the U.S. Embassy, and almost every military fire base throughout South Vietnam, including Cu Chi, Tay Ninh, and Dau Tieng. The history books called this massive attack the Tet Offensive, after the Vietnamese name for the Chinese Lunar New Year celebration. We had a cease-fire in place at the time, and the enemy violated it by attacking, thinking they could win a major victory in the process. With my departure approaching in March, the Tet Offensive couldn't have come at a worse time.

Fucking Charlie! I thought. *Why can't he wait until after March to do this, when I'm safe at home?*

Early on that first morning of the Tet Offensive, I heard mortar rounds and rockets exploding. My hooch and the PX were deep inside the base camp's perimeter, but the mortars and rockets were exploding nearby.

I jumped out of my bunk, grabbed my M16 and a bandolier of magazines, and headed outside for the nearest bunker. I'd never heard so many explosions all at once. Enemy B–40 rockets whistled through the air past the bunker. I began to realize that this storm was shaping up to be much more intense than the mortar attack on our kennel back in November. The only thing any of us could do was to stay inside and look for VC who might breach the base camp's perimeter of defense.

Minutes went by and all I heard was explosion after explosion outside the bunker. From what we could see through the portholes, the stacked sandbags around the bunker and hooches were absorbing shrapnel. At one point, a huge explosion rocked the walls and shook dust from the sandbags around the bunker. My ears were ringing from the loud sounds.

We had no radio inside the bunker, so we couldn't contact anyone to get a status report. Machine guns and artillery fired in the distance. It was clear that the perimeter was under heavy attack. Several men in the bunker who had failed to get their weapons were scared shitless, sitting on the dirt floor, curled up against the sandbagged walls, and covering their bare heads with their hands. I guessed they'd never had the war that close to them. They looked and acted like REMFs and FNGs, and I was sure the only ones in camp that were more frightened were the helpless hospital patients.

A nearby ammunition dump took a direct hit, and there was no way to put out the fire. Several ammunition dumps were strategically located throughout the division's base camp, and they were definitely on Charlie's list of critical targets. So too were the reinforced bunkers that maintained the strategic and tactical communication systems. Charlie would have a hard time taking out those targets without a ground assault. As each wooden crate of ammunition, rockets, artillery, and grenades exploded, it set off another crate, until the entire stockpile of munitions went up in smoke. The army's own rockets and artillery rounds whistled through the air and exploded.

The ammunition dump finally burned out, but there was still sporadic small arms fire in the distance. It was late in the afternoon before I came out of the bunker to check the damage to my hooch. I hadn't fired one round from my M16. None of the nearby hooches were destroyed by shrapnel and the damage inside mine appeared minimal. My personal items were unharmed.

An artillery battery launched flares into the air with howitzers to light up the perimeter, allowing the men in the bunkers to better see their targets and dissuading Charlie from attempting a sneak attack at night. The sky lit brightly as the parachuted flares slowly descended to the ground.

That next morning, the base camp buzzed with activity and I reported to work as usual. The PX and surrounding buildings had only sustained minor damage. A few days after that all-out attack, SGM Kelly summoned me. He told me that General William Westmoreland, Commanding General of the Vietnam Armed Forces, was scheduled to give a speech over the armed forces radio to be broadcast for all the troops stationed throughout South Vietnam.

General Westmoreland's long speech was motivational. He reported that the Tet Offensive, with an estimated seventy thousand enemy troops involved in the attacks, had been a major military defeat for the Viet Cong and the North Vietnamese Army. They'd been repelled overwhelmingly, the American embassy had been secured, and law and order had been restored to the streets of Saigon. Of all the military base camps throughout Vietnam that had been attacked simultaneously, none were in the hands of the enemy.

American casualties were reported as minimal, but the VC and NVA had suffered thousands of dead and wounded. General Westmoreland called the Tet Offensive a great victory for South Vietnam and the American and allied forces. I waited for the general to say that all orders to leave Vietnam for the States were canceled, but he didn't and I breathed a sigh of relief.

I could think only of Dau Tieng and wondered how Clipper and the rest of my pals were getting along. Getting news from there was especially difficult then. I went to see SGM Kelly and pleaded with him to find out what was going on in Dau Tieng. SGM Kelly put me in contact with an SGM buddy of his who worked at division operations. The SGM took me to the communications shed—a heavily fortified bunker with a bunch of antennas sticking out of it. The shed buzzed with radio communication. The SGM got on a radio and patched me through to the 44th Scout Dog Platoon's land line.

Through some static, I could hear Sergeant Barnett on the other end of the handset. He told me that everything was okay; to my relief, there had been no dog or handler casualties. The VC had hit Dau Tieng hard but didn't realize that most of the infantry units were in base camp at the time of the attack. The Americans easily drove back Charlie's attempt to penetrate the wire surrounding the perimeter. He told me that the original dog handlers and Lieutenant Fenner had rotated back to the States already, but that he had extended his tour of duty for six more months.

After asking how my knee was doing, Sergeant Barnett explained that most of the dog teams were out on patrol, supporting the Tet counteroffensive operations. Clipper, however, had not been assigned to another handler; he was my dog until I left Vietnam. Sergeant Barnett asked if I was going to get a chance to come back to Dau Tieng before I rotated to the States in March. I told him I was trying all the time and not to give up on my return. Then the transmission ended.

By the middle of February 1968, the 25th Infantry Division was continuing the Tet counteroffensive throughout Cu Chi's surrounding areas of operation. I was ordered to report to Sergeant Major Kelly. I had a gut feeling that I was in for a butt-chewing, but I didn't know why. Instead, the SGM told me that with all the hell going on with the Tet Offensive, he needed an experienced combat infantryman to ride shotgun on his resupply convoy to Saigon. He'd requested support from the infantry units, but they told him to go blow. They couldn't spare infantry troops for that kind of task. They'd told him to use REMFs for the job—cooks, mechanics, supply clerks, and administrative personnel. Considering the circumstances, SGM Kelly was uncomfortable with that idea. In the past, he'd always had infantry troop support. Several infantry combat veterans were already assigned to PX jobs, but they were all wounded short-timers, so the job landed in my lap.

SGM Kelly said that he needed a good sergeant like me, who had combat experience, to honcho an empty convoy into Saigon and Bien Hoa to pick up supplies for the division. If I accepted the mission, SMG Kelly promised that when I returned, he'd make sure I got a chopper ride to Dau Tieng to see my dog.

Those were exactly the words I wanted to hear. Without hesitation, I volunteered. To be able to see my dog again outweighed the risks of the mission. Despite my previous experience with army promises, I had a good feeling that the SGM wouldn't fuck me on the deal.

What I missed most about Clipper was his loving companionship, how he got excited when I called his name. I wanted to roll around in the dirt with him one more time, have him sit next to me and lean against my leg when he was tired. I missed the simple pleasure of having Clipper by my side. It was tormenting not to be able to see my dog.

After I accepted the mission, SGM Kelly leaned close to my face, looked me in the eye, smiled, and told me that I'd separated myself from all the boys in Vietnam. I figured that was a compliment from a man who'd earned three Combat Infantry Badges, but to me, the incentives simply outweighed the risk of a trip outside base camp. Plus, I didn't have to walk, so I wouldn't be violating my medical profile restrictions. But I decided that I'd better not tell my doctor about the mission, or he might find a way to keep me from going and ruin my chances to see Clipper and my other K-9 brothers.

My orders were to leave at first light. The convoy would be fueled with engines running and waiting at the staging area on the roadside near the PX. That night some new pals I'd met—Freddie and a soldier I'll call Red—paid me a visit. Both worked in the PX for SGM Kelly. Red was supposed to ride shotgun in another one of the convoy's trucks, and like me, I soon learned that Red also had another reason for wanting to go to Saigon. He said that he needed to see his Vietnamese dentist about a tooth problem.

I liked Red and Freddie, but Freddie wasn't scheduled to ride shotgun, so he stayed behind. The trip was scheduled to be a three-day mission. One day to get there, one day to load up, and one day to get back. After a long bullshit session with those guys, I turned in for the evening.

The next morning, I rode in a jeep at the head of the convoy, which was escorted by military police riding in several other equipped jeeps. If we needed them, gunships, artillery, and infantry troops were within immediate striking distance of our route to Saigon. My jeep was equipped with a driver, a mounted M60 machine gun, several thousand rounds of ammunition, a machine gunner, two radios, and a radio operator who could communicate with SGM Kelly and the air strike support. I was responsible for coordinating all tactical decisions with the experienced convoy escort MPs who were in charge. I felt comfortable working with military police who had worked outside the perimeter of a base camp. I considered the MPs to be as highly respectable and capable as infantrymen.

SGM Kelly issued me the Signal Operating Instructions (SOI)—a tiny booklet with the word "Secret" printed on each page. The SOI contained all the call signs and frequencies to get military support, and was attached to a chain I wore inside my shirt. I was responsible for this highly classified military document, and if I was in imminent danger of being captured by the enemy, destroying that book would become my highest priority.

The daylong convoy trip to Saigon put us on a road that went through the middle of the fiercest fighting in our war zone. Cu Chi was near Hobo Woods, where the Viet Cong were heavily concentrated. Charlie fought like hell to keep Hobo Woods to himself, and many Americans and some of the 38th scout dog teams had lost their lives in that dreadful place.

Highway 13 from Cu Chi to Saigon was damaged but clear for our seventy-mile trip. Infantrymen on foot and mechanized and armored tank squadrons had secured the most dangerous sections of the road, which was a vital link to our supply lines and had to stay open during all daylight hours. For obvious reasons, no convoys traveled outside base camp at night during the Tet counteroffensives.

By the time the convoy of flatbed trailers attached to diesel tractors was assembled and prepared to roll, I was also ready to go. I didn't have enough time to check over everything carefully, so I relied on the drivers to ensure their vehicles were serviceable enough to make the three-day journey. But, what the hell, I had learned to live without ever having enough time.

I put my M16 and backpack in the back of the jeep. Each truck had one man riding shotgun inside a canvas-covered cab. One MP jeep rode ahead of me and another one brought up the rear. I was assigned the second vehicle behind the lead jeep. I walked down the line of ten or so flatbed trucks. Motors ran and smokestacks filled the air with the stinking smell of diesel fuel. Since we didn't know what kind of road conditions we'd encounter, we planned to keep the column moving together as tight as possible.

Everybody was ready. I hopped into my jeep and waited for the MPs to signal and start rolling. The machine gunner handed me a set of goggles and said that I'd need them to keep the dust out of my eyes. Red rode shotgun in the first truck behind my jeep.

My radio squawked with chatters of call signs for radio checks. After we were assured that everyone was on the net and right frequency, it was time to go. One by one, we rolled out of the gate into no-man's-land.

I remembered that President Roosevelt had said, "We have nothing to fear but fear itself." Well, I was definitely feeling fear at first, but my stomach soon settled down as we continued on the slow and bumpy ride.

Several miles into that trip, I saw a few burned-out military trucks tipped over on the roadside. They'd apparently been pushed there by bulldozers. Helicopters followed overhead and infantry troops were positioned alongside us near the tree lines.

It looked as if the Americans had broken Charlie's back when he'd tried his all-out attack a few weeks earlier. I figured that he was probably licking his wounds and regrouping, so we had timed our convoy run well. So far, I was feeling okay about the mission.

About twenty miles into the trip and several hours later the convoy still hadn't been attacked. We were going at a snail's pace but making steady progress, and it looked like we would get into Saigon before dark.

Every bridge we needed to use had been damaged, but the engineers had made paths around them where we could cross. About fifteen miles from Saigon, not a shot had been fired at the convoy and all of the trucks were accounted for. During some stretches, the thick jungle closed in on the road. If Charlie was going to hit us, that was where we'd be the most vulnerable.

Maybe Charlie had already seen us and decided not to attack because he thought that the convoy was empty. Or maybe, it was just our lucky day.

Sections of the road were dry and dusty. The goggles came in handy as dust caked around my face. It was a long, hot ride, but I still had plenty of water and snack food. The radios stayed on but remained silent, except for the occasional situation report.

At last, the convoy approached the outskirts of Saigon and headed for a secure staging area within the Cholon district. In Cholon, we were scheduled to park in a fenced and guarded compound and spend the night in a hotel across the street. The next morning the convoy was to roll from the city of Saigon and into the Ben Hoa beer-and-soda yard.

As we entered Saigon's Cholon district, I could see that some fighting had occurred there. Direct hits from tank and artillery rounds had made gaping holes in some of the buildings, and war debris littered the roadsides. Several civilian cars were burned and overturned on the shoulders of the road we traveled. Martial law had been declared, roadblocks were set up all over the place, and very few pedestrians walked the streets. The MP jeep ahead of mine was doing a good job leading the way. So far, we'd kept all the trucks intact and hadn't had to stop along the way for emergencies or maintenance problems.

At about six o'clock in the evening, the convoy reached a large parking lot surrounded by a ten-foot triple barbed-wire fence. South Vietnamese Army troops, wearing burgundy berets, opened the gate to let us pass through. All of the trucks and jeeps fit inside with plenty of room to spare. The South Vietnamese military would handle vehicle security and our hotel expenses had already been paid for. We only had to check in and get a room for the night.

We descended from our vehicles, carrying our gear and weapons, and headed for the hotel. I wanted one of those burgundy berets as a souvenir, so I approached a Vietnamese guard and offered a trade. He couldn't speak English, so I took a dollar out of my pocket and used hand gestures to bargain for his headwear. The soldier smiled, took the money and gave me his beret. I didn't realize it would be that easy. I was prepared to give more if he demanded.

I put the beret away and Red and I walked to the hotel, carrying our M16s, bandoliers of fully loaded magazines, lightly packed backpacks, and .45-caliber pistols. The trucks and jeeps were now under the full protection of the Vietnamese army.

The hotel Mama San greeted and assigned us to rooms. She recognized my stripes and said that she had a special room for me. The hotel was about three stories high and wasn't fancy by any stretch of the imagination. My room had only a single metal-frame bed and a beat-up dresser with a small dirty mirror. I had a window view of the vehicles parked across the street. When I looked outside, I noticed a few Vietnamese troops guarding our vehicles and patrolling the street. Curfew was in effect for everyone except the military.

Later that night, Red came to my room to talk. I knew from previous conversations with him that he had attended an American linguist school somewhere in the States. Red spoke excellent

Vietnamese and had been an interpreter working for military intelligence in Saigon before he'd been transferred to Cu Chi several months earlier. Red had less than thirty days before he'd be going home. When he became a short-timer, he had talked his way into a rear area job in the PX, which was where we had met.

Red told me that he'd broken a tooth two days earlier and that it was infected. After he'd heard about the convoy run to Saigon, he volunteered to ride shotgun because he refused to see an army doctor or dentist. Instead, he insisted on seeing his Vietnamese dentist in Saigon.

Because he could speak fluent Vietnamese and had been well-established in Saigon before coming to Cu Chi, he had a lot of friends there. But he didn't have approval from any military medical personnel to have a dentist in Saigon. Nevertheless, I could see that Red was going to follow his dental preferences into Saigon, and that he was kind of asking my permission to go.

Red told me so many stories about Saigon that I trusted him to know how to get around the city, but I reminded him that we were restricted to the hotel for the night. I told him that the city was under martial law and he was out of his fucking mind to leave the safety of the men and the hotel.

Red argued that there was nothing to worry about. His dentist worked only a few blocks from the hotel. But if he left that shitty little hotel, and something happened it was going to be my ass in trouble.

Red said that he had to at least get some painkillers, and he'd be back before I could miss him. With those words, Red left my room and headed downstairs to the hotel lobby. After he left, I paced back and forth for a few seconds.

Ah, shit, I thought. *I can't let him go by himself and I can't keep his ass here, either. He's a fucking bonehead.*

I quickly grabbed my rifle and bandolier of ammunition and followed after Red. I caught him on the street as he was about to climb into a black covered rickshaw being pulled by a horse.

"Red!" I yelled.

Red turned around, broke into an ear-to-ear grin, and waved and told me to hurry. I caught up with him and climbed into the rickshaw driven by a smiling Vietnamese man. Red gave the driver directions to the dentist's office in Vietnamese. I looked at him, shook my head, and told him that I couldn't let him go alone. So off we went like a couple of war-zone tourists.

The driver headed toward the first Vietnamese-manned road-block, where soldiers stood holding machine guns. When we arrived at the roadblock, Red spoke Vietnamese to the guards, who immediately smiled and let us pass through.

"Shit, your dentist isn't down the street from our hotel, is he, Red? Do you know where the fuck you're going?"

"Sure, I do. We're almost there," he assured me with a big grin.

We turned down some side streets that had no pedestrians on them and eventually pulled over in front of a row of small build-ings. Several Vietnamese citizens were milling around the build-ings, and I noticed that there were no military personnel in sight.

I checked my watch and saw that it was a little after seven o'clock. I advised Red that if his dentist wasn't there, we were heading back to the hotel before it got dark. Red said nothing as he stepped out of the rickshaw and walked to the entrance of a building and knocked on the door. A Vietnamese woman opened it, smiled, and greeted Red as if he were a long-lost friend. They talked in Vietnamese and laughed when Red showed her his tooth.

I was getting nervous sitting outside in the rickshaw. Red finally came back to tell me that his doctor had left, but would be back at six o'clock in the morning. He also said that we had plenty of time for him to get his tooth fixed and get back to lead the convoy by nine o'clock the next morning.

"Trust me," Red said. "The beer-and-soda yard at Ben Hoa is less than an hour away."

"Why did I let myself get into this shit?" I asked myself.

Red told me that that building was a hotel and a dentist office. After I climbed out of the rickshaw, the well-dressed Vietnamese woman greeted me with a smile. She spoke broken English as she bowed and motioned for me to come inside. I didn't smile back, but gave Red a dirty look. I told him to call our hotel to let a member of our convoy team know where we were and when we'd be back. Red made the call, using the Vietnamese woman's phone, and spoke in Vietnamese to someone back at our hotel.

After the phone call, he looked at me and said, "John, we're set, and they expect us back by nine o'clock tomorrow morning. Hey, buddy, I'll take care of you. Isn't this a nicer place to sleep than that rat hole we were in?"

"Uh huh, this is great!" I agreed. "But we're only two people here and I feel safer being in numbers, especially American numbers."

Red was right about one thing, though. The inside of this hotel was upscale compared to where we'd been assigned to spend the night. Aside from the Vietnamese woman and her family, no one else was staying there, which I thought to be a little strange. Also, the dentist's office was locked. I wondered how Red would get the painkillers he said he needed, unless he planned to break into it.

The Vietnamese woman asked if we were hungry. She said that the recent fighting in the streets had chased away her customers. She gave us a bowl of steamed rice with chunks of meat mixed in it.

"Hey, Red, this is pretty good." I said. "It's the first hot meal we've had. The meat tastes a little like beef. Ask her what kind it is."

Red looked at me and said, "It's dog! That's a delicacy within the Vietnamese culture."

I spit out a mouthful on the table.

"I can't eat this shit if it's dog. Why the hell didn't you tell me that before I ate it? You know I'm a dog handler for chrissake! What the fuck is wrong with you, Red?"

Red smiled and said, "I think it tastes great!"

After we ate, Red decided that he wanted to visit a female friend he used to stay with when he lived in Saigon. He told me that she was a beautiful Vietnamese/French girl with round eyes. I opposed leaving the hotel, especially to see a woman. Red was really pressing his luck with me.

Before I knew it, a small black car pulled up in front of the hotel. It became clear that Red had a preconceived plan he was now putting into action. He told me to bring my weapons and get into the car to take a short ride. We were going to pick up the woman, and we'd be back in a half hour.

I wasn't excited about going for a car ride in the dark of night. Red, on the other hand, was totally calm and relaxed, as if there were no martial law or war going on in Vietnam. When he walked to the car, I couldn't imagine staying behind by myself, so I followed. Splitting up now would have been an even worse idea.

I didn't like it that Red had placed me in a totally reactionary mode since arriving in Saigon. He was driving me nuts with his complete disregard for all the danger signs around us. Although we hadn't heard any shooting since we entered Saigon, we had no way of knowing what would happen.

We sat in the backseat of the little black car, and Red spoke Vietnamese to the driver and off we went. Heading down a dark and quiet side road several blocks from the hotel/dentist office, the driver turned left onto another side street, which looked more like an alleyway. Red began to look nervous. He spoke to the driver in a louder than normal tone. The driver turned his lights off and kept driving slowly down the alleyway while he talked to Red. Up ahead, several figures suddenly appeared out of the darkness, and they slowly approached the car. It looked as if they were armed with rifles. Red quickly jumped into the front seat of the car and pointed his .45-caliber pistol at the driver's temple. He was talking fast in Vietnamese. The car's tires screeched to a sudden stop.

The armed men in black clothes continued to walk in our direction with their weapons at the ready. From a distance, I assumed that they were not friendly, so I chambered a round into my M16, moved to the window, and quickly rolled it down. I stuck the barrel out and awkwardly pointed it in the direction of the approaching figures. Red screamed in Vietnamese at the driver. All of a sudden, Red's pistol went off. I flinched and ducked. My ears were ringing like crazy. I looked up quickly to see what had happened. Red had blown out the driver's side window.

The driver slammed the car into reverse and turned the lights back on. The men started shooting at us. Several bullets hit the front of the car. I awkwardly returned fire with my M16. Because the car was jerking; my aim was terrible, but I squeezed off one round after another.

Finally, we backed out of the alleyway. The car screeched on the pavement as the driver spun the steering wheel to straighten it out. And Red was still pointing the barrel of the .45-caliber pistol at the driver's temple.

We sped down the street and made a sharp turn onto a different road. I didn't know where the hell we were. My heart pumped hard inside my chest, but I was relieved that we weren't being chased or fired at anymore.

Red's face was dripping in sweat and his eyes bulged out of their sockets. He looked like an enraged madman, and kept talking to the driver who answered him with terror in his voice. To my surprise, the driver stopped the car suddenly.

I was scared. All I could think of was that we needed to get out of there. The city of Saigon at night was an unfamiliar battleground for me. We had to make it back to that hotel as quickly as possible. The Tet Offensive had brought the war to every nook and cranny throughout Vietnam. We weren't safe anywhere.

Then I heard Red shout, "John! Get the fuck out!"

I didn't hesitate or ask any questions. Once I was outside the car, I nervously looked up and down the street, but saw only darkness. Red scooted over to the door. I pointed my weapon through the windshield at the driver. The driver froze with both of his hands on the steering wheel. Red frantically shouted at him in Vietnamese, then came flying out of the door and told me to follow him and not to look back.

My heart pounded fast as I ran after Red. He turned the corner and ran across the street. To my amazement, we were only a block away from the dentist office/hotel. The streets were bare and totally dark. Red suddenly stopped, turned, and banged a clenched fist on the hotel door, which opened to let us inside. By that time, we were almost completely out of breath.

The nicely dressed Vietnamese woman who managed the hotel looked bewildered as she and Red chattered in Vietnamese. After they finished talking, Red told me the woman wouldn't be letting anyone else come into the hotel that evening. Of course, she'd said more than that. Red wasn't telling me the whole story. It was late and I was upset and not interested in asking anymore questions.

One thing was for certain. My right knee was killing me. I hoped that it wouldn't swell up after I rested it. I didn't want to have to see the doctor with my knee swollen and have him tell me that he was putting a cast on my knee, or worse, scheduling me for surgery.

We locked the door, barricaded ourselves inside the room, and took turns pulling guard duty until the sun came up. Throughout the night, I heard vehicle noises and voices on the street outside the hotel. I was sweating at the thought that someone may have spotted us and knew where we were. I was scared to death and felt trapped.

Neither Red nor I caught a wink of sleep that night. When it was light outside, I heard a man's voice downstairs. Red quickly sat up and smiled. He told me the male voice was his Vietnamese dentist. I looked at my watch and saw that the dentist had arrived on his usual schedule—promptly at six o'clock. Red moved the barricade, unlocked the door, and went downstairs. I was still stunned from the events of the night before. I stayed behind the dresser with my M16 at the ready. From downstairs, I heard the sounds of laughter and friendly voices.

I cautiously made my way to the bottom of the carpeted stairs. Red was already sitting in the dentist's chair and getting his tooth looked over.

When the dentist finished, Red got up from the chair, pocketed some pills, and paid the man. All I wanted to do was to get the fuck out of there and safely back to the hotel where we were supposed to be staying.

As we left, I saw very few people on the street outside. Red flagged a rickshaw and we went back to our hotel. As we approached the first manned roadblock, I got real nervous. Red instructed me not to say anything, but to look tough and hold my weapon where the Vietnamese could see it. I did as instructed and to my surprise the soldiers lifted the arm of the roadblock and let us pass. We crossed through three more roadblocks without incident before reaching the hotel.

We made it back before nine o'clock in the morning. Neither of us talked about our near-fatal encounter with the enemy. I grabbed a can of spaghetti and meatballs from my pack and gulped it down as if I hadn't eaten in a week, and Red disappeared somewhere. After I ate, I washed my face and shaved. Through the window, I saw troops milling around the parked trucks inside the fenced yard. Grabbing my gear, I walked out of the hotel to my jeep. Red was already sitting inside the first truck behind my jeep. He waved at me with a smile on his face.

I was fuming and thinking, *How could that fucker smile at me after putting us through all that shit? The bastard has a death wish and I blame myself for becoming part of it.*

That morning, I walked past each vehicle and checked inside for a head count; ten soldiers per truck. Every man was accounted for and ready to go. After a radio check, the MP jeep slowly led us into the street. The convoy wound its way through the narrow streets of Saigon heading to the Bien Hoa beer-and-soda yard.

I noticed that Red had been right about one thing—Bien Hoa was only an hour from the hotel. And what an incredible sight it was to see so many piled pallets of beer and soda. Vietnamese civilians operated forklifts, lifting pallet after pallet onto the flatbed trucks. They tied down the pallets with handheld metal banding machines, while the Americans watched and directed the loading procedure. It took about five hours for the trucks to be fully loaded. Then the convoy maneuvered back through the streets of Saigon without incident.

The fully loaded convoy pulled into the staging area at Cholon before six o'clock that evening. We stayed at the same hotel across the street for our last evening in Saigon. The second leg of the trip was now over.

Back in the same hotel room, Red and I had a long talk over a few beers. We discussed the details of the incident that we'd barely survived the night before. According to Red, the Vietnamese driver had been a North Vietnamese officer posing as a cab driver, and was trained to capture unsuspecting Americans.

"If it weren't for my background in military intelligence and the fact that I could speak Vietnamese, we'd both be prisoners of war right now." Red blurted out with a serious look on his face.

I quickly responded in anger, "You're full of shit! You almost got us both captured or killed."

I wasn't too happy with myself, because I could have prevented the whole situation from happening. I'd made two bad decisions. First, I let Red leave the hotel. Secondly, I foolishly went with him. How stupid can you get to take such risks with only a month left to serve in Vietnam?

I told Red that we were both out of our fucking minds and that I wanted to forget about the entire trip. Red didn't say another word.

———————————

The next morning we cranked up the engines and headed down the road for the long trip back to Cu Chi. I could hardly wait for our mission to end.

When we arrived back at Cu Chi, SGM Kelly was standing on the side of the road watching his intact convoy pull up to the PX. After I reported to him that the men and trucks were accounted for and the goods were intact, SGM smiled at me.

"Job well-done, Buck Sergeant! Give me that SOI and I'll

have those trucks unloaded. Did anything happen on that mission that I should know about?"

"No, Sergeant Major, nothing but the usual bullshit!"

I intended to remind Sergeant Major Kelly of his promise to let me go see Clipper in Dau Tieng. After that trip, my plan was to never leave base camp until it was time for me to catch a ride on a commercial airliner back to the United States.

Good-bye Clipper

SGM Kelly had kept his end of the bargain and personally coordinated a space for me on a resupply chopper to Dau Tieng. I packed a bunch of goodies for my dog handler friends.

When I arrived at Dau Tieng, I had to walk for about ten minutes from the airstrip to the K-9 compound. With thoughts of seeing Clipper again, the limp in my step seemed unimportant. Once at the base camp, I first stopped at the kennel and met Dan Scott standing at the entrance. He was shirtless as usual. We shook hands and I gave him a bear hug. It had been a long time since we'd seen each other, and Dan knew I couldn't leave Vietnam without coming back to say good-bye. I told him that I'd come to see Clipper, give out some free stuff, and then head back to Cu Chi first thing in the morning.

It felt like Christmas when I handed him a brand-new Zippo lighter with flints and lighter fluid. I showed him a copy of my orders to leave Vietnam, and he was really excited for me. He asked how my gimpy knee was healing and what Cu Chi was like, and after a short bullshit session, I decided to spend some time with Clipper. Dan and I planned to party in the K-9 Klub later that night.

I headed into the kennel, but Clipper wasn't in his run. I should have known that he'd be out under the shade of his tree during the day. As I walked through the kennel, it was great seeing all the other scout dogs and hearing them bark like crazy for attention.

I walked to the rubber trees to find Clipper. In the distance, I spotted him lying on the ground and taking a nap. I quietly whispered his name. Clipper's ears popped up and he canted his head. He looked in my direction, rose to his feet stretching out his legs and back, and turned his head slightly to the left and then to the right. I could tell that he was trying to figure out who had called him.

I walked closer without saying another word. When Clipper recognized me, he went crazy. He charged toward me until his leash fully extended and stopped him in his tracks. I rushed over to him and he jumped up on my chest with his front paws. He licked all over my face, wagged his tail joyfully, and in his immense excitement, he piddled on my leg and boots. It felt great being with him again. I hugged his soft furry body.

What an exhilarating moment! Words can't begin to describe the emotions that poured out of me for that dog. He was my best friend and at last we were together again.

I fastened Clipper's choke chain to the leather leash and took him for a walk to calm us both down. I gave him no commands, so he could be free of thought. Clipper automatically moved to my left side and walked at a slow pace, while constantly staring up at me with love and happiness in his eyes. He remembered exactly what my walking pace was and never once pulled ahead or crossed over my path. After a while, I slowly worked him through some basic commands and scouting positions. It was as if we'd never been separated.

How am I ever going to leave this dog after seeing him again? I wondered. Clipper must have thought I was back to stay. He didn't realize I'd only be visiting him for a short time. We spent the entire afternoon together outside under the shade of the rubber trees.

———————————

Later that night, I joined the rest of the scout dog handlers in the K-9 Klub. Some new guys had arrived since my departure. It was March 1968 and nearly all my old friends from the original 44th had returned to the States. Their twelve-month tour had passed and I hadn't had the chance to say good-bye. Dan Scott was due for rotation in March, so now he was a short-timer like me. After we said our good-byes, I crashed on an empty cot inside my old hooch to sleep one last night in Dau Tieng.

I got up early the next morning to say my last good-bye to a dog that didn't deserve the fate in store for him.

I walked into the kennel to see Clipper. When I opened his run, he ran off to wait under his tree until I caught up and hooked his collar to the twenty-five-foot leash. I filled his water bucket with fresh water and cleaned his run. Afterward, I sat with him under the shade of his tree and stroked his head and back. My mind flashed back to the many combat missions we'd gone on as a team. Clipper had alerted me to danger and saved countless lives on so many occasions. It was hard to believe I was going to have to leave him behind. He was a real American hero, but he would never get to go home and receive the hero's welcome he deserved.

Obviously, Clipper couldn't speak for himself and was at the mercy of people who had recruited him for military life, indoctrinated him for war, shipped him off to Vietnam, and teamed him with a handler. As Clipper's handler, I was the only one who had truly developed an allegiance with him.

Because our government had classified Clipper and all scout dogs as expendable equipment, I had to leave him behind. I felt as if I were abandoning a brother condemned to the dangerous job of walking point for the rest of the war. *How can my country weigh me down with the burden of this lifelong memory?* I wondered. Clipper deserved to live the rest of his life in a peaceful environment away from that war. I wanted Clipper to be treated with the same dignity and respect I expected for myself. He had earned it.

Dogs that served during World War II and Korea were given discharge papers and repatriated with their devoted handlers or original owners after the war. It was not to be for the valiant war dogs of the Vietnam War. For their service, their heroism, their bravery under fire, and risking their lives to save others, the survivors were given to the South Vietnamese Army, or disposed of by other means. They are buried in war dog graves that are all but forgotten.

Since I met him, it had always been my dream to bring Clipper home. He would have made a great pet. Clipper had already served in Vietnam for fifteen months, and I wasn't sure how many more missions or months he would survive. I feared that Clipper's death would be violent, especially after the Tet Offensive had agitated the war into such a frenzy. I could only hope that when Clipper finally did fall, he would die quickly and painlessly.

I knew as I sat under that tree with him leaning against my leg, that I'd never see him again in this life. The tragedy of it all haunted me like a nightmare.

I had noticed that the sign I'd placed above Clipper's tree ten months before was still there. *War is Good Business. Invest Your Dog.* Now that sign disgusted me. I got up, ripped it down and broke it into tiny pieces.

At last, the time had come for me to go. I tried to hold back my tears. I didn't know how to say good-bye to my best friend, so I looked into his big brown eyes and gave him one last loving farewell bear hug. Afterward, I turned and walked away with the bitter and sad truth that Vietnam would become my dog's final resting place.

Clipper stood erect with ears pointed high like the champion he was. I felt him watching me as I eventually vanished down the dirt road away from the 44th Scout Dog Platoon, never looking back.

I knew right then that I truly had no more reason to stay in Vietnam, but every reason in the world to keep Clipper alive in my heart for the rest of my life.

Leaving Vietnam

I left Cu Chi for Saigon to hop on a commercial flight to the States in March 1968. My departure couldn't have been scheduled for a worse time. Because the Americans were in the middle of a fierce counteroffensive with the North Vietnamese Army near the surrounding areas of Cu Chi and Tay Ninh Province, I could have easily had my exit orders rescinded.

Before I left, Sergeant Major Kelly summoned me to his office. He promised me another stripe if I would stay on for six more months. I politely declined his offer by saying, "No fucking way!"

I knew it was time for me to leave the war behind, go home to Colorado, and have a big party with my family and friends. Two years was long enough for me to spend fighting in Southeast Asia.

Under a heavily armed convoy escorted by tanks and helicopter gunships, I made it out of Cu Chi base camp in the back of a troop truck. The road to Saigon was still littered with burned-out vehicles cleared to the side of the road. Along the way, infantry troops were positioned off the road to protect the convoy from attack and to keep the road open. Without incident, the convoy reached the city limits of Saigon, where I saw the devastation that had been brought about by the Tet Offensive and the American counteroffensive.

Buildings bore the scars of these battles, and debris from explosions littered the street and sidewalks throughout the city. Saigon was still under martial law and in chaos. Homeless pedestrians walked on the roadways and filled crowded buses. Armed military police and South Vietnamese Army troops barricaded and manned the major streets' intersections.

My convoy stopped along the road next to Camp Alpha, the U.S. Army Replacement Center where I'd first entered Vietnam. I climbed out of the back of the truck, grabbed my duffel bag, and handed my M16 rifle and bandolier of ammunition to a sergeant who had been riding shotgun. As I entered the gates of Camp Alpha, I handed a copy of my orders to a soldier with a clipboard in his hand. Each step was bringing me closer to returning to the world outside of Vietnam.

I stayed in Camp Alpha for several days to out-process. My name was placed on a manifest, and I was assigned a group number. When I heard my group number called, I reported to a numbered building where I and everyone else in my group were strip-searched. The military police looked for and confiscated any pistols, grenades, knives, and other items that wouldn't be allowed to be brought onboard a commercial plane.

I hadn't tried to bring any of these kind of souvenirs out of Vietnam. Clipper was all I had wanted to take back home with me.

When the strip search was finished, I boarded a bus to Ton San Nhut airfield. During the ride, I sat on a bench seat next to the window and thought about my Vietnam experience, Clipper, and the friends I was leaving behind. Before I realized it, the bus ride ended and I was standing on the runway of Ton San Nhut airfield. Military guards in jeeps surrounded a commercial jetliner in the near distance and waited to receive its passengers. In single file, we walked to the plane, where a military attendant with a manifest checked off our names as we climbed the plane's steps. I found an empty seat next to a window and sat down.

———————————————

When everyone was onboard, the doors closed and the plane slowly moved down the runway. As soon as it lifted off, a roaring cheer from the passengers broke the silence. I settled back into the soft seat and looked out of the window. During takeoff, I watched the airfield and city of Saigon grow smaller as the plane climbed higher. After several minutes, only the South China Sea was visible below us.

Our next stop would be to set foot again on American soil in San Francisco.

Despite the violent counteroffensive taking place, the timing and process to get everyone out of Vietnam had been impeccable. Recent battles must have lit a spark under their butts. They didn't waste any time getting us out of there safely. I only wished that they would apply this same sense of urgency to rescuing our four-legged brothers. In a matter of only twenty-four hours, I was out of harm's way and leaving Vietnam forever.

During the long flight, cute, round-eyed American stewardesses smiled and waited on the passengers. They served coffee, tea, soda, snacks, and hot meals but no alcohol.

I had a lot of time on that flight to think about going home. I couldn't wait to again be part of the Colorado culture I'd left behind two years earlier.

I wondered: *How will the new cars look? Will clothes be different from when I left? I'll see a lot of American girls again; will they like me? Will my friends be different from how I remember them? Who will I take out on my first date when I get home?*

My only fear was from what some of the new guys who'd recently come to Vietnam had said about people back at home starting to reject the war. I didn't remember reading anything about this in the letters I'd received from family and friends. They were always wishing me well and saying how they couldn't wait to see me. I didn't understand how people could say that they knew anything about Vietnam when they hadn't been there.

I thought about some of the first things I'd do when I returned. I knew that I wanted to get a new car. I'd heard that the 1968 Dodge Charger 440 RT had a 300-horsepower engine and ram air and that it could clock thirteen seconds in a quarter mile. I had to have that car. My plan was to find a date one night, drive up to a lookout point in the Colorado Rocky Mountains, and peer down on the city of Denver.

I still had my tiny red address book that listed the names and addresses of family and friends with whom I'd corresponded while I was in Vietnam. I hoped that they hadn't moved or changed their phone numbers, because I wanted to call and see them again.

I couldn't wait to live halfway around the world from the sounds of explosions, machine guns, helicopters, fighter jets, armored vehicles, infantry talk, and the permanent, stinking smell of fish. I felt full of excitement to be finally going home and getting away from everything that had been so hard for a nineteen-year-old to experience.

As the wheels touched down on San Francisco International Airport's runway, a chorus of cheers reverberated throughout the plane. When I touched the runway's pavement with the bottom of my shoe, I bent down and kissed the ground. I was so grateful to be home.

Military policemen greeted and escorted us to several military buses, parked on the runway. They took us past U.S. Customs and directly to Oakland Army Base. After we arrived at the base, we were confined to a warehouse that was a holding area for in-processing, reassignments, and discharging U.S. Army personnel. There were no marching bands or welcome-home parades. It was all quiet on the Western Front, so to speak. However, we were treated to steak dinners in the warehouse mess hall.

At last, I was on American soil, and that was all that mattered to me. During out-processing, I was paid in American greenbacks. I reached into my pocket and felt a coin. When I pulled it out, I saw that it was a South Vietnamese five dong, silver-plated coin, dated 1968. I decided to hold on to it as a keepsake to always remind me of the year that I'd returned home from Vietnam.

Within eight hours after I arrived in Oakland, I was released on furlough. The personnel sergeant told me that I'd soon be receiving a stateside unit of assignment in the mail at my home of record. And that was it. I was now cleared to leave Oakland Army Base.

Taxicabs lined up outside the gate to take us wherever we

wanted to go. Several of us shared a ride to the San Francisco airport so we could continue our journeys home. When a cab pulled up in front of the airport, I hooked up with infantryman George Johnson. We'd met during out-processing in Camp Alpha. George was going home to New York.

George and I couldn't believe that in as little as a day and a half we were out of the jungles of Vietnam and walking on the streets of San Francisco. We agreed that things were happening a little too fast. We decided not to book a flight home right away. We wanted to go into San Francisco, clear our heads a bit, and get used to American soil. So we put our baggage in lockers inside the terminal and took off.

On this day, March 15, 1968, we proudly walked around San Francisco, wearing our Class-A khaki uniforms, combat infantry badges, and Vietnam combat ribbons. The next day would be my twenty-first birthday. It felt so peaceful to be walking on San Francisco's downtown sidewalks.

George wanted to buy our first beers in an American bar, so we stopped at a local downtown bar and sat down to enjoy the scenery. I began to notice that we were the only soldiers in the place. It wasn't crowded and the bartender was friendly to us. I ordered a bottle of Coors beer, but they didn't have any. I figured that I'd have to wait until I got to Denver to get a cold Coors. We ended up ordering bottles of Pabst Blue Ribbon.

Suddenly, our uniforms became targets of some angry Americans who were protesting the Vietnam War. One of the bar's patrons blurted out, "Hey, baby killers! Did you enjoy burning down villages?"

I was outraged by this man's taunts. I gnashed my teeth and

held back my anger. Having gone through what I had in Vietnam taught me how to control my emotions in a heated situation. I realized that the consequences of getting into a bar fight could be police action and jail time.

But I felt perplexed because I didn't understand why this man was so fired up against soldiers who had served in Vietnam. I wondered if the people who had been writing to me while I was over there had held back the truth about how they really felt about the war. It made me feel apprehensive about what unexpected attitudes I might find toward me when I came home to Colorado.

George raised up from his barstool, but I put my hand on his shoulder and told him that fighting this guy wouldn't be worth the consequences. George agreed and we decided to ignore the remarks. A few other men sitting in the joint started to let us know that we weren't welcome there. This caught us by surprise and confused us. We didn't know what to think or say. The longer we stayed at the bar, the more uncomfortable and upset we became. We decided to keep our mouths shut and get the hell out of there. George paid the tab, and we walked out without finishing our beers.

After we left the bar, George suggested that it would be a good idea if we got out of our damn uniforms. We found the closest men's clothing store, bought civilian clothes and shoes, changed in the store's dressing room, and walked away with our uniforms in paper bags. Only our military haircuts now distinguished us from the rest of the American male public. God, how we wished we had long hair so we could blend into the crowd. I felt completely depressed and self-conscious, trying not to appear so military. My dream of coming home and being welcome had been shattered in only one afternoon.

I'd be back in Colorado on furlough for forty-five days. The plans and dreams I'd had while flying home on the plane were already crumbling. I no longer felt enthusiastic about buying a car, having a big party, or hanging out in public places with my friends. I'd spent almost two years in military service and now, back in the States, I felt like an outsider. Soon the army would send me orders to report to another military duty station. It surprised me to realize that the attitudes of my fellow American citizens made me feel safer and more comfortable around military people than civilians.

After I went home, I wanted to believe the incident in San Francisco had been an isolated one, but it wasn't. I was soon to learn that many people my age around the country were protesting the Vietnam War.

From that point on, even in my hometown I had to fight a war of words with people who didn't have any idea what we'd been through over there. Occasionally, I got pushed around and wound up in fights. The television news covered the war every day. Protesters were everywhere and "flower power" was in; draft dodging was acceptable; and "Hell, no, I won't go," was the chant of the day. I began to believe that it was safer to be in the military, where people like me understood one another.

After the initial shock of my homecoming, I worked hard to

reacclimate myself to the American way of life and to appreciate the fact that we all had freedom of speech. I eventually overcame my fear of having some Vietnam protester bust my head wide open.

I endured many nightmares about my war experiences and often woke up from them, unable to go back to sleep. I'd stay up and stare into the darkness of my room, worried about my inability to adjust to a normal life. The feelings and emotions I was confronting at home reminded me of the enemy I'd faced so many times in the Vietnam jungles.

The tables had turned in a direction I hadn't expected. I felt that the people who I thought were supporting me while I was fighting in Vietnam now viewed me as their enemy. In my own backyard, I was having to fight a miniature Vietnam conflict. However, it would be a cold day in hell before I would let anyone drive me out of the country I loved or to deprive me of the freedom I'd fought to preserve.

Epilogue

After Vietnam, I decided to make a career out of the military. My goal was to become the Command Sergeant Major of the Army (CMA), the highest ranking enlisted position of power, with a special office in the Pentagon. I knuckled down and worked determinedly at every task that career path required and I completed a 4-year college degree from National-Louis University.

In 1978, I left my Army assignment in a military personnel office in San Francisco and traveled to Washington, D.C. to manage the training program I had since created to support the Army's personnel information management system.

In 1980, I was awarded a personal letter of appreciation from former president Jimmy Carter at a special Pentagon awards ceremony for saving the government $5.6 million with my program. Subsequently, the Army instituted a special administrative personnel career path training course after validating the success of my training program.

As time went on, I quickly climbed the enlisted ranks and was promoted to Master Sergeant (E8) in 1983 and placed on a fast track to attend the Sergeants Major Academy. But one morning in the fall of 1983, my whole world changed when I woke up with blurred vision in my left eye. The attending ophthalmologist readily diagnosed my eye condition as a retinal vein occlusion. I was immediately taken to Walter Reed Army Medical Center for emergency treatment.

After many lengthy tests and physical examinations by several eye specialists including an expert from John Hopkins University, the doctors couldn't pinpoint the reason why it had occurred nor could they promise that they could stop the loss of vision in my left eye. In less than one month, my sight in that eye had deteriorated to total blindness. I was shocked and depressed thinking that the vision in my right eye would soon be gone too, but the doctors assured me that my right eye was in no danger.

My dreams of becoming the Sergeant Major of the Army were destroyed when the Army's medical regulations disallowed me from continued military service and a medical discharge was ordered under honorable conditions with full military retirement benefits. At my retirement ceremony, I was awarded the Legion of Merit medal, which is the highest peacetime award for military service. I was an emotional wreck, unable to speak without choking up, in front of a large audience of well-wishers. But I was never a quitter and I soon got over my self-pity.

As the years have passed by, my right eye has remained healthy. I have also maintained a full-time civilian job and an excellent employment record. My doctor has advised me that when I can no longer stand the pain of the advanced stages of degenerative arthritis—from that old punji stake wound in my right knee—that I could get it replaced. As of this writing, I still have my original knee and excellent vision in my right eye.

I remember the news on TV and in the papers about Paris on January 27, 1973, and America signing a peace agreement with the North Vietnamese government. I couldn't believe it at the time. It actually called for the release of all U.S. prisoners, withdrawal of U.S. forces, limitation of both sides' forces inside South Vietnam, and a commitment to the peaceful reunification of North and South Vietnam. And when Saigon fell on April 30, 1975, two years after the American military forces pulled out the last American troops on March 29, 1973, I wondered, as did so many other Vietnam veterans, *How could we have lost this war or fought so hard only to end it with an agreed-upon stalemate?*

As I went on with my life after Vietnam, there hasn't been one day that has gone by when I haven't thought about my dog, Clipper, and the men I served with in Vietnam. Memories of them have been very important to me because *they* are why I survived Vietnam. Each year, I honor them during Memorial Day and Veterans Day.

During the Vietnam War, our military war dogs never gave up on the battlefield while scouting, patrolling, tracking the enemy, or guarding Americans from danger. After the war, their records were shipped to Lackland Air Force Base, Texas and archived. Research of those records indicated that approximately 4,000 dogs served during the Vietnam War. It has also been estimated that about 250 dogs made it through a quarantine program and were reassigned to other U.S. military installations outside of Vietnam. The rest of the several thousand surviving four-legged soldiers were either given to the South Vietnamese Army or euthanized by order of the U.S. military to close down the quarantine program in its haste to withdraw from South Vietnam.

Official military records document that Clipper served with the 44th Scout Dog Platoon in South Vietnam, but his final disposition was never recorded. What finally happened to Clipper is anyone's guess. I know that he was healthy when I left him, and I do think that because Clipper was such an exceptional scout dog, he may have died in combat. I try not to think about his demise because I always want to remember Clipper as the valiant and loyal soldier he was. I want to remember that I had the privilege and honor to serve with him during the Vietnam War, and that if it hadn't been for him, I'd be another name on the Vietnam Veterans Memorial.

The sad truth is that Clipper, Timber, Prince, Shadow, Ringo, Erik, Sergeant, Buckshot, and thousands more war dogs died in Vietnam. The American base camps they had once occupied throughout the Republic of South Vietnam are now abandoned and littered with war dog cemeteries, once maintained by the surviving war dog handlers as hallowed ground. As of this writing, no war dog remains have ever been recovered from Vietnam and returned to American soil for proper burial.

Clipper was just one of the tens of thousands of war dogs that have served our country in wars across the globe with unconditional loyalty and bravery. If it were not for their courageous service, there would be a lot more human tombstones planted from WWI, WWII, Korea, Vietnam, Desert Storm, Bosnia, and now Afghanistan.

On Memorial Day Sunday in 1991, my life took a dramatic turn. That Sunday, I had reunited with Kenny Mook who was my first best friend in Vietnam. Our reunion inspired me to write this book.

On a summer day in northern Virginia in 1998, a neighbor handed me a copy of *DOGWORLD* magazine, pointing out an article about war dogs written by Mary Thurston and listing the

Vietnam Dog Handler Association (VDHA) website *(www.vdhaon-line.org)*. I immediately joined the VDHA and searched for members that I had served with in the 44th Scout Dog Platoon. To my surprise, there were only two members listed—Ollie Whetstone and Dan Scott. But what blew me away was that I had just completed the first draft of my manuscript and both of these men were significant characters in the chapter titled, "Death in the Kennel," which was later reenacted for the TV documentary *War Dogs*. Before long I had located and contacted "Mac" MacClellan, Dan Barnett, Van Wilson, Marlin Doreman, Doctor Bogumill, and LTG (ret). Hal Moore, all of whom are key characters in this book. Each person helped me validate some of the details I had written before this book was published.

In late 1998, I was recruited as a Technical Advisor during the filming of a TV documentary produced by GRB Entertainment which resulted in the following comment:

> I want to thank you for the relentless expertise, concern, and creativity you've brought to your role as technical advisor for our production of *War Dogs*. When we invited you to play this special role, we knew we were getting someone who could ensure verisimilitude in myriad ways. What we didn't fully appreciate is how compassionately you would guide us all—the director, writer, actors, and crew—to a deep resonant understanding of the bond between animal and man and the experience of being a young soldier in Vietnam. —John Drimmer, Supervising Producer, *War Dogs* Documentary.

Since 1998, my war dog stories have been featured in the following TV documentaries:

War Dogs, America's Forgotten Heroes (Discovery Channel)
Dogs of War (CNN TIME Magazine News Feature)
Dogs With Jobs (PBS TV Documentary)
Hero Dogs (The History Channel)

In January 2001, I was elected President of the Vietnam Dog Handlers Association by popular vote. My first major act was to launch a National War Dog Memorial Fund in *Parade* magazine after only a few months in office. It was a huge risk, but when *Parade* hit the Sunday newsstands (April 1, 2001) across the country (33+ million copies), public support for a national war dog memorial in Washington D.C. was overwhelming. That support continues to grow today.

Some of the most exciting times I've had recently have been traveling to numerous cities and towns across America telling Clipper's story to people of all ages, raising money for a National War Dog Memorial, and working with our nation's congressional leaders to sponsor a bill of resolution mandating a National War Dog Memorial in Washington, D.C.

I hope that my story will help fellow Vietnam veterans, Vietnam war dog handlers, and their families to heal from the lingering pain of the Vietnam war experience. I also hope that my story will give everyone a better understanding of what it was like to be a young man with a dog serving in one of the most unpopular wars in our country's history.

And if the war dog memorial gets turned down by a final-approval oversight committee that manages our country's hallowed Memorial Mall, I'll personally organize and lead "The Million Dog March" on Washington, D.C.!

So, as long as I have my memory, I will think of all my brother veterans every day. And I am sure that when I leave this world, my last thoughts will be of my family, my comrades, and my war dog, Clipper.

Glossary

Acronym	Definition
AK-47	Enemy Military Rifle
AO	Area of Operation
APC	Armored Personnel Carrier
ARVN	South Vietnamese Army
CAR15	American Military Rifle
CMB	Combat Medical Badge
CG	Commanding General
CIB	Combat Infantry Badge
CO	Commanding Officer
CP	Control Point
C Rations	Canned Food
FNG	Fucking New Guy
JWS	Jungle Warfare School
KIA	Killed in Action
LAW	Lightweight Anti-tank Weapon
LRRP	Long Range Reconnaissance Patrol
LTC	Lieutenant Colonel
LZ	Landing Zone
M16	American Military Rifle
M60	American Machine Gun
M79	American Grenade Launcher
MOS	Military Occupational Specialty
MP	Military Police
NCO	Noncommissioned Officer
NVA	North Vietnamese Army

Acronym	Definition
OCS	Officer Candidate School
OD	Olive Drab
P38	C Ration Can Opener
PAVN	Peoples Army of Vietnam
PFC	Private First Class (E-3)
PSP	Perforated Steel Plating
PX	Post Exchange
	Queen/King of Battle
RA	Regular Army Volunteer
REMF	Rear Echelon Mother Fucker
RPG	Enemy Rocket-Propelled Grenade
RTO	Radio/Telephone Operator
RVN	Republic of Vietnam
S & D	Search-and-Destroy
S2	Military Intelligence
SGM	Sergeant Major (E-9)
SOI	Signal Operating Instructions
SOP	Standard Operating Procedure
Top	First Sergeant (E-8)
VC	Viet Cong
VDHA	Vietnam Dog Handler Association
WIA	Wounded in Action

Acknowledgments

I could not have written this book without the support, advice, and friendship of many people. I would like to express my gratitude to Mark Hart and his family for locating my Vietnam War buddy Kenneth L. Mook after twenty-five years; to Kenny L. Mook, whose reunion with me inspired this book. To Ollie Whetstone, Mike "Mac" McClellan, and Dan Barnett, former German shepherd scout dog handlers with the 44th Scout Dog Platoon in Vietnam, whose advice and friendship gave me the guidance and the determination to see this project through; to my editor, Keith Wallman, who helped me to become a better writer; to Caleb Adoin, a gifted young man with an optimistic future for military service; and finally to my daughter, Jennifer, and granddaughter, Ariana, who needed a clearer understanding of what life was like for me when I was nineteen years old.

Appendix:
Gone But Not Forgotten

The Vietnam Dog Handler Association (VDHA) supplied the following names and supporting data for each dog handler and war dog who died during the war in South Vietnam. The VDHA Web site is at: *www.vdhaonline.org*.

Congressional Medal of Honor

The Congressional Medal of Honor is the highest military decoration for bravery that can be bestowed upon a military service member by our great country.

Staff Sergeant Robert W. Hartsock, 44th Infantry Platoon Scout Dogs, 3rd Brigade, 25th Infantry Division, was the only war dog handler to receive such an award during the Vietnam War. Staff Sergeant Hartsock was born on January 24, 1945, in Cumberland, Maryland. He entered the service at Fairmont, West Virginia.

Staff Sergeant Hartsock earned the Congressional Medal of Honor for extraordinary heroism in the Hau Nghia province, Republic of Vietnam, on February 23, 1969.

> **Citation:** For conspicuous gallantry and intrepidity in action at the risk of his life above and beyond the call of duty. Staff Sergeant Hartsock distinguished

himself in action while serving as section leader with the 44th Infantry Platoon Scout Dogs. When the Dau Tieng Base Camp came under a heavy enemy rocket and mortar attack, Staff Sergeant Hartsock and his platoon commander spotted an enemy sapper squad, which had infiltrated the camp undetected.

Realizing the enemy squad was heading for the brigade tactical operations center and nearby prisoner compound, they concealed themselves and, although heavily outnumbered, awaited the approach of the hostile soldiers. When the enemy was almost upon them, Staff Sergeant Hartsock and his platoon commander opened fire on the squad. As a wounded enemy soldier fell, he managed to detonate a satchel charge he was carrying.

Staff Sergeant Hartsock, with complete disregard for his life, threw himself on the charge and was gravely wounded. In spite of his wounds, Staff Sergeant Hartsock crawled about 5 meters to a ditch and provided heavy suppressive fire, completely pinning down the enemy and allowing his commander to seek shelter. Staff Sergeant Hartsock continued his deadly stream of fire until he succumbed to his wounds. Staff Sergeant Hartsock's extraordinary heroism and profound concern for the lives of his fellow soldiers were in keeping with the highest traditions of the military service and reflect great credit on him, his unit, and the United States Army.

War Dogs Killed in Action in Vietnam

(Note: All were German shepherds except

for the Labrador retrievers that served

with the Combat Tracker Teams.)

Name	Died	Unit	Military Branch	Name	Died	Unit	Military Branch
Ago	9/20/68	49th Scout	A	Blackie	3/21/69	49th Scout	A
Alex	9/16/69	47th Scout	A	Blackie	9/9/70	47th Scout	A
Andy	1/9/70	50th Scout	A	Blaze	2/28/67	12th Sec.	AF
Anzo	9/23/68	Unknown	Unk			Police Squad.	
Apache	1/11/69	Unknown	Unk	Blitz	10/4/67	43rd Scout	A
Arko	7/15/67	Unknown	Unk	Blitz	5/31/71	59th Scout	A
Arko	12/12/68	45th Scout	A	Blitzen	7/1/69	Unknown	Unk
Arko	6/5/69	Unknown	Unk	Blitzer	3/17/69	Unknown	Unk
Arras	1/12/68	45th Scout	A	Bo Bear	11/12/68	58th Scout	A
Arras	11/27/70	57th Scout	A	Bobo	12/26/70	43rd Scout	A
Arry	1/29/69	Unknown	Unk	Bo-Bo	7/24/69	40th Scout	A
Artus	12/11/70	42nd Scout	A	Bodie	11/16/66	Unknown	Unk
Astor	11/10/70	39th Scout	A	Bodo	7/1/68	Unknown	Unk
Axel	4/13/69	Unknown	Unk	Bootsy	9/19/67	48th Scout	A
Axel	3/31/70	58th Scout	A	Bounce	2/14/71	43rd Scout	A
Axel	1/29/71	39th Scout	A	Bozo	9/12/67	377th Sec.	AF
Bark	6/16/67	42nd Scout	A			Police Squad.	
Baron	2/23/67	25th Scout	A	Brandy	6/25/71	42nd Scout	A
Baron	6/30/68	Unknown	Unk	Britta	11/27/68	25th Scout	A
Baron	1/30/69	Unknown	Unk	Bruno	7/16/67	48th Scout	A
Baron	4/7/69	39th Scout	A	Bruno	1/30/69	35th Scout	A
Baron	9/23/70	47th Scout	A	Brutus	3/17/69	43rd Scout	A
Bizz	3/21/69	47th Scout	A	Buck	11/24/68	47th Scout	A
Black Jack	9/23/71	48th Scout	A	Buck	6/2/70	Marine Scout	M
Blackie	12/7/67	25th Scout	A	Buck	9/1/71	58th Scout	A

Name	Died	Unit	Military Branch	Name	Died	Unit	Military Branch
Buckshot	5/13/68	44th Scout	A	Duchess	9/13/67	Unknown	Unk
Buddy	12/15/68	43rd Scout	A	Dug	6/1/71	Marine Sentry	M
Buddy	9/2/70	59th Scout	A	Dugan	7/18/69	Unknown	Unk
Buddy	11/12/70	48th Scout	A	Duke	1/15/67	41st Scout	A
Bummer	7/4/67	Unknown	Unk	Duke	4/7/68	35th Scout	A
Butch	11/8/70	38th Scout	A	Duke	6/13/68	25th Scout	A
Caesar	5/19/68	38th Scout	A	Duke	2/23/69	49th Scout	A
Caesar	10/31/70	Unknown	Unk	Duke	12/6/69	57th Scout	A
Caesar	3/4/68	39th Scout	A	Duke	3/24/70	57th Scout	A
Cap	6/27/71	34th Scout	A	Duke	1/3/71	48th Scout	A
Casey	9/17/71	58th Scout	A	Duke	1/21/72	3rd Sec. Police Squad.	AF
Ceasar	4/10/70	50th Scout	A				
Charger	6/2/70	Unknown	Unk	Dusty	7/28/70	37th Scout	A
Chase	8/20/68	57th Scout	A	Dusty	4/27/71	58th Scout	A
Chief	4/17/69	Unknown	Unk	Dutchess	8/1/70	981st MP	A
Chief	12/9/69	57th Scout	A	Egor	6/23/69	41st Scout	A
Chief	7/1/70	Unknown	Unk	Eric	11/9/67	44th Scout	A
Chooch	4/28/70	48th Scout	A	Erich	1/18/70	35th Scout	A
Claus	6/18/69	40th Scout	A	Fant	10/28/70	47th Scout	A
Colonel	3/1/71	981st MP	A	Feller	11/8/68	39th Scout	A
Commander	4/26/69	41st Scout	A	Flare	7/26/69	42nd Scout	A
Cookie	9/28/68	50th Scout	A	Frico	1/13/67	41st Scout	A
Country Joe	1/23/71	Mine & Booby Trap	M	Fritz	10/18/68	57th Scout	A
				Fritz	11/7/68	57th Scout	A
Cracker	8/19/68	49th Scout	A	Fritz	2/28/69	12th Sec. Police Squad.	AF
Crazy Joe	2/13/70	Marine Scout	M				
Crypto	2/23/69	45th Scout	A	Fritz	10/6/69	Marine Scout	M
Cubby	12/4/66	3rd Sec. Police Squad.	AF	Fritz	10/15/69	47th Scout	A
				Fritzie	1/26/69	35th Sec. Police Squad.	AF
Danny	4/29/70	42nd Scout	A				
Deno	5/22/69	41st Scout	A	Gallo	4/13/67	Unknown	Unk
Diablo	1/31/68	3rd Sec. Police Squad.	AF	Gar	3/9/70	37th Scout	A
				Gretchen	11/18/68	44th Scout	A
Dix	2/15/70	57th Scout	A	Gretchen	5/29/70	42nd Scout	A

Name	Died	Unit	Military Branch	Name	Died	Unit	Military Branch
Gretchen	9/3/70	39th Scout	A	King	7/1/68	43rd Scout	A
Gunder	8/13/67	34th Scout	A	King	7/4/68	57th Scout	A
Hannabel	11/22/69	Unknown	Unk	King	9/13/68	34th Scout	A
Hanno	2/16/67	33rd Scout	A	King	12/23/68	41st Scout	A
Hasso	6/18/69	41st Scout	A	King	2/16/69	48th Scout	A
Hector	5/14/69	40th Scout	A	King	3/20/69	33rd Scout	A
Heidi	10/16/68	58th Scout	A	King	5/18/69	49th Scout	A
Heidi	9/1/70	Mine & Booby Trap	M	King	8/1/69	Unknown	Unk
				King	8/14/69	37th Scout	A
Heidi	11/12/70	63rd Com. Tracker Team	A	King	11/13/69	39th Scout	A
				King	1/13/70	8th Sec. Police Squad.	AF
Heidi	2/19/71	43rd Scout	A				
Heidi	4/23/71	57th Scout	A	King	2/13/70	59th Scout	A
Hunde	2/28/68	3rd Sec. Police Squad.	AF	King	4/8/70	39th Scout	A
				King	5/19/70	42nd Scout	A
Husky	11/11/68	Unknown	Unk	King	6/28/71	47th Scout	A
Ikar	7/2/69	40th Scout	A	King I	2/20/70	Unknown	Unk
Irish	3/20/68	Unknown	Unk	Krieger	6/2/71	42nd Scout	A
Jack	10/18/68	57th Scout	A	Kurt	6/22/68	34th Scout	A
Jack	12/17/69	34th Scout	A	Lance	1/26/71	42nd Scout	A
Jack	9/5/70	Unknown	Unk	Lighting	5/11/70	981st MP	A
Joe	6/15/70	45th Scout	A	Little Joe	2/22/70	47th Scout	A
Kaiser	7/6/1966	Unknown	Unk	Lobo	2/15/69	43rd Scout	A
Kaizer	1/18/69	Com. Tracker Team-2	A	Lodo	6/25/70	37th Scout	A
				Lucky	10/17/66	44th Scout	A
Kaizer	1/18/69	Unknown	Unk	Lucky	9/1/70	Mine & Booby Trap	M
Kat	4/30/70	48th Scout	A				
Kazan	6/15/68	57th Scout	A	Ludwick	8/22/66	377th Sec. Police Squad.	AF
Keechie	12/10/67	34th Scout	A				
Kelly	12/10/67	34th Scout	A	Lux	8/19/68	43rd Scout	A
Kelly	5/18/70	34th Scout	A	Mac	11/5/68	Unknown	Unk
Kelly	1/23/71	Unknown	Unk	Machen	3/31/68	39th Scout	A
King	1/10/68	43rd Scout	A	Max	7/1/67	Unknown	Unk
King	2/10/68	981st MP.	A	Max	6/4/70	42nd Scout	A

Name	Died	Unit	Military Branch	Name	Died	Unit	Military Branch
Mesa	8/24/69	49th Scout	A	Rebel	5/26/70	Unknown	Unk
Mike	7/2/67	41st Scout	A	Reggie	3/10/68	981st MP	A
Mike	11/10/69	57th Scout	A	Rennie	9/1/70	Mine &	M
Ming	5/11/68	45th Scout	A			Booby Trap	
Mister	6/1/70	58th Scout	A	Renny	1/11/68	35th Sec.	AF
Mitzi	12/5/67	Unknown	Unk			Police Squad.	
Money	1/24/69	50th Scout	A	Rex	5/25/67	33rd Scout	A
Notzey	4/25/70	33rd Scout	A	Rex	2/7/68	43rd Scout	A
Paper	6/26/69	42nd Scout	A	Rex	2/7/68	43rd Scout	A
Peanuts	4/13/69	Unknown	Unk	Rex	5/4/68	40th Scout	A
Penney	10/5/70	34th Scout	A	Rex	1/26/69	Unknown	Unk
Pirate	12/2/68	34th Scout	A	Rex	2/22/69	35th Sec.	AF
Prince	12/9/65	3rd Sec.	AF			Police Squad.	
		Police Squad.		Rex	3/6/70	48th Scout	A
Prince	3/2/67	48th Scout	A	Rex	5/29/70	34th Scout	A
Prince	9/2/67	44th Scout	A	Ringo	2/6/68	44th Scout	A
Prince	2/20/68	Unknown	Unk	Rinny	7/4/68	212th MP	A
Prince	7/10/68	Unknown	Unk	Rip	10/16/67	Unknown	Unk
Prince	9/1/68	Unknown	Unk	Rolf	6/17/70	42nd Scout	A
Prince	1/2/69	Unknown	Unk	Rommell	6/10/70	50th Scout	A
Prince	3/15/69	37th Scout	A	Rover	9/7/68	57th Scout	A
Prince	7/27/69	Marine Scout	M	Rover	9/19/70	33rd Scout	A
Prince	6/12/70	37th Scout	A	Royal	9/27/70	Marine Scout	M
Prince	10/26/70	981st MP	A	Rusty	8/30/69	42nd Scout	A
Princess	2/2/69	39th Scout	A	Saber	11/30/68	Unknown	Unk
Princess	4/13/69	47th Scout	A	Sam	4/11/68	Unknown	Unk
Princess	8/3/69	39th Scout	A	Sam	4/6/70	57th Scout	A
Princess	4/19/70	39th Scout	A	Sam	9/24/70	62nd Com.	A
Ranger	3/16/69	37th Scout	A			Tracker Team	
Reb	2/23/67	48th Scout	A	Sam	12/16/70	635th Sec.	AF
Rebel	12/4/66	377th Sec.	AF			Police Squad.	
		Police Squad.		Sarge	11/1/66	Unknown	Unk
Rebel	7/9/69	47th Scout	A	Sarge	10/29/69	34th Scout	A
Rebel	3/8/70	50th Scout	A	Sarge	1/12/71	57th Scout	A

Name	Died	Unit	Military Branch	Name	Died	Unit	Military Branch
Sargeant	1/27/67	44th Scout	A	Stormy	7/17/70	Unknown	Unk
Sgt. Bilco	10/25/68	Unknown	Unk	Suesser	1/21/68	42nd Scout	A
Satch	1/31/68	212th MP	A	Taro	8/30/71	59th Scout	A
Savage	9/28/68	49th Scout	A	Tasso	5/26/70	25th Scout	A
Shack	1/28/69	Marine Scout	M	Tempo	1/19/71	48th Scout	A
Shadow	11/9/67	Unknown	Unk	Teneg	3/12/70	62nd Com. Tracker Team	A
Shadow	8/26/68	Unknown	Unk				
Shadow	5/27/70	Unknown	Unk	Thea	11/8/68	Unknown	Unk
Shane	12/1/68	Unknown	Unk	Thor	1/1/65	Unknown	Unk
Sheba	8/27/71	58th Scout	A	Thor	6/3/70	42nd Scout	A
Shep	1/24/69	50th Scout	A	Thor	4/9/71	63rd Com. Tracker Team	A
Shep	1/27/69	Unknown	Unk				
Shep	1/29/70	47th Scout	A	Thunder	5/15/68	42nd Scout	A
Sheps	1/13/67	41st Scout	A	Tiger	8/9/1966	25th Scout	A
Silber	11/27/68	25th Scout	A	Tiger	8/14/70	57th Scout	A
Silver	7/24/68	59th Scout	A	Tim	9/11/68	44th Scout	A
Sissy	1/26/71	43rd Scout	A	Toby	12/4/66	377th Sec. Police Squad.	AF
Skipper	7/25/70	50th Scout	A				
Smokey	9/18/66	25th Scout	A	Toby	1/25/70	63rd Com. Tracker Team	A
Smokey	5/27/68	Unknown	Unk				
Smokey	6/1/68	43rd Scout	A	Toto	9/12/67	Unknown	Unk
Smokey	1/27/69	57th Scout	A	Troubles	12/30/67	25th Scout	A
Smokey	5/13/69	57th Scout	A	Tye	9/29/70	42nd Scout	A
Smokey	4/26/70	47th Scout	A	Willie	7/27/68	47th Scout	A
Spade	12/17/68	Marine Sentry	M	Wolf	5/22/68	Marine Scout	M
Spike	3/1/71	981st MP	A	Wolf	1/7/69	49th Scout	A
Stark	11/16/68	Unknown	Unk	Wolf	2/26/71	33rd Scout	A
Storm	4/23/69	39th Scout	A	Ziggy	4/10/69	41st Scout	A

War Dog Handlers Killed in Action in Vietnam

Name	Died	Age	Unit	Military Branch
Ahern, Robert Paul	3/30/69	27	37th Sec. Police Squad.	AF
Alcorn Jr., Dale Robert	9/6/69	19	60th Mine & Booby Trap	A
Amick, Richard Michael	5/12/69	19	57th Scout	A
Anderson, William Allison	11/6/69	21	66th Com. Tracker Team	A
Armstrong, Robert Dale	1/16/69	20	Marine Scout	M
Atkins III, Joshua Abraham	4/26/67	19	Army Scout	A
Baker, Donald Lee	9/6/67	20	Marine Sentry	M
Baker, Gary Paul	5/11/70	21	Army Scout	A
Baldoni, Lindsay David	8/22/67	21	39th Scout	A
Banaszynsk, Richard Michael	10/25/68	22	59th Scout	A
Barkley, Earl Duane	11/9/71	21	Army Scout	A
Beauregard, Richard Mauric	4/24/71	19	Army Scout	A
Beaver, James Harold	3/16/68	20	50th Scout	A
Beck, Terrence Daniell	2/20/67	18	Marine Scout	M
Beesley, Gary Evans	6/22/67	21	43rd Scout	A
Behrens, Peter Claus	12/4/70	26	1st Provisional	M
Belcher, Robert Winslow	4/11/68	22	Marine Scout	M
Bell, Mark Wayne	6/9/69	19	Marine Scout	M
Bennett, John Willie	10/14/69	20	Army Scout	A
Berge, James Maynard	1/23/68	24	50th Scout	A
Best, Billy Howard	3/3/69	18	Marine Scout	M
Beuke, Dennis Arthur	10/11/67	21	Com. Tracker Team -8	A
Bevich Jr., George Michael	12/4/66	22	377th Sec. Police Squad.	AF
Blaauw, James Evart	3/22/68	21	Army Scout	A
Blair, Charles Douglas	5/14/70	20	64th Com. Tracker Team	A

Name	Died	Age	Unit	Military Branch
Bost, Michael James	5/14/67	20	44th Scout	A
Bowman, Stephen Wesley	6/2/68	18	49th Scout	A
Boyd, James	2/28/68	22	3rd Sec. Police Squad.	AF
Boyer, James Roger	9/22/67	20	Com. Tracker Team -2	A
Bozier Jr., Willie	7/9/70	21	Army Scout	A
Brede, Robert William	11/16/67	24	Com. Tracker Team-2	A
Brophy, Martin Earl	5/5/68	24	41st Scout	A
Brown, Charles Paul	3/9/67	21	40th Scout	A
Browne, Walter D.	8/2/69	21	41st Scout	A
Buckingham, Keith Charles	2/25/69	22	43rd Scout	A
Bullwinkel, Alden John	9/11/69	20	61st Com. Tracker Team	A
Burdette Jr., Hilburn M.	7/12/70	19	Army Scout	A
Burk, Jimmy Rea	11/30/69	21	43rd Scout	A
Burlock Jr., Kenneth George	9/17/69	23	Army Scout	A
Burnette Jr., Archie	1/31/68	20	Army Scout	A
Cabarubio, James	6/18/69	20	Marine Scout	M
Cain, Douglas Michael	7/14/68	23	43rd Scout	A
Camp, Anthony Lorin	6/4/69	21	Marine Scout	M
Campbell, William Ladd	3/3/67	21	49th Scout	A
Carinci, Joseph A.	12/30/70	20	Mine & Booby Trap	M
Carrillo, Melvin	3/3/68	19	48th Scout	A
Carter, Merle Keith	10/22/67	20	Navy Sentry	N
Castle, Russell Leonard	7/2/67	34	40th Scout	A
Chisholm, Ronald Lee	5/11/67	21	Marine Sentry	M
Clark, Walter Levon	10/29/67	20	Army Scout	A
Clokes, Robert	12/4/68	21	40th Scout	A
Colford, Darrell Lee	11/8/70	25	38th Scout	A
Collier, Steven Edward	10/27/68	19	Army Scout	A
Conklin, Michael Lee	6/24/70	22	Army Scout	A
Conner, Jack William	4/4/70	25	557th Com. Tracker Team	A

Name	Died	Age	Unit	Military Branch
Conners Jr., Ralph Wilson	5/22/69	22	41st Scout	A
Connors, Jack Lee	8/21/69	23	557th Com. Tracker Team	A
Cox Jr., Edward Erlin	2/15/69	20	76th Com. Tracker Team	A
Crawford, Bobby Dean	1/10/68	22	43rd Scout	A
Crawford, Gordon Lee	2/1/71	24	Army Scout	A
Cumbie, William Thomas	2/9/69	19	Marine Scout	M
Currier Jr., Gordon Leroy	1/31/68	22	212th MP	A
Czarnota, Christopher Zeno	3/22/71	20	Army Scout	A
Davis, Abron Earl	1/11/69	20	Marine Scout	M
Davis, Eligah Lamar	4/5/70	19	Mine & Booby Trap	M
Davis, Alan Eunice	3/21/71	21	48th Scout	A
Deitrick, George Douglas	6/23/69	19	41st Scout	A
Dell, Kenneth John	11/5/68	21	49th Scout	A
Detrick, Gary Gene	4/13/69	20	47th Scout	A
Dillinder, Randy Eugene	12/10/67	19	34th Scout	A
Doria, Richard Albert	8/19/69	21	48th Scout	A
Doyle, John Francis	8/25/68	19	59th Scout	A
Drobena, Michael James	2/23/69	23	Marine Scout	M
Drum, Thomas	3/4/70	21	62nd Com. Tracker Team	A
Drysdale, Charles Douglas	1/26/69	19	Marine Scout	M
Ducote Jr., Lonnie Joseph	8/13/67	22	34th Scout	A
Duff, Phillip Randall	7/7/72	20	Army Scout	A
Duke, Douglas Ovyle	12/20/68	23	Veterinarian	A
Dunning, William Martin	6/22/70	24	66th Com. Tracker Team	A
Elliott, Robert William	8/9/70	24	Mine & Booby Trap	M
Erickson, Russell Martin	7/24/68	24	59th Scout	A
Esterly, Lawrence Alan	7/18/69	20	Marine Scout	M
Eubanks, George F.	12/7/67	21	25th Scout	A
Evans, Ronald Lee	4/29/71	24	44th Scout	A
Farley, Marshall Colin	9/19/67	20	44th Scout	A

Name	Died	Age	Unit	Military Branch
Fisher, Thomas William	9/4/67	20	Marine Sentry	M
Ford, Richard Edward	1/18/70	22	35th Scout	A
Fox, Gary Wayne	4/30/67	18	37th Sec. Police Squad.	AF
Fraley, Eugene Thomas	1/21/68	28	Navy Seal Team	N
Fraser, William George	12/28/67	20	Marine Scout	M
Freeman, David Michael	8/11/69	20	34th Scout	A
Freeman, Jeffrey Alexander	4/8/70	23	39th Scout	A
Freppon, John Dennis	2/2/69	20	35th Scout	A
Fuller, Gary Leroy	2/27/67	21	Army Scout	A
Fuller, Stanley Carl	12/12/68	21	76th Com. Tracker Team	A
Gaspard Jr., Claude Joseph	5/20/68	21	33rd Scout	A
Giberson, Jerry Guy	6/20/70	21	Army Scout	A
Glenn, Livingston	12/9/67	28	57th Scout	A
Goudelock, William Roger	3/18/68	19	57th Scout	A
Green, Billy Monroe	6/24/66	22	Scout	A
Grieve, Michael A.	1/31/68	21	Army Scout	A
Grifasi, James Anthony	3/26/70	22	Army Scout	A
Griffin II, William Donald	12/15/70	23	63rd Com. Tracker Team	A
Groves, William E.	11/30/67	20	Army Scout	A
Grundy, Dallas George	11/5/66	23	Army Scout	A
Gyulveszi, Theodore Louis	2/10/69	24	41st Scout	A
Hales, Raymon Draper	7/19/69	27	58th Scout	A
Harding, John H.	10/8/67	19	557th Com. Tracker Team	A
Harris, Jessie Earl	1/31/68	22	212th MP Vet.	A
Hartsock, Robert Willard	2/23/69	24	44th Scout	A
Hartwick Jr., Floyd Wayne	7/15/67	20	Marine Scout	M
Hatcher, David Lee	11/12/70	21	63rd Com. Tracker Team	A
Henshaw, Patrick Lee	12/19/67	21	Army Scout	A
Hernandez, Victor Reyes	10/18/68	24	57th Scout	A
Hicks, Larry David	9/24/70	22	Army Scout	A
Hilerio-Padilla, Luis	11/13/69	20	Army Scout	A

Name	Died	Age	Unit	Military Branch
Hilt, Richard Michael	2/13/69	20	Army Scout	A
Holland, Wayne Bizzle	10/26/68	21	Army Scout	A
Holley, Glynn Byron	12/26/69	20	Army Scout	A
Holt, Herschel Cyle	8/3/66	23	Marine Scout	M
Hoppough, Dennis Karl	7/16/69	22	Marine Scout	M
Howard, James Ray	11/9/67	20	44th Scout	A
Howard, Mark Thomas	11/16/67	21	Com. Tracker Team-2	A
Huberty, William M.	10/17/66	21	44th Scout	A
Hughes III, Edward Cowart	11/27/67	19	44th Scout	A
Hurksman Jr., Wilhelm S.	7/22/68	20	43rd Scout	A
Ireland, Elmer Glenn	7/1/69	21	44th Scout	A
Jenkins, Steven Lee	1/15/69	21	981st MP	A
Jenkins, Clayton Dean	6/3/69	21	Marine Sentry	M
Jenks, Robert James	3/2/68	20	45th Scout	A
Jesko, Stephen Edward	10/16/70	20	Army Scout	A
Joecken, Richard Kenneth	8/28/69	22	44th Scout	A
Johnson, Freddie Lee	12/7/66	26	1st Com. Tracker Team	A
Johnson, Arnold Edward	11/16/67	20	Com. Tracker Team-2	A
Johnson, Carl Irving	6/22/68	19	34th Scout	A
Johnson, Herbert Burton	7/5/68	19	Army Scout	A
Johnson, Larry Lee	11/14/68	19	Army Scout	A
Johnson, James Allen	7/1/69	22	39th Scout	A
Karau, Ronald Dean	3/20/71	21	Army Scout	A
Kiefhaber, Andrew John	2/23/69	20	65th Com. tracker Team	A
Kimbrough, Golsby	7/6/69	20	35th Scout	A
King, Alexander	1/20/69	21	557th Com. Tracker Team	A
Kobelin, John William	3/6/69	24	40th Scout	A
Koon, George Kenneth	11/16/67	20	Com. Tracker Team-2	A
Kuefner, John Alan	8/14/69	20	35th Scout	A
Kuehn, Lloyd Martin	3/9/67	20	40th Scout	A
Kunz, Anthony Edmond	5/4/67	21	Army Scout	A

Name	Died	Age	Unit	Military Branch
Lagodzinski, Roger Thomas	5/19/70	22	57th Scout	A
Land, David Alfred	6/7/67	19	Marine Scout	M
Lane, Richard Arthur	6/16/68	23	Army Scout	A
Lawton, Edward Lester	9/27/68	19	75th Com. Tracker Team	A
Lebrun, Robert Normand	3/22/71	21	Army Scout	A
Lee, Edward Gilbert	5/13/68	20	44th Scout	A
Levins, Frederick Richard	6/16/70	23	76th Com. Tracker Team	A
Lindholm, Dan Victor	9/8/68	20	Army Scout	A
Lindsay, Stephen Lee	1/24/71	23	Marine Scout	M
Lipton, Joseph Price	5/1/67	18	Marine Scout	M
Lockhart, Harlan Nathan	11/9/66	23	35th Scout	A
Loftis, Joel Conrad	6/7/69	22	35th Sec. Police Squad.	AF
Lovellette, Gary Vaughn	12/29/69	23	45th Scout	A
Lumsden, William Wayne	5/21/67	19	Com. Tracker Team-3	A
Magruder, David Byron	5/16/70	21	Army Scout	A
Mahurin, Elmer Wain	10/11/67	19	Com. Tracker Team -8	A
Mansfield, John Montague	3/9/67	21	Army Scout	A
Marasco, Joseph Allen	7/22/69	22	62nd Com. Tracker Team	A
Marchant, Paul Lafontaine	10/18/69	22	Army Scout	A
Markey Jr., James Paul	1/26/71	23	63rd Com. Tracker Team	A
Marrufo Jr., Rodney Elmer	5/23/68	20	66th Com. Tracker Team	A
Marshall, Mark Duane	3/29/69	18	Marine Scout	M
Marshall, Clifford Wayne	2/19/71	21	43rd Scout	A
Martin, Kenneth	3/5/69	20	40th Scout	A
Martinez, Juan Patricio	5/5/68	25	41st Scout	A
Mason Jr., Benjamin H.	9/4/67	18	Marine Scout	M
Matel, Ronald James	6/9/69	20	1st Com. Tracker Team	A
Mattson, Paul Edward	4/20/68	23	59th Scout	A
Maurer, Walter Lawrence	11/1/70	20	Army Scout	A
May, Robert Walter	2/12/68	20	34th Scout	A
Mazzone, Joseph Mark	9/22/68	23	Army Scout	A

Name	Died	Age	Unit	Military Branch
Mc Carty, Glenn Weldon	2/20/71	21	Army Scout	A
Mc Fall, Gary Richard	9/13/68	24	34th Scout	A
Mc Grath, Edward Charles	10/6/67	20	43rd Scout	A
Mcintosh, Donald William	11/8/70	19	Army Scout	A
Mclaughlin, James Bruce	4/16/71	23	Army Scout	A
Merschel, Lawrence James	5/1/68	20	Army Scout	A
Meyer, Leo Roland	10/5/68	20	61st Com. Tracker Team	A
Michael, James Albert	2/13/71	21	Army Scout	A
Miller, Timmy Larry	11/24/68	21	Marine Scout	M
Mills, Rodney Kenneth	5/5/70	22	Army Scout	A
Montano, William Andrew	11/19/70	19	Marine Scout	M
Morrison, James John	2/2/69	20	39th Scout	A
Mugavin, Martin M.	2/23/67	20	48th Scout	A
Munch, Michael R.	5/13/69	20	57th Scout	A
Munoz, Jose	12/7/66	19	1st Com. Tracker Team	A
Murray, Harry Walter	12/7/66	20	1st Com. Tracker Team	A
Myers, Richard Vaughn	11/13/67	20	39th Scout	A
Newell, Tim Edwin	9/9/70	24	47th Scout	A
Nicolini, Peter Joseph	5/16/67	21	44th Scout	A
Norris, Robert Norman	12/19/69	18	44th Scout	A
Nudenberg, David Alan	11/12/70	24	63rd Com. Tracker Team	A
Nurzynski, Joseph Anthony	5/12/69	24	59th Scout	A
Oaks, Robert Larry	11/11/69	20	Army Scout	A
Ohm, David James	7/20/68	20	Army Scout	A
Olmstead, John Paul	7/15/67	21	48th Scout	A
Orsua, Charles David	7/15/69	19	Army Scout	A
Palacio, Gilbert Gonzales	5/6/69	21	34th Scout	A
Park, Irving Geon	3/6/70	23	12th Sec. Police Squad.	AF
Parker Jr., Carter	10/24/70	23	Army Scout	A
Parrish, Billy Joe	5/23/68	32	66th Com. Tracker Team	A
Payne, Robert Paul	3/18/68	24	Marine Scout	M

Name	Died	Age	Unit	Military Branch
Payne, Terry John	8/5/70	22	Army Scout	A
Payne III, Howard David	4/27/71	24	59th Scout	A
Pearce, Marvin Robert	8/25/68	19	47th Scout	A
Petersen, Harry Thomas	11/9/70	21	Army Scout	A
Piasecki, John Michael	11/29/69	22	Army Scout	A
Pierce, Oscar Wayne	3/9/67	23	40th Scout	A
Plambeck Jr., Paul Wandling	11/13/69	22	39th Scout	A
Plattner, Ernest Melvin	11/8/68	23	44th Scout	A
Poland Jr., Leon Lovell	3/26/67	20	Marine Scout	M
Porter, Richard Charles	1/24/71	21	Mine & Booby Trap	M
Pretter, Thomas	6/8/67	20	38th Scout	A
Pulaski Jr., Peter	1/4/70	23	44th Scout	A
Quinn, Thomas Wayne	4/4/69	21	45th Scout	A
Randolph, Michael James	3/29/70	20	1st Com. Tracker Team	A
Ratliff, Billy Harrison	9/24/70	20	76th Com. Tracker Team	A
Ray, William Clayton	7/4/70	21	58th Scout	A
Rhodes, Robert David	5/27/70	19	Marine Scout	M
Rivera, James	3/9/68	20	62nd Com. Tracker Team	A
Roberts, Virgil Jessie	1/22/69	21	557th Com. Tracker Team	A
Robinson, Charles John	1/7/69	21	49th Scout	A
Rosas, Jose Antonio	5/8/67	27	Marine Scout	M
Roth, John Howard	3/9/67	21	50th Scout	A
Rowe, Michael Thomas	2/19/69	20	Army Scout	A
Sandberg, Charles H.	5/13/68	30	44th Scout	A
Schachner, David Brennan	5/14/69	20	40th Scout	A
Schmid, Robert Anthony	8/16/66	23	Army Scout	A
Schossow, Dennis Robert	1/22/71	21	Mine & Booby Trap	M
Schwab, Richard Michael	9/6/70	21	57th Scout	A
Schyska, Leroy Floyd	12/6/67	18	46th Scout	A
Scott, Dave Russell	1/24/68	21	Army Scout	A
Segundo, Pete Sprule	9/5/69	22	Marine Scout	M

Name	Died	Age	Unit	Military Branch
Selix, James Michael	10/30/71	44	47th Scout	A
Severson, Paul Roy	8/25/68	23	Army Scout	A
Sheldon, William Charles	5/5/68	19	Navy Sentry	N
Shelton, Bobby James	9/29/67	23	38th Scout	A
Shepard, Raymond Andrew	8/3/66	24	Marine Scout	M
Sheppard, Ronald Eugene	9/20/68	22	49th Scout	A
Simpson, Edward Monroe	5/11/68	19	45th Scout	A
Sims, William Jess	7/16/69	21	60th Mine & Booby Trap	A
Smith, Gary Kenneth	2/27/67	21	39th Scout	A
Smith, Ronald C.	3/3/67	20	212th MP	A
Smith, Michael Francis	4/28/68	19	59th Scout	A
Smith, Winfred Lee	6/8/70	22	Army Scout	A
Smith, Stephen Jay W.	6/21/70	22	Army Scout	A
Smoot, Robert Gene	1/5/68	19	557th Com. Tracker Team	A
Soto Concepcion, Jose	5/6/69	20	25th Scout	A
Southwick, John Paul	10/19/69	19	Marine Scout	M
Spangler, Max Ray	1/12/68	19	45th Scout	A
Spencer Jr., Daniel Eugene	11/12/68	23	Army Scout	A
Steptoe, Raymond	8/15/66	20	35th Scout	A
Sturdy, Alan Macdonald	7/2/67	22	41st Scout	A
Sullivan, Donald Sherril	1/29/67	22	40th Scout	A
Sullivan, Jeremiah Joseph	10/23/67	21	38th Scout	A
Sunday, James Michael	9/29/67	22	43rd Scout	A
Sweat Jr., Herbert Hoover	2/21/69	20	34th Scout	A
Sweatt, Theodore A.	11/27/68	22	25th Scout	A
Tallman, George	4/9/67	21	Army Scout	A
Taranto, Robert Joseph	11/29/68	21	57th Scout	A
Taylor, Mark Randall	6/2/71	20	44th Scout	A
Teresinski, Joseph Alvin	2/6/71	20	557th Com. Tracker Team	A
Thibodeaux, Michael L.	7/19/70	19	Army Scout	A
Tosh III, James C.	8/21/69	23	25th Scout	A

Name	Died	Age	Unit	Military Branch
Triplett, James Michael	4/17/69	22	Marine Scout	M
Truesdell, John Leroy	3/20/71	21	Army Scout	A
Van Gorder, William Joseph	6/21/68	20	57th Scout	A
Vancosky, Michael Anthony	5/4/70	19	Marine Scout	M
Vogelpohl, Rex Alan	1/11/71	21	57th Scout	A
Waddell, Larry Jonathan	3/9/67	20	Army Scout	A
Ward, Danny Edward	6/1/68	21	43rd Scout	A
Ward, David James	7/4/68	20	981st MP	A
Webb, Howard Lee	6/8/67	24	44th Scout	A
Whetham, Vernon E.	11/30/67	25	43rd Scout	A
White, John Oliver	1/22/68	21	57th Scout	A
White, Garson Franklin	2/13/69	21	Marine Scout	M
Whitehead, Alfred Evarts	6/16/68	25	44th Scout	A
Whitten, Robert Eugene	5/8/68	21	Army Scout	A
Wickenberg, Erik Bernard	7/6/67	20	43rd Scout	A
Winningham, Richard Daniel	1/7/69	20	Army Scout	A
Wood, Robert Helm	4/9/68	21	Marine Scout	M
Yeager, Michael Joseph	4/8/70	19	Mine & Booby Trap	M
Yochum, Lawrence Wayne	2/13/70	19	59th Scout	A
Young, Jon Michael	4/4/68	22	43rd Scout	A

Index

Afghanistan, 330

Aldridge (SP4), 99

American counteroffensive, 318

American embassy, 293

American grenades, 242

American lightweight antitank weapon (LAW), 150

American Military Assistance Command Vietnam (MACV), 272

America's Forgotten Heroes (Discovery), 332

ammunition, conserving, 16

An Khe, 7, 38, 71, 73

APCs, 152–153, 155, 156, 157, 158, 159, 160, 161, 162–163, 165, 167, 168, 169

Archates, 147

area of operation (AO), 198

Arlington National Cemetery, 195

Armored Personnel Carriers (APCs), 149–150, 151

Army Achievement Medal, x

Army Corp of Engineers, 139–140

Army Republic of Vietnam (ARVN), 129, 272

Ballantine beer, 262–263

ball with bamboo spikes, 131

Barnett, Sergeant Dan, 186, 190–191, 194, 294, 295, 331

Beau, 263

Ben Cui rubber tree plantation, 130, 227–228, 271–272

Ben Hoa, 295, 300, 310

Bible, 225

"Big Red One," 260

Black Virgin Mountain, 256

blood stripes, 284

11B Military Occupational Specialty, 39

Bogumill, George, 85, 87–88, 91, 113, 282, 331

Bong Son mission (Operation Davy Crockett), 41–42, 49, 126, ix

Bong Son plains, 45, 53–54, 71, 72

Bosnia, 330

Brigade S2 (military intelligence), 232, 256

British Jungle Warfare School (JWS), xiii

Bronze Star medal, 254, x

Buck Sergeant, 285

Buckshot, 330

Buddhist, 276

Burnam, John
  arriving at Dau Tieng, 127–132
  assignments/missions, 23, 41, 75–76, 197, 231–233, ix
  background, 2
  back home
    fighting war of words, 325
    nightmares of war, 326
    shock of homecoming, 326
  best friends, 239
  at Camp Alpha, 2–6
  at Camp Radcliff, 7–8, 9–10
  and Club Lucky, 109–112
  convoy
    back to Cu Chi, 311–312
    at hotel, 309–311
    hotel Mama San, 301
    and Red's girlfriend, 305–308
    and Red's toothache, 301–305
    to Saigon, 297–299
    Saigon's Cholon district, 300
  Dau Tieng, training at, 129–130
  first Christmas in South Vietnam, 276–279
  getting homesick, 116
  good-bye Clipper, 313–317
  Hans
    attack process with, 108
    first tour of guard duty with, 112–115
    quality time with, 99–100
    training, 101, 102–103
  Ia Drang valley mission, 22–37
  joining K-9 platoon, 134–135
  at kennels, 97–99
  and Kenny Mook, 4–5

and Kiko, 116–117
knee injury, 209, 235, 253, 274, 279–283, 308
leaving for America, 320–321
life after Vietnam
  dreams destroyed, 328
  Legion of Merit medal, 328
  retinal vein occlusion, 327–328
medals, x
meeting decent girls, 111
military dog-training manual, 102
mission with 2/12, 233
needles, fear of, 283
new accommodations, 286
new job, 287
NVA captured, 259–261
Operation Davy Crockett, 41–50
overview of experience, ix–xi
paratrooper wings, 39
promised assignment, 124
promotion to sergeant, 284
punji stake, 80–83
recommended for medal, 255
reenlisting, 119–120
rotation month, 278
rubber gas masks, 114–115
scout dog handlers, presentation of, 132–134
searching hamlet, 249–250
and Tena, 117
"The Mennen Boy," 31
training sessions with platoon, 103–108
trip wire training with Clipper, 228–231
walking point, 133–134
weapons squad, 13–14

California Boy, 194–195
Cambodia, 126, 128, 197, 198, 272
Cambodian border, 125, 197, 210, 223
Camp Alpha, 2–4, 121–122, 319, 323
Camp Radcliff, 7–8, 72
  meeting 2nd Platoon, 11–12
  mess hall, 10
  quarters, 9–10
  showers, 22
  supply sergeant at, 10–11
CAR15, 154, 216, 266

Carter, Jimmy, 327, x
Charlie, 14, 41–42, 59, 62, 64, 75, 85–86, 146, 153, xi
cherry jumper, 39
Chinese grenades, 241–242
Chinese Lunar New Year, 291
Cholon district, 300, 310
Christmas in Vietnam
  American Christmas vs. Vietnamese culture, 276
  cease-fire, 278
  fruitcakes, 276–277
  homemade goodies, 277
  manning defensive perimeter, 278
Chu Pong Mountains, 27, 31–32
CIB (Combat Infantry Badge), 283
claymore mine, 29
Cleveland, 263
Clipper, 264, 274, 275, 294, 296, 312, 313, 333, ix
  in animal snare, 244–245
  during attack on kennels, 188
  as best friend, 239
  and booby traps, 252–254
  capturing NVA, 259–261
  chance to visit, 286
  character of, 173
  in charge, 252–254
  and Christmas, 278
  and combat infantry patrol, ix
  crossing log, 246–247
  good-bye, 313–317
  honoring, 329
  hugging, 254
  insects on, 236–237
  and local Vietnamese, 174
  mission with 2/12, 233
  under rubber tree, 314
  saying good-bye to, 283
  searching hamlet, 249–250
  story of, 332
  tactics and solution in chopper, 200–201
  training, 174–177
  tree of, 195–196
  trip wire training, 228–231
  Vietnamese afraid of, 250

walking point, 175–179
war records, 329–330
and wood ticks, 237
Club Lucky, 102–103, 109
Club Texas, 116–117
Colorado, 321
Colorado Rocky Mountains, 321
Combat Infantry Badge (CIB), 39–40, 41, 96,
    296, x
Combat Medical Badge, 41
Combat Tracker Team (CTT), 137, 138
Command Sergeant Major of the Army
    (CMA), 327
Company A, 2nd Battalion, 12th Infantry, 256
Company B, 2nd Battalion, 22nd Mechanized
    Infantry, 148
Company B, 1st Battalion, 7th Cavalry Regi-
    ment, 9
composition C-4, 243
Cong, 14
control point (CP), 243
Coors beer, 323
Cox, Randy, 263
C rations, 25, 30
CTT (Combat Tracker Dog Teams), xii–xiii
Cu Chi, 130, 191, 257, 265, 280, 281, 286,
    291, 298, 302, 318
    heading back to, 313
    hospital, 282, 283
    Tet counteroffensive, 295
Custer, George Armstrong, 9

Dau Tieng, 125, 127, 128, 129, 130, 137–138,
    180, 182, 233, 250, 274, 281, 284, 286, 291,
    294, 295, 313
    airstrip, 200
    base camp, 253, 271
    death certificate for Beau, 264
    field hospital, 280
    last night in, 315
    during mortar attack, 269
    NVA courier, 256
    reason for occupying, 271–272
    road march, 269–271
    rubber tree planttations, 227
    supple channels, 266

25th Infantry Division in, 257
VC buildup around, 232
Vietnamese bakery, 273–274
village, 272
village of, 271
"Death in the Kennel" (chapter in manu-
    script), 331
DeBarros, Fred, 180–181
Denver, 116, 321, 323
Desert Storm, 330
Dinks, 14
Doc Bell, 40–41, 58, 59, 63, 65, 66, 82
1968 Dodge Charger 440 RT, 321
dog handler. See war dog handlers
Dogs of War (CNN TIME Magazine News
    Feature), 332
dogs serving in WWII and Korea, 316
Dogs With Jobs (PBS TV Documentary), 332
DOGWORLD, 330–331
Dorman, Sergeant Marlin, 95, 96, 331
    in An Khe, 73–74
    Bong Son, 41–42
    at Camp Radcliff, 13–14
    CIBs, 39–40
    friendly fire, 52
    hill jumping, 75
    platoon leader, 50
    rear guard, 70
    respect for, 38
    returning to Ia Drang valley, 22–23, 26, 27,
        28, 30
    story of Ia Drang valley, 17–21
    "The Mennen Boy," 31
    wounded and dead, 66–67, 68, 69
Drimmer, John, 332
Dunn, Bob, 14, 15, 16
    in Bong Son, 43, 49, 50, 52, 53, 54, 55, 56,
        57, 62, 66, 68–69, 73
    team leader, 22
    in Ia Drang valley, 27–29, 30
    napalm, 59
    respect for, 56
Durbach (Sergeant), 222, 223, 224, 225, 226

Engles (Specialist Four), 56, 63, 68
enlisted structure, 9

Eply, Mike, 194, 224, 225
Erik, 136, 147, 189–190, 191, 271, 330
Expert Rifle Badges, 15–16

Fenner, Lieutenant Robert, 170, 184, 185,
    187, 223, 224, 265, 266
    after VC barrage, 184, 185, 187
    breaking up altercation, 194
    Ed's dog, Sergeant, 225–226
    and knee injury, 279
    and Major General Mearns, 191
    road march, 269–270
    44th Scout Dog Platoon, 136–137
    and war stories, 139
firefight, 265
fire team, 257
flashback, 240–241
FNGs, 292
Fort Benning, Georgia, 136, 137, 145, 180,
    263, 264, xii
Fred, 95, 96, 97, 102, 103, 109–112, 114
Freddie, 296–297

Garden Grove, California, 226
"Gary Owen," 9, 10
Geneva Convention, 59
German shepherds, 97–98, 132, 136, 137, 138,
    146, 263, 265, 270
    in mine, booby trap, and tunnel dog teams,
        xiii–xiv
    in patrol dog teams, xiii
    as scout dogs, x–xiii
    in sentry dog teams, 1, 94, xiii
    tasks well-suited for, x
    as water dogs, xiv
German shepherd(s)
    sentry dog, ix
German shepherd scout dog handler, ix
Glydon, Robert, 139, 145, 169, 170, 173,
    188–189, 190, 264, 265, 271
Good Humor man, 287
Gooks, 14, 224
GRB Entertainment, 331
grease gun, 266–267
grunt, 73, 228, 242, 271
gunships, 29

Hanoi, 277
Hans, 99–102, 103, 118, 132, 133, 138, ix
Hardcore, 142–143, 271
H.E., 50
Headquarters, Company A, 196, 197
Headquarters Company, 25th Supply and
    Transportation Battalion (S & T), 283
head shed, 285
Hero Dogs (The History Channel), 332
Hobo Woods, 298
Ho Chi Minh Trail, 197, 210
hot, 42
Hughes, Ed
    bad eulogy, 276
    remembering, 284
Hughes, Edward Cowart, 194–195, 196, 199,
    207, 208, 222–224, 225, 226

Ia Drang valley, 17, 207, ix
    loading plan, 26–27
    returning to, 22–23
igloos, 113–114
Indian Wars, 232
infantry division's organizational structure, 9
infantrymen, 287–288
infantry war dog handlers, x
IPSD (Infantry Platoon Scout Dogs), xi–xii

Japan, 116, 282
John Hopkins University, 328
Johnson, George, 323
Johnson, SP4, 34
Jones, Nancy, 85, 87, 91
Jones, Roger, 264–266
Jump Wings, 283
JWS (British Jungle Warfare School), xiii

Kadena Air Force Base, 120
Kaiser Coffin, 172
Kashini Barracks, Yokohama, Japan, 84
K-9 compound, 136, 192, 232, 271, 313
    attack on, 182–187
Kelly (Sergeant Major), 285, 286, 294, 295,
    296, 297, 311, 312, 318
Kenosha, Wisconsin, 132
Kentucky, 186–187, 191, 263

Kiko, 116–117
killed-in-action (KIA), 69
King of Battle, 233
K-9 Klub, 141, 142, 182, 191, 192, 194, 208, 224, 262, 284, 313, 315
Knutson, 63
Kool-Aid, 263
Korea, 286, 330
K-9 platoon, 148, 228
K-9 units
    Combat Tracker Dog Teams (CTT), xii–xiii
    Infantry Platoon Scout Dogs (IPSD), xi–xii
    Mine Booby Trap, and Tunnel Dog Teams, xiii–xiv
    Patrol Dog Teams, xiii
    Sentry Dog Team, xiii
    Water Dogs, xiv

Labrador retrievers, 137–138
    as combat tracker dog, xii–xiii
    tasks well-suited for, x
Lackland Air Force Base, 329, xiii, xv
Lang, Robert, 85, 86
LAW (American lightweight antitank weapon), 150
LBJ (Long Bin Jail), 287
Leg, 5
Legion of Merit medal, x
letter of appreciation from Jimmy Carter, x
lieutenant colonel (LTC), 2–3
lifers, 279
Little Big Horn, 9
Littleton, 116
Littleton, Colorado, 283
Littleton High School, 4, 117
Long-Range Reconnaissance Patrol (LRRP), 148, 256
L-shaped ambush, 159, 171
Lucky, 97
LZ, 27, 47, 75, 76, 202, 232
LZ Gold, 128, 129, 137
LZ Victor, 23, 35–36
LZ XRAY, 23, 27

MacClellan, Mike (Mac), 146, 147, 168, 169, 172, 183, 189, 194, 264, 331

MACV (American Military Assistance Command Vietnam), 272
mad minute, 129
malaria, 282–283
Malaysia, xiii
Mama San, 110, 268
marijuana, 242
Master Sergeant (E8), 327
Mearns, Major General, 191, 192, 193, 206, 207, 208
medals earned, x
Mekong Delta, 85
Memorial Day, 329, 330
Meritorious Service Medals, x
M79 grenade launcher, 154
Michelin rubber tree plantations, 127, 136, 227–228, 233, 271–272
Mike, 97
Milanowski (First Sergeant), 283, 285
Military Occupational Specialty (MOS), 4
Military Police detachment, 271
Military Policemen (MPs), 1
military war dogs
    outcome of, 330
    records, 329
M60 machine gun ammunition, 24
M60 machine guns, 14, 46, 77, 201
105mm Howitzers, 233–234
Mook, Kenny, 78, 92, 125–126, 330
    background, 4–5
    Bong Son, 38, 47, 48, 52, 53, 57, 58, 59, 64
    at Camp Radcliff, 7, 9, 10, 12, 15–16
    CIB and Purple Heart, 73
    Ia Drang valley
        to LZ Victor, 35
        returning to, 22–26, 27–28
        Sergeant Dorman's war story, 17–21
    as replacement, 5–6
    supply sergeant, 11
    wounded, 65–66, 68, 69
    writing to parents, 71, 74
Moore, Lieutenant Colonel Hal, 17, 35, 36, 76, 331
mortar attacks, 268–269
Morton, Gary, 86–87
MP night patrols, 272

MPs (Military Policemen), 1
M16 rifle, 15, 52, 53, 77, 129, 154, 266
M14 rifles, 5, 15

napalm, 59
National Geographic, 45, 231
National-Louis University, 327
National War Dog Memorial, xvi
National War Dog Memorial Fund, 332
2nd Battalion, 7th Cavalry, 17–21
2nd Battalion of the 22nd Infantry, 129
2nd Battalion of the 12th Infantry, 129, 231–232
2nd Platoon, 47, 48
   Lost Platoon, 19
   war story, 17–21
2nd Platoon of Company B, 1st Battalion, 7th Cavalry "Gary Owen," ix
New York, 323
New York soldier, 170
no-fire zone, 198, 199
noncommission officers' (NCO) quarters, 284
North Vietnam, 197
North Vietnamese Army (NVA), 41, 128, 197, 291, 293, 318, xi
North Vietnamese officer, 311
Nui Ba Den, 256, 257
NVA (North Vietnam Army), 14, 42, 156

Oakland, 322–323
Oakland Army Base, 322
Officer Candidate School, 266
Okinawa, 93–94, 116, 134, 228, ix
   culture, 116
   and Kiko, 117–118
   and sentry dog handlers, 93–94, 275
   sentry dog training in, 134
Operation Davy Crockett, 41
Operation Junction City, 264
Orthopedic Ward D, 84–89, 91–92

P38, 155
Pabst Blue Ribbon beer, 262–263, 323
Parade magazine, 332
Paratrooper Wings, x

PAVN (Peoples Army of Vietnam), 14
peace agreement with North Vietnam, 328–329
Pentagon, 327
Pettingill, Tony, 271
PFC (private first class), ix
Phillips, Mike, 263–264, 267, 281
point man, xi–xii
PRC/25 radio, 272
President Roosevelt, 299
Prince, 271, 330
private first class (PFC), ix
punji pits, 131
punji stake, 80–83, 131–132, 206, 209, 280, 328
Purple Heart medal, 73, 94, x
PX, 285, 286, 295, 302

Queen of Battle, 233
Qui Nhom, 72, 83

radio/telephone operator (RTO), 70, 246, 247
Rat Patrol, 272–274
   173rd Airborne Brigade, 119–120, 121, 122, 123, 135
   3rd Brigade, 4th Infantry Division, 44, 122, 123, 125, 126, 128, 129–130, 142, 271
   3rd Brigade, 25th Infantry Division, 137, 192, 206, 271, 280
   3rd Brigade's combat missions, 138
Red, 296–297, 301–311
REMFs, 236, 292, 295
replacement centers, 6
replacements, 3, 5
Report of Survey, 265
Republic of South Vietnam, 330
Rex, 97, 99
rice-paddy-racers, 22
Ringo, 264–266, 330
Rocky Mountains, 116
Rodriguez (Rod), 40, 61, 62, 68

Saigon, 2, 121, 141, 264, 265
   convoy to, 297–311
   fall of, 329

leaving for, 318–320
under martial law, 319
military district, 291
morgue in, 225–226
Saigon River, 130, 272
Saipan, 136
San Francisco, 327
changing uniforms, 324–325
protesters in, 323–324
San Francisco International Airport, 322
Santa Claus, 276
Savage (Sergeant), 13
S-2 (Battalion Intelligence), 41, 75
Scott, Dan, 194, 266, 267, 281, 331
background on, 190–191
centipede and monster scorpion, 267
CG and, 192–193
chaplain's eulogy for Ed, 225
and Clipper, 281
grease gun, 266–267
humor, 267
saying good-bye, 313, 315
training, 266
scout dog(s), 132
bounty on, 182
handlers, 270
teams, 278
Scout Dog Training Center, 137, 263, 264
sentry dog(s), 93, 96
handlers, 93, 95, 97, 103
platoon, 95, 96, 275
training, 138, 148
Sergeant, 195, 196, 199, 207, 208, 222–224,
225, 226, 271, 330
Sergeant Major of the Army, 328
Sergeants Major Academy, 327
SGM (E-9), 285
Shadow, 190–191, 271, 330
short-timer, 288–290
shrapnel, 264
Signal Operating Instructions (SOI), 297, 311
skoshi cabs, 109, 112
slicks, 71, 248
South China Sea, 55, 60, 61, 320
Southeast Asia, 278
South Vietnam, 130, 198, 291

infantry war dog handlers and war dogs, x
serving with 44th Scout Dog Platoon, ix
flight to, 1
military policemen (MPs), 1
returning to, 121–124
Vietnam war dog, 1
South Vietnamese Army (ARVN), 300, 319, xv
South Vietnamese five dong, 322
Specialist-4 (SP4), 95
spider holes, 54, 241
spies, 94
spotter round of artillery, 243
standard operating procedure (SOP), 205
standing down, 278
Stars and Stripes, 262, 265
1st Battalion, 7th Cavalry Regiment, 42, 45
1st Cavalry Division, 5, 7–8, 119, 130
1st Infantry Division, 260

Tan Son Nhut airport, 1
Tay Ninh, 130, 256, 257, 260, 291, 318
Tena, 117
Tet counteroffensive operations, 294–295, 298
Tet Offensive, 293, 295, 307, 316, 318
in the bunkers, 292
General Westmoreland, 293–294
launching howitzers, 293
mortars and rockets exploding, 291–292
267th Chemical Company, 93, 94, 275
"The Million Dog March," 333
"The Pussy That Swallowed Vietnam," 267
25th Infantry Division, 280
signal corps VHF and FM, 256–257
Tet counteroffensive, 295
44th Infantry Platoon Scout Dogs (IPSD),
132, 133, 135, 136, 168, 170, 180, 182, 222,
255, 272, 283, 294, 317, 331, ix
811th Military Police Company, 136
38th Scout Dog Platoon, 265, 298
Thurston, Mary, 331
Timber, 330, ix
background on, 144
mission, 149–151, 154–162
recuperating, 169–171
training, 145, 147, 148
wounded, 163, 165–166

Tinzer, 180–181
Tomb of the Unknown Soldier, 195
Ton Son Nhut airfield, 319–320
Ton Son Nhut Air Force, 121
Top, 94–95, 284–285
tracers, 24
Trainee of the Cycle award, 264
training, 77
trip flares, 29–30
triple deuce, 148

2/12. See 2nd Battalion, 12th Infantry
University of Colorado, 117
U.S. Army Officer Candidate School (OCS), 137
U.S. Army Recruiting Station, 76
U.S. Army Replacement Center, 319
U.S. Army 5th Special Forces Group, 256
U.S. Embassy, 291
U.S Army 25th Infantry Division (Tropical Lightning), 130
US declaring war on North Vietnam, 277
106 US General Hospital, 84–89, 91–92, 93

VC rocket-propelled grenade (RPG), 150
VC (Viet Cong), 294
Vestal, Don, 120
Veterans Day, 329
Viet Cong (VC), 14, 57, 62, 63, 64, 148, 197, 293, 298, xi
    base camps, 241
    finding hidden base camps, 233
Vietnam, 136, 148, 263, 270, 286, 330
    war, 329
    war dog handlers, 332–333
Vietnam Dog Handler Association (VDHA), 331, 332, xv, xxii
Vietnamese Cross of Gallantry ribbon, x
Vietnamese culture, 276

Vietnamese laborers, 140
Vietnam Veterans Memorial, 330
Virginia, 330
volleyball, 268

wait-a-minute vines, 236
Walter Reed Army Medical Center, 328
war dog(s)
    handlers, 132–134, 137
    as military surplus equipment, xiv
    outcome of, xiv–xv
    serving, x
    teams, xi–xiv
War Dogs (TV Documentary), 331, 332
War Zone C, 264
Washington D.C., 327
weapons squad, 13–14
Westmoreland, General William, 293, 294
We Were Soldiers, ix
Whetstone, Oliver (Ollie), 136, 146, 331
    background, 132
    and dog Erik, 147
    dog training, 174, 176
    Erik's burial, 191
    Erik's wounds, 189–190
    rotation date, 192
    Timber, 144
Wildman (Private), 14
Willy Peter, 50
Wilson, Van, 76, 77, 78, 83, 89, 95–96, 331
Wolf, 97
World War II, .45-caliber machine gun, 266
wounded-in-action (WIA), 69
WWI, 330
WWII, 136, 286, 330

Yokohama, Japan, 90–91, 93

Zantos, Bill, 268